Comparative Executive Clemency

Virtually every constitutional order in the common law world contains a provision for executive clemency or pardon in criminal cases. This facility for legal mercy is not limited to a single place in modern legal systems, but is instead realized through various practices such as a law enforcement officer's decision to arrest, a prosecutor's decision to prosecute, and a judge's decision to convict and sentence. Doubts about legal mercy in any form as unfair, unguided, or arbitrary are as ubiquitous as the exercise of mercy itself.

This book presents a comparative analysis of the clemency and pardon power in the common law world. Andrew Novak compares the modern development, organization, and practice of constitutional and statutory schemes of clemency and pardon in the United Kingdom, United States, and Commonwealth jurisdictions. He asks whether the bureaucratization of the clemency power is in line with global trends, and explores how innovations in legislative involvement, judicial review, and executive consultation have made the mercy and pardon procedure more transparent. The book concludes with a discussion on the future of the clemency and pardon power given the decline of the death penalty in the Commonwealth and the rise of the modern institution of parole.

As a work concerned with the practice of mercy in the common law world, this book will be of great interest to researchers and students of international and comparative criminal justice and international human rights law.

Andrew Novak is Adjunct Professor of Criminology, Law, and Society at George Mason University, where he teaches Law and Justice Around the World. He has previously taught African law at American University Washington College of Law. He has written extensively on comparative and international criminal justice issues, including three books: *The Global Decline of the Mandatory Death Penalty: Constitutional Jurisprudence and Legislative Reform in Africa, Asia, and the Caribbean*; *The Death Penalty in Africa: Foundations and Future Prospects*; and *The International Criminal Court: An Introduction*.

Routledge Research in Human Rights Law

Available titles in this series include:

The Right to Development in International Law
The case of Pakistan
Khurshid Iqbal

Global Health and Human Rights
Legal and philosophical perspectives
John Harrington and Maria Stuttaford

The Right to Religious Freedom in International Law
Between group rights and individual rights
Anat Scolnicov

Emerging Areas of Human Rights in the 21st Century
The role of the universal declaration of human rights
Marco Odello and Sofia Cavandoli

The Human Right to Water and its Application in the Occupied Palestinian Territories
Amanda Cahill

International Human Rights Law and Domestic Violence
The effectiveness of international human rights law
Ronagh McQuigg

Human Rights in the Asia-Pacific Region
Towards institution building
Hitoshi Nasu and Ben Saul

Human Rights Monitoring Mechanisms of the Council of Europe
Gauthier de Beco

The Positive Obligations of the State under the European Convention of Human Rights
Dimitris Xenos

Vindicating Socio-Economic Rights
International standards and comparative experiences
Paul O'Connell

The EU as a 'Global Player' in Human Rights?
Jan Wetzel

Regulating Corporate Human Rights Violations
Humanizing business
Surya Deva

The UN Committee on Economic, Social and Cultural Rights
The law, process and practice
Marco Odello and Francesco Seatzu

State Security Regimes and the Right to Freedom of Religion and Belief
Changes in Europe since 2001
Karen Murphy

The European Court of Human Rights in the Post-Cold War Era
Universality in transition
James A. Sweeney

The United Nations Human Rights Council
A critique and early assessment
Rosa Freedman

Children and International Human Rights Law
The right of the child to be heard
Aisling Parkes

Litigating Transnational Human Rights Obligations
Alternative judgements
Mark Gibney and Wouter Vandenhole

Reproductive Freedom, Torture and International Human Rights
Challenging the masculinisation of torture
Ronli Noa Sifris

Applying an International Human Rights Framework to State Budget Allocations
Rights and resources
Rory O'Connell, Aoife Nolan, Colin Harvey, Mira Dutschke and Eoin Rooney

Human Rights Law in Europe
The influence, overlaps and contradictions of the EU and the ECHR
Kanstantsin Dzehtsiarou, Tobias Lock, Theodore Konstadinides and Noreen O'Meara

Nomadic Peoples and Human Rights
Jérémie Gilbert

Children's Lives in an Era of Children's Rights
The progress of the convention on the rights of the child in Africa
Afua Twum-Danso Imoh & Nicola Ansell

China's Human Rights Lawyers
Advocacy and resistance
Eva Pils

The Right to Equality in European Human Rights Law
The quest for substance in the jurisprudence of the European courts
Charilaos Nikolaidis

Business and Human Rights in South East Asia
Risk and regulatory turn
Mahdev Mohan & Cynthia Morel

Indigenous Peoples, Title to Territory, Rights and Resources
The transformative role of free prior and informed consent
Cathal M. Doyle

Challenging Territoriality in Human Rights Law
Building blocks for a plural and diverse duty-bearer regime
Wouter Vandenhole

Care, Migration and Human Rights
Law and practice
Siobhán Mullally

Comparative Executive Clemency
The constitutional pardon power and the prerogative of mercy in global perspective
Andrew Novak

Forthcoming titles in this series include:

Jurisdiction, Immunity and Transnational Human Rights Litigation
Xiaodong Yang

Extraterritoriality and International Human Rights Law
The spatial reach of African human rights treaties
Takele Soboka Bulto

Human Rights Law and Personal Identity
Jill Marshall

In Pursuit of Human Rights
NGOs, pedagogy and praxis in grassroots Africa
Joanne Coysh

The Law and Practice of the European Social Committee
Francesco Seatzu and Amaya Ubeda de Torres

Reconciling Cultural Diversity and International Human Rights Obligations
The compatibility approach in the practice of international human rights institutions
Michael K. Addo

Social and Economic Rights in Theory and Practice
A critical assessment
Helena Alviar Garcia, Karl Klare & Lucy A. Williams

The Human Rights Approach to Disability
Cases and materials
Andreas Dimopoulos

Socio-Economic Rights in Emerging Free Markets
Comparative insights from India and China
Surya Deva

Capturing Caste in Law
The legal regulation of caste discrimination
Annapurna Waughray

The Protection of Vulnerable Groups under International Human Rights Law
Ingrid Nifosi-Sutton

Human Dignity and Degrading Treatment in the European Convention on Human Rights

The ends of Article 3 of the European Convention on Human Rights

Elaine Webster

Comparative Executive Clemency

The Constitutional Pardon Power and the Prerogative of Mercy in Global Perspective

Andrew Novak

Routledge
Taylor & Francis Group
LONDON AND NEW YORK

First published 2016
by Routledge
2 Park Square, Milton Park, Abingdon, Oxon, OX14 4RN

and by Routledge
711 Third Avenue, New York, NY 10017

First issued in paperback 2017

Routledge is an imprint of the Taylor & Francis Group, an informa business

Library of Congress Cataloging in Publication Data
A catalog record for this book has been requested

ISBN 13: 978-0-8153-5536-6 (pbk)
ISBN 13: 978-1-138-81382-3 (hbk)

Typeset in Garamond
by FiSH Books Ltd, Enfield

Contents

Abbreviations

Print reporter citations

A.H.R.L.R.	African Human Rights Law Reports
C.H.R.L.D.	Commonwealth Human Rights Law Digest
D.L.R.	Dominion Law Reports (Can.)
F.L.R.	Fiji Law Reports
S.A.C.R.	South African Criminal Law Reports

Medium-neutral citations

EWHC	England and Wales High Court
IACommHR	Inter-American Commission on Human Rights
PTCC	Constitutional Court of Portugal
SBHC	High Court of the Solomon Islands
SCSL	Special Court of Sierra Leone
SGCA	Singapore Court of Appeal
SZHC	Swaziland High Court
VUSC	Vanuatu Supreme Court
ZWBHC	Zimbabwe High Court in Bulawayo

General abbreviations

CCSU	Council of Civil Service Unions
ICAC	Independent Commission Against Corruption
ICAC	Independent Commission Against Corruption (Hong Kong)
ICCPR	International Covenant on Civil and Political Rights
NEC	National Executive Council
NEC	National Executive Council (Papua New Guinea)
UNAMI	UN Assistance Mission for Iraq

Acknowledgements

This book grew out of my first book on the global decline of the mandatory death penalty. Clemency and the mandatory death penalty were codependent through much of modern legal history, and the decline of one has inevitably resulted in the decline of the other. The people who helped me on the first book by extension contributed to this one. This included the attorneys of the Death Penalty Project in London, including Parvais Jabbar, Saul Lehrfreund, Annette So, and Nicola Goldfinch-Palmer. I received timely updates from Kenya by Azania Legal Consultants' Timothy Bryant and Gerry Gitonga in Nairobi. The idea for this book originally stemmed from a conversation with barrister Joseph Middleton at Doughty Street Chambers in London who was working on a clemency petition for a Ghanaian national in Britain. As always, I would like to thank Dr. Jesse Fecker and Dr. Jay Michaelson for helping with my law review articles on the death penalty. Others who helped me answer questions that came up in the course of writing or who forwarded me useful sources include William Schabas, Jens David Ohlin, and Michael Loatman.

I must also thank a number of new colleagues. Professor Lill Scherdin at the University of Oslo engaged me in several helpful conversations about the pardon and clemency power during my visit to Norway in February 2015, where she introduced me to her colleagues at the Department of Criminology and Sociology of Law and served as a fantastic tour guide. Professor Sarah Lucy Cooper at Birmingham City University provided me with a draft paper on clemency and wrongful convictions in the United States and gave me helpful insight into the operations of state parole and pardon boards. Bikram Jeet Batra, a researcher on clemency and the death penalty in India, shared a helpful working paper that he wrote on constitutional clemency in India. Carolyn Hoyle at the University of Oxford provided me great feedback on my previous book and looked over the contents for this one. I had the opportunity to meet all four of them at a conference organized in London by Professor Michael Radelet and the team at the Death Penalty Project.

The students of my Spring 2015 Law and Justice Around the World class at George Mason University were instructed to find newspaper articles on executive clemency worldwide; many of them found topics and cases that contributed to the depth of this book.

Finally, I would like to dedicate this book to the memory of two lawyers: David Messerschmitt and Shelley D. Hayes.

1 Introduction

Executive clemency in global perspective

Most of the world's legal systems have a provision for mercy in criminal cases to temper the overly harsh application of law without undermining the law's deterrent potential. In the common law world, this power was traditionally exercised by the monarch, and delegated to colonial governors. Outside the common law world, however, constitutional mechanisms for mercy vary more widely. In most of continental Europe, the traditional manner of dispensing mercy was through a legislative amnesty, though many civil law countries today also have at least a limited means of executive pardon. Variations include requiring legislative approval of mercy decisions or requiring a minister accountable to the legislature to countersign a pardon in countries where the head of state is not directly elected. Clemency also existed in non-Western legal traditions, including under Islamic and precolonial law, where it was viewed as a traditional power of a chief or ruler.

Legal mercy is not limited to a single place in modern legal systems: it exists in a law enforcement officer's decision to arrest, a prosecutor's decision to prosecute, and a judge's decision to convict and sentence, to name a few. Doubts about legal mercy in any form as unfair, unguided, or arbitrary are as ubiquitous as the exercise of mercy itself.[1] The mercy power possesses an inherently contradictory nature: it is a discretionary instrument, often subject to the control of a single individual, yet used simultaneously to proclaim the law's impartial, determinate, and otherworldly nature. To be merciful is to forgive, a concept central to many global religious traditions. This book is about a specific type of mercy: the clemency and pardon power. Punishments are often delineated by legislatures and imposed by judiciaries; the clemency power, by contrast, is typically exercised by the third branch, the executive. The opacity of an executive clemency decision, outside of public view, allows a harsh sentence to be modified after the fact without undermining any deterrence

1 Austin Sarat, *When Can or Should Legal Judgment Be Merciful? An Introduction*, *in* Merciful Judgments and Contemporary Society: Legal Problems, Legal Possibilities 1 (Austin Sarat ed., 2012).

impact of the original sentence.[2] Although the traditional exercise of the clemency and pardon power has declined in world-historical terms over the past several centuries, the use of parole – a bureaucratized form of sentencing mercy – has become more common, despite occasional attempts to restrict it.[3] In many developed countries, the most commonly used form of "mercy" is dispensed by correctional authorities and parole boards in decisions that are mostly invisible.

Mercy tempers justice. Historically, mercy had powerful resonance where the rigors or harsh applications of the law were perceived to cause injustice. Although it plays a small role in modern criminal law, the pardon looms large in historical memory as evidenced by the quest for posthumous pardons, especially in cases with overt political overtones such as sympathetic rebellious leaders or wrongfully convicted political prisoners.[4] The philosophical underpinnings of mercy have been explored in Western popular culture, not least through William Shakespeare's three plays *The Merchant of Venice*, *Measure for Measure*, and *The Tempest*. Shakespeare famously provides a nuanced portrait of mercy, one in which legalism or leniency may triumph with a fair amount of unpredictability thrown in.[5]

As Sarat writes, clemency exists on the borderland between monarchical privilege and democratic rule of law. The United States constitution, for instance, imports the prerogative of the British monarch into a document otherwise constructing a government of limited powers. Alexander Hamilton's defense of clemency in the US constitution included recognition that the law of England was too harsh, where even minor offenses carried death sentences. He highlighted the awesome responsibility of the constitutional pardon power concentrated in one person and the possibility of restoring order after civil strife through pardons and amnesty, even for treasonous conduct.[6] Still the debate rages. Crouch argues that the clemency power is being abused by modern presidents in the United States, who have used it to protect themselves or their subordinates, or to reward supporters. The most famous pardon in modern history – US President Gerald Ford's pardon of President Richard Nixon – initiated a recent trend

2 Anthony N. Doob, *Punishment in Late-Twentieth-Century Canada: An Afterword*, *in* QUALITIES OF MERCY: JUSTICE, PUNISHMENT, AND DISCRETION 166, 172–3 (Carolyn Strange ed., 1996).

3 Paul J. Larkin, *Clemency, Parole, Good-Time Credits, and Crowded Prisons: Reconsidering Early Release*, 11 GEO. J. L. & PUB. POL'Y 1, 7 (2013).

4 Barry Wright, *"Harshness and Forbearance": The Politics of Pardons and the Upper Canada Rebellion*, *in* QUALITIES OF MERCY: JUSTICE, PUNISHMENT, AND DISCRETION 77, 77 (Carolyn Strange ed., 1996).

5 Robert A. Ferguson, *The Place of Mercy in Legal Discourse*, *in* MERCIFUL JUDGMENTS AND CONTEMPORARY SOCIETY: LEGAL PROBLEMS, LEGAL POSSIBILITIES 19, 43 (Austin Sarat ed., 2012).

6 Austin Sarat, *At the Boundaries of Law: Executive Clemency, Sovereign Prerogative, and the Dilemma of American Legality*, 57 AMERICAN Q. 611, 614–17 (2005).

toward use of the pardon not merely as an act of grace or for the public welfare, but as a political weapon used to interfere in the justice system.[7]

The mercy power also triggers philosophical reflection. Any discussion of the mercy power must rest on the fundamental tension between a conception of clemency as a rarely used "act of grace" within the sole discretion of an executive, or a routine, rule-bound process, publicly transparent and amenable to judicial review. Max Weber's distinction between legitimate charismatic authority and bureaucracy may be relevant here: is a grant of clemency a form of charisma, an other-worldly power outside the rational world of legal rules, or a routine administrative decision that is repetitive, subject to explicit criteria, and consistent?[8] Different legal systems have resolved this fundamental tension in different ways, and both have merits. Conceiving of clemency as a charismatic "act of grace" recognizes that clemency is a departure from the legal letter, an awesome power that can reverse or undo a decision of a court of law – a power that should be used sparingly and with flexibility. By contrast, imagining clemency as a routine, bureaucratic process ensures that grants of clemency are fair, impartial, and non-discriminatory, subject to due process rights and decision-making criteria.[9] Whether an executive should use the clemency power as a form of curative legislation by making policy-based pardons, or whether this is best left to the legislative and judicial branches is a subject of perennial debate in many legal systems.

Discretionary executive clemency sits uncomfortably in a legal system of objective rules and distinctions, and the pardon power has triggered different philosophical objections. For utilitarians like Cesare Beccaria, the penal code itself should be lenient, not the penal code's agents. If a pardon is just, the law must be wrong; if the law is just, a pardon must be wrong. For retributivists, the questions posed by Saint Anselm of Canterbury about the consistency of clemency might be more relevant: if God is merciful to some sinners, why not to all whose sins are similar?[10] These philosophical questions about mercy have been fiercely debated over centuries. This includes the very nature of a pardon. Who or what is pardoned? The offender or the offense? Philosopher Jacques Derrida argued that the pardon power is intentionally ambiguous on this point and requires reference to both the act and the person.[11] Is it "merciful" to nullify a criminal punishment that is genuinely deserved? Is it right? This book explores the practice of clemency and not the theory, but the practice never completely escapes the moral and theoretical plane.

7 Jeffrey Crouch, THE PRESIDENTIAL PARDON POWER 4 (2009).

8 Max Weber, author, Hans H. Gerth and C. Wright Mills, trans., eds., FROM MAX WEBER: ESSAYS IN SOCIOLOGY 196–97, 245–50 (1946).

9 Margaret Colgate Love, *Fear of Forgiving: Rule and Discretion in the Theory and Practice of Pardoning*, 13 FED. SENT'G REP. 125, 127–28 (2000).

10 Nigel Walker, *The Quiddity of Mercy*, 70 PHILOSOPHY 27, 27 (1995).

11 Sarat, *supra* note 6 at 614–15.

Defining terms

The royal prerogative of mercy is the residue of royal power that traditionally resided in the English sovereign, once expansive though today limited by convention and principles of administrative law, and, in the former colonies, by constitutional provision. In this book, "clemency" will be used as an umbrella term encompassing the four traditional forms of executive mercy: pardons, reprieves, commutations of sentence, and remissions of fines and forfeitures. The word "pardon" indicates a sentence or punishment that is fully cancelled, either freely or conditionally. A "reprieve" is a delay or suspension of punishment, while a "commutation of sentence" is a substitution of a greater sentence with a lesser one. In short, the mercy power allowed the sovereign unlimited discretion to replace one form of punishment with another, or none at all. Where all forms of clemency are being discussed, this book will frequently use the word "pardon," the broadest form of clemency, as shorthand for the full mercy power. However, as many constitutional systems make distinctions among the four traditional mercy powers, or otherwise provide for slightly different definitions, these will be carefully noted throughout the text. Amnesty is a slightly different conception, one similar to the common law clemency power but with different origins in the civil law world. The word "amnesty" originates from the ancient Greek, in which it referred to amnesia or oblivion. Amnesties have sought to provide soldiers, rebels, and authoritarian government officials, for example, with incentives to stop fighting, surrender their might, and begin participating in a new political system. In this way, amnesties have historically been a frequent component of peace settlements and negotiated transitions.[12]

The clemency power in the common law world

Despite its uncomfortable and often controversial role in modern legal systems, virtually every common law jurisdiction has a constitutional provision for executive mercy, and even those few that do not nonetheless typically have a statutorily-enacted scheme that allows some executive input into criminal sentencing. The survival of executive clemency into the twenty-first century may be attributed in part to the fact that the power derives from the same source in the common law world, rooted in the British monarch's royal prerogative of mercy. Because the King was the sovereign, crime against the state was crime against the King himself, and he alone had the power to reprieve it.[13] As the British Empire expanded

12 Roman David, *Transitions to Clean Government: Amnesty as an Anticorruption Measure*, 45 Aust. J. Pol. Sci. 391, 395 (2010).

13 C.H. Rolph, The Queen's Pardon 16–17 (1978).

globally, the pardon power followed, delegated to colonial governors on the King's behalf and later claimed by independent heads of state.[14] Slowly, however, the prerogative of mercy became bureaucratized in Great Britain and later in most of its former colonies partially as a protection against arbitrary decision-making and partly to cope with the vast numbers of cases in large and complex societies. The United States is no exception here: a former British colony itself, it inherited the pardon power from the British sovereign, where the power was enshrined in the US constitution after vigorous debate by the constitutional drafters; today, all 50 state constitutions also possess some form of mercy mechanism.[15] Although early US state constitutions expressed skepticism of executive power, nineteenth century state constitutions typically conferred the clemency power on a governor acting alone; in yet another shift, during the twentieth century, the trend was to delegate this power to an external pardons board.[16]

Clemency has declined in world-historical perspective, and today plays only a minor role in most criminal justice systems. This neglects its heretofore illustrious and robust history.[17] One reason for the decline of the pardon power is the global decline of the death penalty. This is particularly true with regard to the common law mandatory death penalty, in which sentencing discretion was removed from the trial judge in favor of an automatic death sentence upon conviction for certain offenses under the penal code.[18] The sweeping scope of the mandatory death penalty and the potential for enormous bloodshed placed great importance on a functioning clemency mechanism. The clemency power may also be endangered because of changes in public preferences and cultural mores. Writing of the United States, Crouch explains that pardons rarely provide any political benefit to presidents, and often involve some risk to the incumbent's political capital. In the modern era, mass media and an emphasis on government transparency create the expectation that the President would provide rhetorical justifications for controversial decisions. He concedes: "[t]he current political environment rewards – or at least does not punish – a president who is sparing with the pardon power."[19] Commutations and pardons have become rarer over the past several decades, especially since 1980, largely as a consequence of a "tough on crime" attitude and a chief

14 *Id.* at 120–139.

15 Crouch, *supra* note 7 at 27.

16 Leslie Elazar Sebba, *Pardon and Amnesty: Juridical and Penological Aspects*, LL.D. Thesis, Hebrew University of Jerusalem at iv (June 1975) (*hereinafter*, "Sebba, *Pardon and Amnesty*").

17 Carolyn Strange, *Introduction, in* QUALITIES OF MERCY: JUSTICE, PUNISHMENT, AND DISCRETION 3, 14–15 (Carolyn Strange ed., 1996).

18 Andrew Novak, THE GLOBAL DECLINE OF THE MANDATORY DEATH PENALTY: CONSTITUTIONAL JURISPRUDENCE AND LEGISLATIVE REFORM IN AFRICA, ASIA, AND THE CARIBBEAN 166 (2014).

19 Crouch, *supra* note 7 at 5.

executive's fear of making a mistake that could damage his or her public image. The hostility of federal prosecutors also plays a significant role.[20]

Although the clemency power has declined in recent years, especially over the last century, the primary reason why the clemency power survives at all in most common law constitutional systems may be because it serves an important societal function. As Moore explains, an increase in fixed punishments such as mandatory minimum sentences may lead to a revival of the pardon power. "Since there are only so many levels of punishment, and since the levels of culpability are infinite and the human capacity for causing harm is boundless in its variety, there will necessarily be 'hard cases' in which the predetermined sentence is wrong."[21] Pardons may have life left. Nonetheless, the decline of executive clemency at the federal level in the United States has attracted a great deal of academic scholarship, far more than any other country in the English-speaking world. The presidency of Barack Obama is following this trend: of the more than 1,866 requests for pardon and 16,362 requests for a commutation of sentence received between 2009 and 2015, Obama granted only 64 pardons and 21 commutations of sentence, the least of any chief executive thus far.[22] The first of these commutations was for Eugenia Marie Jennings, who served less than half of her sentence for a crack cocaine violation. Jennings, who had three children and a recent cancer diagnosis, had a long 22-year prison sentence due to two minor prior convictions and mandatory minimum sentencing guidelines.[23] Even these rare cases underscore the role that clemency plays in rectifying injustices that fall through the cracks.

The clemency power in global perspective

Executive mercy existed in legal regimes as varied as under the Code of Hammurabi in the Babylonian Empire, in the Roman Empire during Biblical times, and during the Han dynasty in China.[24] Nonetheless, not every society entrusted the mercy power to a single executive. In ancient Athens, mercy decisions were made democratically, requiring signatures of 6,000 Greek citizens, in effect limiting clemency to those with celebrity status. "Perhaps the most famous Roman pardon was Pontius Pilate's release of Barabbas instead of Jesus Christ" in the Christian Scriptures, as part of a Passover tradition of granting clemency on special occasions.[25]

20 Jeffrey Crouch, *The President's Power to Commute: Is It Still Relevant?*, 9 U. St. Thomas L.J. 681, 694 (2011).

21 Kathleen Dean Moore, Pardons: Justice, Mercy, and the Public Interest 85 (1989).

22 US Department of Justice, *Clemency Statistics*, www.justice.gov/pardon/clemency-statistics (last accessed March 22, 2015).

23 Crouch, *supra* note 20 at 681.

24 David Tait, *Pardons in Perspective: The Role of Forgiveness in Criminal Justice*, 13 Fed. Sent'g Rep. 134, 134 (2000).

25 Crouch, *supra* note 7 at 10–11.

Judeo-Christian traditions emphasize the personal virtues of forgiveness and compassion, with followers placing their faith in the mercifulness of God's justice and the justice of God's mercy, in this life or the next one. The common law tradition secularized these religious notions by prescribing punishment (justice) and providing a mechanism to modify those punishments (mercy). The link between God and temporal power through the divine right of the king ensured that the mercy power became a semi-divine one. Since then, it has been remarkably resilient, reconstituted as an attribute of democratic rule in the newer republics.[26]

Outside of the common law world, the clemency power does not follow a single model and may have different historical origins. Rolph writes that outside of the English-speaking world (as well as the United States), the pardon power is not a vague and traditional "prerogative" power, but rather has clear authority in the constitution or civil code.[27] In many countries, the head of state is the pardon authority. However, some constitutional systems provide that the clemency and pardon power is to be reserved for the legislature or for multiple branches of government acting together. Under the constitutions of Nicaragua, Switzerland, Turkey, and Uruguay, to name several examples, the pardon power is vested primarily in the legislature or shared among the branches.[28] Greece requires the president to follow the recommendation of the Justice Minister and to consult with a council composed primarily of judges; in addition, pardon of a government minister requires parliamentary consent, also a feature of Denmark's system. Some countries such as Portugal, Finland, or Indonesia require the government in pardoning to act in conformity with a Supreme Court opinion.[29] As Sebba writes, the traditional European continental equivalent of the pardon power was the amnesty, which implied a legislative measure applying to a category of unnamed offenders. Today, a legislative amnesty is referred to in some legal systems as a "general pardon," as in Israel, though in the English-speaking world a "general pardon" was still typically granted by the executive. Unlike the common law prerogative power, however, the civil law amnesty is today an institution of less than universal acceptance and does not enjoy the same recognition in common law countries, though the British Crown has used general pardons in a manner similar to the continental amnesty many times in its history.[30]

26 Strange, *supra* note 17 at 4.

27 Rolph, *supra* note 13 at 75.

28 Leslie Sebba, *The Pardoning Power: A World Survey*, 68 J. Crim. L. & Criminology 83, 112 (1977) (*hereinafter*, "Sebba, *Pardoning Power*").

29 Claudia Ilona Dascălu, *Elements of Comparative Law on the Individual Pardon, Between Constitutional Constraint and Discretionary Prerogative of the Head of State*, 2(2) Union of Jurists of Romania L. Rev. 1 (2012), www.internationallawreview.eu/fisiere/pdf/04-Claudia-Dascalux.pdf (last accessed May 13, 2015).

30 Sebba, *Pardon and Amnesty*, *supra* note 16 at i-iii.

The exercise of the clemency power varies based on the political system, and countries outside the common law world tend to show greater variation in political institutions than those derived from the Commonwealth framework. In countries governed by a collective body rather than an individual, for instance, such as previously the German Democratic Republic or the Soviet Union, the pardoning power vests in the collective body rather than in an individual head of state as such.[31] Countries that have separate heads of state and government may require both to countersign a pardon. In Romania, the president is entitled to grant pardons only for custodial sentences and only after conviction, but the prime minister must countersign a presidential pardon as a check on the president's authority. The president is also entitled to request (but is not bound by) a recommendation by the justice minister.[32] By contrast, the president of Poland may issue a pardon without countersignature from the prime minister, even though other presidential powers require such assent.[33]

France is an example of a country that relies primarily on legislative rather than executive mercy. France today makes frequent and regular use of the amnesty power, which is now incontrovertibly in the hands of the legislature. As late as the nineteenth century, however, claims were still made to the executive to issue general pardons, and such a power was expressly held by Emperors Napoleon I and III. Under the present constitutional order, however, even executive participation in the amnesty process derives from the provisions of the legislative amnesty law.[34] During pre-revolutionary times, only the pardon power existed. It was firmly in the hands of the absolute monarch, who, as God's representative on earth, had inherent power to judge and pardon crimes. After the Revolution, this conception of sovereignty was rejected, with the power henceforth transferred from the king to the legislature. In this period, the pardon power was temporarily abolished, and restored only under Napoleon and thereafter coexistent and in tension with the legislative power under succeeding constitutions.[35] In this sense, the ideals of the French revolution rejected the theoretical basis of executive clemency such as that exercised by the English King as a result of skepticism toward a single authority figure.

In modern France, the president retains the power to commute a sentence or reprieve an offender of a punishment, which is a truncated

31 Sebba, *Pardoning Power, supra* note 28 at 112.

32 Dascălu, *supra* note 29 at 3.

33 Irina Tanasescu, *The Presidency in Central and Eastern Europe: A Comparative Analysis Between Poland and Romania*, Paper presented to the Contours of Legitimacy in Central Europe: New Approaches in Graduate Studies Conference, European Studies Centre, St. Anthony's College, Oxford (24–26 May 2002) at 8–10.

34 Sebba, *Pardon and Amnesty, supra* note 16 at v.

35 René Lévy, *Pardons and Amnesties as Policy Instruments in Contemporary France*, 36(1) CRIME & JUSTICE 551, 554 (2007).

form of the clemency power. By contrast, the legislative amnesty completely erases both the conviction and the punishment. While historically the purpose of the pardon was to individualize an ordinary offender's sentence and an amnesty had a collective and political character, designed to restore harmony and expunge events from collective memory, this distinction today is somewhat anachronistic. Today, the two categories overlap substantially, and both have become routinized policy instruments aimed at reducing prison overcrowding. Pardons have been extended to entire categories of offenses and offenders, and since 1988 have become annual events. The corrections department relied on the pardon power for its prison population forecasts in order to reduce overcrowding in prisons during the hottest part of the year to prevent prison revolts. Similarly, amnesties have become a regular feature of presidential elections, aimed at ordinary crimes. The convergence of the pardon and amnesty powers in France and their prolific use do not generate widespread controversy among political elites or the general public, and are not the subject of hostile media coverage. They have become expected events, a necessary evil.[36] This bureaucratization of the clemency power is in line with global trends and is a central theme of this book. In addition, this book will identify additional examples where mass clemency or commutations can be an effective policy tool independent of the merits of individual cases.

The president of France exercises his right of pardon in his personal capacity and cannot delegate it. He also does not have to communicate his reasons, and he may consider petitions for reprieve from anyone with a material or moral interest in the matter – not just from the offender. Typically, an amnesty does not depend on the individual characteristics of the offender, but on the type of the offense, the nature and severity of the sentence, and the date of the judgment. The legislature is subject to no limits when determining the acts to which amnesty applies, and in the case of political offenses, these can be serious crimes. Amnesties apply not only to criminal convictions, but to professional malpractice and disciplinary sanctions. Recent practice reveals confusion between the two types of measures, because both are used in a category-specific way. Amnesty has to some degree lost its solemn and political character, while pardon, having become a collective measure, has lost its individual and exceptional character, though their legal effects remain distinct.[37]

By contrast, the Russian president retains a broader clemency power than France, though the legislature, like France's, may additionally exercise the traditional continental European amnesty power. In Russia, a country with a long history of autocratic rule, the presidential pardon power in the 1993 Constitution provides full and unlimited pardon power to the

36 *Id.* at 552–554.
37 *Id.* at 559–561.

president.[38] Since 1992 a 15-member Presidential Pardon Commission composed of prominent artists, writers, and citizens, reviews and submits recommendations to the president. Prior to the abolition of the death penalty in Russia after its entry into the Council of Europe in 1996, much of the Commission's work dealt with commutation of death sentences.[39] The Russian constitution also contains a novel feature in which the lower house of parliament, the State Duma, has the power to grant legislative amnesties without being subject to a presidential veto. Since 1994, the Duma has granted several highly controversial amnesties, including to former Chechen rebels and political leaders, insurrectionists of the 1993 uprisings, and deserters from the Russian army. The Duma has also granted full or partial amnesties for thousands of prisoners in squalid Russian prisons.[40] Although the presidential pardon power in Russia is unlimited, so is the Duma's amnesty power, allowing the legislature its own unchecked version of justice.

Twentieth century Germany had a long history of mass amnesties, though these were comparatively rare during imperial times except in the form of sovereign mercy to commemorate important occasions, such as a royal wedding or jubilee. During World War I, however, mass amnesties helped reduce acute labor shortages, though even these were insignificant to the postwar amnesties of 1918 and successive years, which were deeply destabilizing to the Weimar Republic and ended only with the rise of Adolf Hitler.[41] Soviet occupation and subsequent communist rule in the German Democratic Republic (East Germany) revived the use of amnesty as a policy instrument, including a large amnesty of 20,000 prisoners in 1951, intended to resolve labor shortages and stem the brain drain of skilled workers. In addition to several smaller amnesties, another mass amnesty in 1972 resulted in the release of more than 25,000 convicts and the release of another 6,000 prisoners from pre-trial confinement, nearly half the total number of prisoners and detainees in the East German prison system. In 1979, on the German Democratic Republic's thirtieth anniversary, 21,928 criminals were freed, as were another 1,272 criminals who had been convicted but not yet sentenced; another 31,000 non-custodial sentences were cancelled. The primary motivation for such large amnesties was likely to reduce chronic prison overcrowding, but the amnesties also served primary socialist goals such as showing the power and paternalism of the State.[42] For its part, the Federal Republic of Germany (West Germany) had

38 Russia Const. art. 89(c) (executive pardon power); art. 103(g) (legislative amnesty power) (1993).

39 Jody C. Baumgartner and Mark H. Morris, *Presidential Power Unbound: A Comparative Look at Presidential Pardon Power*, 29 Politics & Pol'y 209, 220–21 (2001).

40 *Id.* at 224–25.

41 John C. Palenberg, *Mass Amnesty: The East German Answer to Prison Overcrowding*, 11 Am. J. Crim. L. 369, 369–71 (1983).

42 *Id.* at 372–82.

a fragmented pardon power, exercised by the federal president and the prime ministers of the eight West German states, as well as the senate in the city-states of Bremen and Hamburg and the state government in Saarland. Here, the use of clemency served a different purpose than in the German Democratic Republic. Prior to the development of modern parole procedures, pardons were the only procedure for reducing a life sentence and were granted regularly.[43]

As in the common law world, the trend in civil law countries has been to limit the unchecked or unguided power of the executive to override final decisions of courts of law. The constitution of Austria empowers the president to grant partial pardons in extraordinary cases, limited to commuting the penalty, modifying other legal consequences, cancelling previous convictions, or withdrawing charges before a final judgment.[44] In Finland, the president only may grant a pardon when the conviction was justified, as this leaves the record intact and does not cancel it; where a conviction was wrongful and an offender was innocent of the crime, the remedy is to seek a rescindment of the conviction in court.[45] Unlike Great Britain or other European monarchies, the King of Sweden does not have a pardon prerogative. Rather, this power is given to the elected government through the Chancellor of Justice, who may pardon or reduce criminal sanctions or other legal consequences of an offense (though not absolve guilt) once the Supreme Court has pronounced on a case.[46]

In a detailed study of Serbia, Dušica Miladinović explains that the pardon power dates back to the Middle Ages, though it was restricted to criminal sanctions for a person convicted of a crime. Removing a criminal from the scope of investigation and prosecution required a legislative body in the form of an amnesty, as it necessitated an exception from prevailing law, though Miladinović acknowledges that the two concepts have overlapped in many European continental countries over time. In the 2005 Serbian criminal code, the distinct legal concepts of pardon and amnesty are virtually synonymous, recalling the situation in the Kingdom of Yugoslavia when the monarch could exercise both amnesty and pardon powers.[47] As in the common law world, the comparative pardon and amnesty power in the civil law tradition is pockmarked with exceptions. The constitution of Norway allows a person to refuse an individual pardon unless he or she is a juvenile, while Argentina excludes pardons for persons who commit acts against the constitutional order or the democratic regime. Turkey's pardon

43 K.C. Horton, *Life Imprisonment and Pardons in the German Federal Republic*, 29 Int'l & Comp. L.Q. 530, 531 (1980).

44 Rolph, *supra* note 13 at 71.

45 *Id.* at 71–72.

46 *Id.* at 72.

47 Dušica Miladinović, *An Overview of the Concept of Pardon in the Serbian Criminal Legislation*, 5 Facta Universitatis: L. & Pol. 47, 47–49 (2007).

power may not be used for crimes of forest destruction or burning, and the King of Belgium cannot pardon criminal sentences of government ministers or other government officials.[48]

In the developing world, especially in emerging democracies and socialist states, the existence of a broad clemency power may reinforce an authoritarian or state-centric power structure, one in which political considerations play a role. In Taiwan, once a death sentence is judicially confirmed, only the president can release a person from death row by exercising the amnesty power, which can include general or individual pardons under Article 40 of the constitution of Taiwan. As elsewhere, general or mass amnesties have been carried out to commemorate historic events such as the anniversary of the founding of the republic, reducing a number of death sentences to life imprisonment.[49] However, Taiwanese law still does not guarantee the right to seek pardon or commutation of sentence even though Taiwan has adopted as constitutional principles the provisions of the International Covenant on Civil and Political Rights (ICCPR).[50] None of the three presidents between 1986 and 2008 ever granted an individual amnesty or pardon.[51] Like Taiwan, the People's Republic of China lacks a special amnesty or clemency procedure for death penalty cases outside of the ordinary judicial appeals process, as required by Article 6(4) of the ICCPR. Some observers have suggested that such a modified clemency procedure be delegated to an organ other than the Supreme Peoples' Court, the highest judicial tribunal, such as the Standing Committee of the National Peoples' Congress, the central legislative organ, or to a special pardons or clemency board.[52]

Japan, with a hybrid legal tradition, has a clemency authority that possesses unusual characteristics. Article 73 of the constitution of Japan states that the cabinet shall decide on "general amnesty, special amnesty, commutation of punishment, reprieve, and restoration of rights."[53] The Pardon Act provides that the National Offenders Rehabilitation Commission make recommendations as to individual pardons and remissions of sentence, while the implementing ordinance has established procedures for allowing the warden of a penal institution to petition the commission on

48 Dascălu, *supra* note 29 at 5.

49 Fort Fu-Te Liao, *Why Taiwan's* De Facto *Moratorium Was Established And Lost, in* Capital Punishment: A Hazard to a Sustainable Criminal Justice System 175, 190–1 (Lill Scherdin ed., 2014).

50 Nigel Li, Wei-Jen Chen and Jeffrey Li, *Taiwan: Cutting the Gordian Knot – Applying Article 16 of the ICCPR to End Capital Punishment, in* Capital Punishment: New Perspectives 209, 223 (Peter Hodgkinson ed., 2013).

51 Liao, *supra* note 49 at 190–91.

52 Liu Renwen, *Recent Reforms and Prospects in China, in* Confronting Capital Punishment in Asia: Human Rights, Politics, and Public Opinion 107, 118–20 (Roger Hood and Surya Deva eds., 2013).

53 Japan Const. art. 73 (1947).

behalf of an incarcerated prisoner.[54] As a consequence, incarcerated persons in Japan cannot apply directly to the commission for amnesty or pardon; they must do so through an intermediary. No death sentence has been commuted in Japan since June 1975.[55] Like Japan, Israel is another hybrid legal tradition, possessing characteristics of both common and civil law traditions. This is reflected in the mercy power. In Israel, the Amnesty ("General Pardon") Ordinance was enacted in February 1949, as one of the last acts of the Provisional Council prior to its dispersal and replacement by the first Knesset. Under the British mandate, the power conferred upon the High Commissioner included the power to grant pardons on the basis of the 1918–1922 Order in Council, which served as Mandatory Palestine's constitutional framework during the colonial period. The High Commissioner had the ability to issue full and conditional pardons; remission of sentences, fines, and forfeitures; respites from punishment; and pardons of unconvicted accomplices, a delegation of the British Crown's powers that could in theory still be exercised from Westminster. In addition to the legislative amnesty power established in 1949, the Israeli President still retains the power to pardon, as clarified in an amendment to the Israeli Basic Law in 1964.[56] Under Israel's current Basic Law, the pardon power is the only specific, practical power that the president has. The routine involvement of the minister of justice in the pardoning process has evolved into a process whereby all pleas for pardon or clemency are forwarded directly to the minister, who then submits the petition along with his recommendation to the president.[57]

Many civil law countries, like their common law counterparts, have wrestled with the question of whether the clemency power lends itself to judicial review and in particular whether it is constrained by constitutional principles. In 2008, the Constitutional Court of Portugal determined that a general pardon passed by the legislature, conditional upon the payment of a civil penalty, did not breach the equality provision of the constitution

54 Saul Lehrfreund, *The Impact and Importance of International Human Rights Standards: Asia in World Perspective*, *in* Confronting Capital Punishment in Asia: Human Rights, Politics, and Public Opinion 23, 44 (Roger Hood and Surya Deva eds., 2013).

55 *Id.*

56 Sebba, *Pardon and Amnesty*, *supra* note 16 at iv-vi. Sebba notes that in Israel, although the prerogative of the pardon belongs to the President alone, a minister (typically the minister of justice) countersigns the pardon documents so that the minister is answerable to the legislature and the public. This is an odd procedure, and subjects the minister to accountability for an act over which he or she has no control. The President's pardon power is exclusive; this is so even if the legislature passes a law directing the President to issue a pardon. *Id.* at viii-ix.

57 Leon Sheleff, *Pardoning Policy: Key Constitutional Implications and Some Theoretical Considerations*, 33 Isr. L.Rev. 638, 640 (1999). Sheleff also notes that the minister of justice and the president must be in agreement for a pardon to be given, and as the two staffs work closely, they almost always are. In the event of a disagreement, the president would likely need to seek another minister to provide the counter-signature. *Id.* at 640–41.

when an indigent defendant was unable to pay. According to the Constitutional Court, the general pardon was imposed in an abstract manner and treated all persons sentenced to prison for the same crime in a similar way. Because the general pardon cancelled the punishment for the offense but did not negate the criminal unlawfulness itself, the decision to require payment of civil compensation to an injured party was a rational one. One judge voted against the ruling due to the lack of a safeguard for those who could not pay, finding that the legislation violated the equality provision because it treated dissimilar situations the same way (that is, in treating pecunious and impecunious defendants alike).[58]

Clemency also existed in non-Western legal traditions. Among the Kuba people of modern-day Democratic Republic of the Congo, a supreme council could impose the death sentence for murder, but the king could exercise his royal rights in granting mercy as only he could ultimately take a human life. He was not directly involved in the judicial process.[59] Similarly, among the Banyarwanda and Barundi of the Great Lakes region of Africa, the *Mwami* (king) could exercise his right of mercy and overturn a death sentence for murder by commuting it to compensation. The *Mwami* exercised this power to prevent blood feuds between the victim's clan and the perpetrator's clan.[60] Mercy has a long tradition in Islamic law, grounded in the divine mandate God gave to the Prophet Mohammed and Muslims in their primary duty, the pursuit of justice. The Qur'an recognizes and extols the acts of pardon and amnesty in several verses (2:178, 3:134, 5:45).[61] In Iran, mercy as a legal device exists as part of a retributive system of justice, as it is the victim's family who must grant the pardon.[62] The practice of the Prophet was to encourage forgiveness and repent for offenders; in Islam, clemency is the superior option.[63]

As in the common law world, European mechanisms for clemency – like other political constructs and institutions – were broadly received into postcolonial legal orders. In the colonies as in the metropole mercy was not consistently applied, waxing and waning as political circumstances changed. Although the death penalty virtually died out in French West Africa after World War II, clemency was rare in French Algeria even when death sentences were frequently imposed for minor crimes. Of 272 requests for mercy in 1960, 200 were granted – an extraordinarily high number for the region – and similar patterns continued in 1961 and 1962.[64] In the

58 Generic Pardon of Sentences, Ruling No. 488/08, [2008] PTCC 10 (Oct. 7, 2008).

59 Aimé Muyoboke Karimunda, The Death Penalty in Africa: The Path Towards Abolition 21 (2014).

60 *Id.* at 22.

61 Arzoo Osanloo, *The Measure of Mercy: Islamic Justice, Sovereign Power, and Human Rights in Iran*, 21 Cultural Anthropology 570, 584 (2006).

62 *Id.* at 588.

63 Abu Zayd, The Face of Mercy in Islamic Law 5 (2005).

64 Karimunda, *supra* note 59 at 121.

Belgian Congo, offenders enjoyed automatic appeal in all capital cases and the right to request mercy from the king of Belgium. Despite a more extensive use of the royal prerogative to grant mercy than in Algeria, Belgian colonial judges still were visibly reluctant to pass death sentences.[65] The post-independence period of authoritarian rule and weak democratic institutions, however, was not kind to this tradition of mercy. In independent Zaire, for instance, the system for pleading mercy was especially troubling. Although the condemned was entitled to be considered for mercy, he or she did not have the right to petition for it; rather, the prosecutor was required to introduce such a plea to the head of state for all death sentences, creating an obvious conflict of interest. The incoherence of this system led Mobutu to keep inmates on death row for decades.[66]

The organization of this book

This book will compare the modern development, organization, and practice of constitutional and statutory schemes of clemency and pardon throughout the common law world. Chapter 2 traces the development of the royal prerogative of mercy from early modern England to the present, including its diffusion to the former Empire and its inclusion in postcolonial legal orders. During the colonial period, the monarch delegated the prerogative of mercy to colonial governors, subject to the oversight of the Colonial Office, and at independence this mercy power became a constitutional power delegated to the new heads of state. Similarly, the origins of the pardon power in the United States federal and state constitutions derives from the King's prerogative of mercy at common law.

Chapter 3 turns to the constraints international law poses on the exercise of the clemency and pardon power, including the requirement for a clemency process in all death penalty cases and an emerging international trend to discourage amnesty and pardons for systemic human rights violations. In treaties, state practice, and the jurisprudence of international courts and tribunals, the international legal order requires certain minimum procedural guarantees in clemency processes. This chapter also explores the pardon power as exercised by international criminal tribunals.

Chapter 4 compares constitutional frameworks for the mercy power, including requirements, if any, for consultation with the cabinet, a board or committee, or another minister, as well as federalism structures and provisions specific to the death penalty. Some jurisdictions also have novel features such as automatic pardons or a prohibition on pardons by lame-duck or transitional executives.

65 *Id.* at 124, 127.
66 *Id.* at 154.

Chapter 5 is on the scope of the pardon power, including constitutional exclusions or limitations on the exercise of clemency in specific cases such as self-pardons, posthumous pardons, pardons for impeachment or treason, pardons for corruption and Islamic law offenses, and others. Some of these exclusions from the pardon power are specific to local constitutional contexts, but a number are drawn from British conventions in the exercise of the pardon power, such as the limitation on pardoning prior to conviction.

Chapter 6 is on comparative structures of mercy committees or boards, including whether a committee is purely advisory or whether its decisions are binding, as well as the makeup of such committees and the terms and conditions of appointment. The membership of such committees may be determinative of the ultimate grant or denial of clemency, particularly the degree to which they are independent or political patronage positions. A board overly aligned with law enforcement or the prosecution, for instance, behaves quite differently than a board of experts or *ex officio* officeholders.

Chapter 7 is on comparative mercy procedure, from the application process through to the ultimate decision by the executive. This chapter explores the two general "models" of the clemency process: the committee structure, emphasized in Chapter 6, and the bureaucratic structure in use in, among others, the United Kingdom, United States, and India. In these countries, the clemency application process is an institutional one, subject to the benefits and constraints of an administrative agency. Where the executive is the ultimate decision-maker, however, the actual grant or denial of clemency remains a deeply personal decision, one that resists guidance and transparency.

Chapter 8 turns to the traditional conception of the prerogative of mercy as unreviewable by courts. As the clemency power is subordinated to principles of administrative law and procedure, the process for granting clemency is becoming increasingly rule-bound. This chapter assesses the grounds on and the extent to which a judge may inquire into the clemency decision. In addition, provisions for legislative pardons and amnesties and efforts by legislative bodies to impose criteria or guidelines on the exercise of executive clemency are explored.

Finally, Chapter 9 explores the future of clemency, especially as it declines due to the development of modern parole mechanisms and the general demise of capital punishment. The chapter will additionally consider the role of victims in the clemency process in the context of the restorative justice movement.

2 The origins of the common law prerogative of mercy

The royal prerogative is the residue of royal power that derives from the ancient rights, privileges, and powers of the Sovereign, including the prerogatives of mercy and conferment of national honors, political prerogatives such as declaring war and peace, and financial prerogatives such as reclaiming and disposing of unowned property. Each of these powers has, over time, become limited by convention and later defined by regulation, and the traditional royal powers are primarily exercised by ministers responsible to Parliament rather than the sovereign personally.[1] As a prerogative power, the mercy power descends from the traditional royal powers exercised by British monarchs since the early modern period. In the United Kingdom and Commonwealth countries that recognize the Crown as the head of state, executive authority derives from the Crown, though the Crown is typically subordinate to the political executive.[2] In those countries where the Crown is no longer the head of state, the mercy power is typically constitutionalized as a power of the republican executive or the local monarch. Though the common law mercy power descends from a single source – the King's prerogative of mercy – today, the conceptual definition and practical realities of executive clemency are not uniform throughout the English-speaking world. Like in the United Kingdom, however, in most former colonies including Australia, Canada, South Africa, and the United States, executive clemency is today governed by principles of administrative law rather than existing solely as an executive's "act of grace."

The origins of the royal prerogative of mercy

Sir William Blackstone traced the royal prerogative of mercy to the laws of Edward the Confessor (1042–66), noting that the power derived from the sovereign's "pure grace" to pardon an offender by mitigating or removing

1 Noel Cox, *The Gradual Curtailment of the Royal Prerogative*, 25 Denning L.J. 1, 1–2 (2012).

2 *Id.* at 1.

the consequences of conviction.[3] Others have gone back further, suggesting that the pardon power has Teutonic origins, or at least to the kings of Wessex in the 600s to 800s C.E.[4] The prerogative of mercy was extended to supplicants in the form of letters patent of pardon, authorized by the monarch or his chancellor, to whom administrative authority over pardons was delegated and who issued pardons from the royal chancery. Monarchs delegated the mercy power to other judicial or political actors by the fourteenth century, but they still personally intervened in the mercy decision from time to time.[5] The prerogative of mercy was wide-ranging: at any point in the legal process, the King could pardon any charges brought in his name. Historians and legal theorists have often dismissed the royal pardon as an example of corruption and nepotism endemic in the medieval courts of justice, a personal discretionary judgment in an otherwise law-based system.[6] Despite the fact that the Magna Carta of 1215 forbade sales of justice, pardons were a dependable source of income for the church and the state, and monarchs could and did accept money for pardons.[7]

Kings attempted to claim for the Crown itself the power to punish in life or limb, but the Anglo-Saxon practice by which perpetrators paid compensation to victims of homicide (*wergild*) persisted for some centuries even after the Norman conquest in 1066 in order to prevent vigilante revenge killings. Kings recognized the wisdom of tempering the increasingly harsh sanctions of a centralizing legal system with the possibility of mitigation. The monarch's attempts to strengthen criminal punishments and the system of courts in lieu of private resolution of justice encouraged extension of the mercy power.[8] Since pardoning homicide was a royal prerogative, no hard and fast rules governed how it was sought and bestowed. Supplicants used various methods to bring cases to the King's attention, though formalities increased by the thirteenth century. Outlaws or fugitives from justice typically required an intermediary to seek a pardon from the King, though recommendations for clemency could also come from judges. A recipient would be required to plead the pardon in court in the event of a subsequent prosecution, and therefore needed a copy. The process of obtaining a pardon involved payment of fees to the chancery in the days before the chancellor earned a salary, though the fees could be reduced for those without means; nonetheless, the cost involved "was a grave defect in the

3 David Caruso and Nicholas Crawford, *The Executive Institution of Mercy in Australia: The Case and Model for Reform*, 37 U.N.S.W. L.J. 312, 314 (2014).
4 Stanley Grupp, *Some Historical Aspects of the Pardon Power in England*, 7 Am. J. Legal Hist. 51, 52–53 (1963).
5 Helen Lacey, Royal Pardon: Access to Mercy in Fourteenth-Century England 1–2 (2009).
6 *Id.*
7 Kathleen Dean Moore, Pardons: Justice, Mercy, and the Public Interest 18–19 (1989).
8 Naomi D. Hurnard, The King's Pardon for Homicide Before A.D. 1307 at 23, 2–3, 11–13 (1969).

system and meant that many people who fully deserved pardon were unable to take advantage of it."[9]

As Saxon warlords became English kings, they possessed growing authority over secular and religious matters, though it was not until Norman times that the King used the maintenance of law and order (including through his prerogative powers) to extend royal power.[10] The King's use (or misuse) of the royal prerogative powers was an important antecedent to the establishment of parliamentary supremacy and the development of a constitutional tradition of limited royal powers in Great Britain. Abuses of the prerogative powers by Charles I fuelled the grievances that led to the English Civil War. While Charles II's coronation in 1660 temporarily revived the broad prerogative powers of the monarchy, the Glorious Revolution of 1688, resulting in the exile of Charles's successor James II, entrenched parliamentary supremacy over the Crown. Although the prerogative powers still existed, Parliament began to curtail them.[11] By the seventeenth century, the conditional pardon was used to ease the chronic labor shortage in the colonies, and reprieved offenders were sometimes offered pardons on the condition that they agreed to go to the New World (and later Australia and New Zealand) and work on plantations for a term of years.[12]

The prerogative of mercy descends from a paradox of the common law: the law provides for strict personal liability for broadly-defined offenses, yet officials needed to accommodate human frailty and criminal deviance in order to maintain the public's respect for the law.[13] From the very inception of the English legal system, a widespread societal attitude toward liability for homicide failed to completely align with the rules of the law, distinguishing stealth from sudden homicide and acquitting self-defense.[14] The majority of people who received pardons in the Middle Ages did not petition for one directly; in most instances, the trial judge recommended the prisoner for mercy. As in earlier times, no single procedure for obtaining a pardon existed as the decision was solely a matter of royal grace. Recommendations for mercy by the trial judge to the King's chancellor were highly influential and often approved as a matter of course upon payment of a fee.[15] Although this accounted for a majority of pardons, grants of

9 *Id.* at 31–35, 45–46, 55, 58, 60, 65–66 (1969).

10 David Feldman, *The King's Peace, the Royal Prerogative and Public Order: The Roots and Development of Early Binding Over Powers*, 47 CAMBRIDGE L.J. 101, 107 (1988).

11 Philippe Lagassé, *Parliamentary and Judicial Ambivalence Toward Executive Prerogative Powers in Canada*, 55 CAN. PUB. ADMIN. 157, 160 (2012).

12 Moore, *supra* note 7 at 19.

13 George Roger Chadwick, *Bureaucratic Mercy: The Home Office and the Treatment of Capital Cases in Victorian England*, Ph.D. Dissertation, Rice University 3–4 (1989).

14 Thomas A. Green, *Review of* The King's Pardon for Homicide to A.D. 1307 *By N.D. Hurnard*, 47 SPECULUM 774, 776 (1972).

15 Lacey, *supra* note 5 at 21.

clemency could also be awarded based on petitions from individuals, often those who were awaiting trial or facing prosecution. More commonly a patron intervened on a prisoner's behalf. Several members of the royal family or servants of the Crown were particularly active in securing grants of mercy; the intercession of an influential person increased the odds of a pardon.[16] Petitions for mercy were most effective from men of means. A plea for mercy was frequently passed upward through increasingly higher levels of the social scale among men bound by patronage and obligation, such as by gentlemen on behalf of their laborers.[17] In this way, the pardon process reinforced class divisions and concessions to special interests. However, the most common grounds for pardon – for youth, elders, the infirm, the potentially reformable, the poor, the potentially innocent – conformed to broader social norms and were not necessarily indicative of political patronage or class privilege.[18]

Because of the frequency with which mercy was used, the royal pardon gave rise to certain customs in which the monarch intervened as a matter of course after conviction in order to grant a reprieve, a kind of common "law" of pardons. If a convict were a pregnant woman, for example, execution would not be carried out until after the birth of a child, and the mother might be pardoned altogether. Botched or failed executions in which a prisoner survived an initial execution attempt could trigger a reprieve. More esoteric was the custom in which the King would pardon a person about to be executed if he happened to be passing by and "looked upon" the condemned man. Monarchs often issued pardons on Good Friday or other important holidays, and royal pardons could be issued in public ceremonies in order to display the sovereign's benevolence.[19] Pardons were instances of public ritual and performance that showcased the power of the state and the grace of the sovereign. As Hay wrote, the prerogative of mercy allowed the class that passed one of the bloodiest penal codes in European history to congratulate itself on its humanity.[20]

General pardons and group pardons, such as political amnesties, military service pardons, and remissions of debt, were initiatives taken by the Crown itself, often on the advice of Parliament, rather than on the petition of an individual intercessor to a judge or cabinet minister. Some of these pardons were issued in response to acts of defiance, while others were designed to bolster the ranks of the royal army as when King Edward I invited any man charged with a felony to volunteer for paid service in Gascony in 1294. By

16 *Id.* at 27, 44–45.

17 Douglas Hay, *Property, Authority and the Criminal Law*, *in* ALBION'S FATAL TREE: CRIME AND SOCIETY IN EIGHTEENTH-CENTURY ENGLAND 17, 45 (Douglas Hay *et al.* eds., 1977).

18 Peter King, CRIME, JUSTICE, AND DISCRETION IN ENGLAND, 1740–1820, 322 (2000).

19 Lacey, *supra* note 5 at 69–73.

20 Hay, *supra* note 17 at 48.

the fourteenth century, the anachronistic practice of levying feudal dues led to group pardons for remissions of debt. General pardons, unlike group pardons, were comprehensive amnesties passed after governmental crises, often made available to any individual who wished to purchase a copy, though typically treason, murder, rape, and theft were excluded.[21] Kings gave group and general pardons to curry favor, reduce tensions among competing factions, and even to punish or manipulate opponents through selective grants of mercy, as Richard II notoriously did in the 1390s.[22]

In the seventeenth and eighteenth centuries, Britain transformed from a rural-based society to an urban-based one in which high crime rates and the proximity of rich to poor created pressure for harsh criminal punishments. The Bloody Code expanded the mandatory death penalty to more than 300 crimes, though in practice the number of capital convictions and executions did not increase as the number of capital offenses did.[23] Capital punishment and punishments of the body reached their zenith in England during the 1700s upon the decline of transportation to a penal colony as a criminal sanction and immediately prior to the ascendancy of incarceration.[24] The mandatory nature of the death penalty was by far the most important contributor to the high rate of clemency and pardon in early modern England. Because a trial judge did not have discretion to substitute a lesser sentence, executive mercy was the only mechanism that allowed for consideration of mitigating factors in individual cases.[25] A harsh penal system with a prominent place for executive clemency was perhaps the "least bad solution" under the circumstances and lasted several centuries, but it was a system that no one – neither hard liners nor reformers – supported.[26]

The reign of King Henry VIII (1509–47) helped crystallize the pardon power exclusively as a monarchical prerogative. The Jurisdiction in Liberties Act was passed in 1535 to ensure that no pardon could be given by any person other than the monarch, preserving the prerogative right as

21 Lacey, *supra* note 5 at 85–89. Many of these general pardons were purchased as precautions; records appear to show that they were only rarely presented in court. *Id.* at 91.

22 *Id.* at 127, 160. *See also* Grupp, *supra* note 4 at 59 (noting that Richard II granted pardons upon large sums of money and then held possible revocation over the recipients in order to extort more money). Grupp states that while Richard II was the most notorious, he was not alone: the purchase of a pardon was common practice in pre-modern times. *Id.*

23 David Plater and Sue Milne, *The Capital Case of Sarah McGregor and Mary Maloney in New South Wales in 1834: 'Justice Is Due Even to Them'*, Paper Presented to the Legal Histories of the British Empire Conference 7 (July 2012).

24 J.M. Beattie, Policing and Punishment in London, 1660–1750, 362–3 (2001).

25 Andrew Novak, The Global Decline of the Mandatory Death Penalty: Constitutional Jurisprudence and Legislative Reform in Africa, Asia, and the Caribbean 5 (2014).

26 Barry Mitchell and Julian V. Roberts, Exploring the Mandatory Life Sentence for Murder 26 (2012).

a manifestation of royal power.[27] Prior to 1535, the prerogative of mercy had many contenders: the Church, the great earls, and the feudal lords to name a few, in part because there was no national legal system and because the distinction between crimes and torts was not yet clearly demarcated. Early monarchs generally exercised the prerogative of mercy only to those offenses that threatened their authority and royal power.[28] The reign of Elizabeth I (reigned 1558–1603) saw even more intense battles over the power of the pardon, not only because a woman was on the throne but also because of the continuing centralization of legal power in the hands of the monarchy. She nonetheless was seen as, and cultivated the image of herself as, merciful – though perhaps her infamous treatment of Mary, Queen of Scots was anything but. "Given that women's supposedly merciful dispositions could be regarded as a sign of feminine weakness, it is somewhat surprising that depictions of Queen Elizabeth as a loving and merciful monarch abound during her reign," suggested by the medieval adage "if the king is law, the queen is mercy."[29]

This conception of the royal prerogative dominated for the next 300 years, despite parliamentary efforts to curtail this power for certain cases, including for treason and impeachment. In 1721, the King allowed Parliament itself to exercise the pardon power.[30] By the next century, Henry VIII's broad conception of the prerogative of mercy eventually yielded to the rise of the complex bureaucratic state. In 1837, when Queen Victoria ascended the throne, Parliament delegated the mercy prerogative to the Home Secretary, who was to exercise the power in the monarch's name, believing that Queen Victoria was too young and of the wrong gender to properly preside over a "hanging cabinet." The modern bureaucratization of the mercy power in Great Britain descends from this decision. Generally speaking, monarchs have not interfered with this delegation of the prerogative right, though several occasionally discussed death sentences in audiences with the Home Secretary.[31] A pardon, to be effective at common law, had to be granted under the Great Seal of the Realm, a wax seal attached to official documents that required authorization of the monarch. A recipient of a pardon had to plead the pardon at the appropriate stage of a legal proceeding or he or she could be held to have waived the pardon.[32]

27 C.H. Rolph, The Queen's Pardon 19–20 (1978).
28 Grupp, *supra* note 4 at 55.
29 Mary Villeponteaux, The Queen's Mercy: Gender and Judgment in Representations of Elizabeth I 9–10 (2014).
30 Grupp, *supra* note 4 at 57–58.
31 A.T.H. Smith, *The Prerogative of Mercy, The Power of Pardon and Criminal Justice*, 1983 Pub.L. 398, 426.
32 Peter Brett, *Conditional Pardons and the Commutation of Death Sentences*, 20 Mod. L. Rev. 131, 132 (1957).

After 1967, the Queen's handwritten signature (known as the royal sign-manual) on a pardon was required to be countersigned by a secretary of state, by convention the Home Secretary in England or the Secretaries of State for Scotland or Northern Ireland in those jurisdictions. These conventions are not sacrosanct: in at least one prominent espionage case, the Foreign Secretary accepted responsibility for a grant of clemency in lieu of the Home Secretary.[33]

In addition to the flexibility it offered in criminal sentencing, the clemency power also remained an important part of the nineteenth century justice system because England still lacked a modern system of criminal appeals to right legal error. The prerogative of mercy served as the primary means of righting jury errors in extreme cases even until the establishment of the English Court of Criminal Appeal in 1907.[34] Judges and civil servants engaged in the confidential exchange of opinion in making ad hoc and case-specific decisions, but slowly built up a body of "precedential" rules to determine when clemency should be granted.[35] The clemency process, outside of public view, reinforced the social divisions of the time period. Women were less likely than men to be executed in seventeenth and eighteen century England, but criminal proceedings made assumptions about female character, portraying women as either depraved or irredeemable on the one hand or victims of emotion on the other. Only about one-quarter of women were executed from 1660 to 1800, compared to 43 percent of men.[36] While women tended to be punished less harshly in the overall criminal justice system, women were also more likely to carry out certain gendered crimes, such as infanticide or concealment of birth. Petit treason, in which a woman killed her husband in a betrayal of trust, was rarely reprieved and treated more harshly than murder because it challenged patriarchal social norms.[37]

Because the death penalty was still mandatory in Britain and most colonies even by the time the Royal Commission on Capital Punishment was first created in 1949, the only way of confining hanging to the worst murders was through exercise of the royal prerogative of mercy. In the first half of the twentieth century, half of those sentenced to death were reprieved. As Turrell notes, the Royal Commission profoundly understood that not all murders were equally heinous and deserving of death, but the members were nonetheless skeptical of the primary alternative to this

33 Smith, *supra* note 31 at 426–27.
34 Caruso and Crawford, *supra* note 3 at 315.
35 *Id.*
36 John Beattie, CRIME AND THE COURTS IN ENGLAND, 1660–1800, 404 (1986).
37 Plater and Milne, *supra* note 23 at 8–9.

system, which was to adopt an American-style distinction between first- and second-degree murder.[38] The Commission believed that premeditation did not necessarily divide the worst of the worst murders from the rest, as even a sudden and unplanned killing could be the expression of an "incorrigibly vicious nature," while a deliberate murder could be excusable.[39]

Exercise of the royal prerogative of mercy waxed and waned in its consistency. Extensive scholarship on mercy petitions to the King and colonial governors have identified some rough parameters. "A tension between discretion and consistency runs through any study of mercy," Turrell writes, adding that even as the Home Office became more bureaucratic and rational in its assessment of mercy, it continued to claim a free hand in the mercy decision.[40] The Home Office may in practice have distinguished between two degrees of murder in granting mercy, even if no such provision existed in law, by generally restricting the death penalty to murders that contained elements of deliberation and planning.[41] Mercy decisions may also have been made through an assessment of the social and moral circumstances of a murder, but not one governed by fixed rules or forms of procedure. Numerous considerations factored into the process, including motive, degree of premeditation, amount of provocation, state of mind, offender's character, or a recommendation from a judge or jury. The ultimate decision was closely tied to the circumstances of the case.[42] In time, an archive of rules and precedents made it possible to decide mercy petitions very quickly, including reprieves for juveniles, new mothers guilty of infanticide or abortion, survivors of suicide pacts, and persons who were insane or suffering from mental illness. Cases of provocation and intoxication were circumstantial, but so long as the case did not involve revenge or deliberation, the Home Secretary was apt to respond leniently.[43]

Scholarship from the colonies in particular has suggested that the mercy process was potentially more arbitrary and unguided than this, subject to even to discriminatory considerations. Carolyn Strange, in her comparison of executive mercy in Ontario, Canada, and New South Wales, Australia,

38 Rob Turrell, *"It's A Mystery": The Royal Prerogative of Mercy in England, Canada, and South Africa*, 4 CRIME, HIST. & SOCIETIES 83, 85 (2000) (hereinafter, Turrell, *"It's a Mystery"*).

39 *Id.* at 85–6, *citing* Ernest Gowers, A LIFE FOR A LIFE? THE PROBLEM OF CAPITAL PUNISHMENT 37 (1956). Gowers was the chairman of the Royal Commission on Capital Punishment.

40 Robert Turrell, WHITE MERCY: A STUDY OF THE DEATH PENALTY IN SOUTH AFRICA 15–16 (2004) (hereinafter, Turrell, WHITE MERCY).

41 Turrell, *supra* note 38 at 86–87, *citing* Leon Radzinowicz and Roger Hood, 5 A HISTORY OF ENGLISH CRIMINAL LAW AND ITS ADMINISTRATION FROM 1750: THE EMERGENCE OF PENAL POLICY 677–681 (1986).

42 Turrell, *supra* note 38 at 87, *citing* Chadwick, *supra* note 13 at 386–87.

43 As explained in Turrell, *supra* note 38 at 87–8, *citing* Edward Troup, THE HOME OFFICE 55–71 (1925).

writes that "political, cultural, legal, and historical factors modulated capital case outcomes, rendering discretionary justice volatile, partial, and inevitably contingent."[44] In commuting sentences, politicians suggested that only those who *really* deserved the death penalty would actually be executed, insisting that they weighed all possible factors, reviewing each case in its own right, and considering every potential mitigating factor. Executives "tried to justify a secret, highly discretionary process of case disposition as fair," free from the passions and prejudices of the courtroom.[45] Her research documents how racial, gender, and class hierarchies influenced the clemency decision. Women killers were transformed into pitiful creatures worthy of mercy, while new immigrants to Canada tended to have their sentences commuted at a higher rate than the general population for paternalistic reasons. In Australia, whites were spared most frequently, while foreign men and aboriginal Australians fared worse.[46] The discretionary nature of mercy made it simultaneously a necessary pressure valve in an overly formalistic system and a tool of arbitrary or discriminatory application.

The prerogative of mercy in the colonies

Although the sovereign once had a comparatively free hand to act according to the royal prerogatives, these powers became limited by legal conventions, that is, rules of political practice regarded as binding but not enforceable in court. In the colonial period, letters patent delegated the prerogative of mercy throughout the Empire, where colonial governors then carried out their own mercy decisions with only rare intervention from Whitehall.[47] More recently, principles of administrative law govern clemency decisions. This trend is not limited to the United Kingdom: in many Commonwealth realms the modern tendency is toward replacing royal prerogative powers with statutory authority.[48] In the colonial period, the administration of justice in far flung corners of the British Empire faced enormous pressures not present in the metropolis: large and latently-hostile populations, dizzying cultural and linguistic diversity, durable local traditions

44 Carolyn Strange, *Political Culture and the Death Penalty in New South Wales and Ontario, 1890–1920, in* Qualities of Mercy: Justice, Punishment and Discretion 130, 161 (Carolyn Strange, ed., 1996).

45 *Id.* at 160.

46 *Id.* at 142–43.

47 Caruso and Crawford, *supra* note 3 at 314.

48 Noel Cox, *The Importance of the Royal Prerogative in Contemporary Governance*, 18(3) Commonw. Law. 25, 25–35 (2009).

of authority and punishment, and only a skeletal colonial state.[49] Consequently, execution rates in the colonies tended to be much more unstable than in Great Britain, especially where the process of colonialism involved the conquest and incorporation of indigenous peoples and the suppression of working class struggles. Hangings of rebels and strikers distorted the statistics, as did multiple hangings for a ritual murder.[50]

Close to home, the prerogative of mercy in Scotland was in frequent use by Scottish monarchs up to the Act of Union in 1707, primarily for the pardoning of treason and other political crimes often due to successional disputes and the Protestant Reformation. Under the peculiar procedures of Scottish law, only questions of law were appealable, while factual disputes were not; consequently, a defendant in Scotland who was wrongly convicted had little legal recourse. Apparently few, if any, pardons were granted in Scotland after the mercy power was transferred to the English Home Secretary after 1746. Not until 1926 was the office of the Secretary of State for Scotland finally revived, with the same mercy powers of the English Home Secretary; the Secretary of State could also send difficult cases to the Scottish Court of Criminal Appeal to hear new evidence.[51]

In Australia prior to Federation, the prerogative of mercy was vested in the colonial governors of each state, who consulted with their colonial executive councils in exercising the mercy power. Until the end of the nineteenth century, this advice was purely advisory. In the colony of New South Wales, the executive frequently exercised the pardon power because New South Wales was specifically a penal colony, and most convicts were freed at some point in their lives. Many citizens became beneficiaries of clemency and in the early colonial period the governor had no limitations on his discretion to grant pardons. In addition, prior to the rise of modern law enforcement, pardons were widely used in order to facilitate accomplice testimony.[52] What was true for New South Wales was also true for Victoria, where executions declined precipitously, especially for non-murder crimes, during the nineteenth century despite the presence of a large number of capital offenses in the penal code. In deciding mercy petitions, the

49 *See generally* A. Arthur Schiller, *Law, in* The African World: A Survey of Social Research 166, 192 (1965). As Schiller describes, "British administration of justice during the early years was solely concerned with the preservation of law and order in the territories under British control and with the settlement of disputes of the merchants and settlers in these outposts," noting that the British did not begin to exercise real control over indigenous administration of justice until the end of the nineteenth century. The administration of justice for African populations was usually under a department of native affairs, not a department of justice, well into the twentieth century. "There was very little contact between the native tribunals and the British courts." *Id.*

50 Turrell, *supra* note 38 at 94.

51 Rolph, *supra* note 27 at 78–79 (1978).

52 Caruso and Crawford, *supra* note 3 at 314.

governor-in-council would review the recommendations for mercy from the judge or the jury and manifestations of public opinion through letters, mass petitions, and noisy demonstrations. A substantial minority of death row prisoners (41 percent) were hanged, of whom women represented only a tiny number, though aboriginal Australians were somewhat more likely than whites to be executed.[53]

Upon unification of the Australian colonies, the governor-general of the Federation of Australia was also vested with the prerogative of mercy, which, by constitutional convention, was exercised on the advice of the federal cabinet.[54] After 1900, the governor-general of Australia and the state governors no longer possessed the prerogative power to pardon before conviction, which limited the potential for accomplice pardons.[55] The 1900 Letters Patent and instructions for the governor-general limited the clemency power to convicted criminals and remained in force until they were superseded by Australian legislation in 1987.[56] Writing of Australia, Plater and Milne write that colonial authorities took the prerogative of mercy seriously, even as to the worst offenders. The governor and cabinet "often strained to find grounds upon which to reprieve the condemned prisoner," and considered factors as various as the safety of the verdict, the conduct of the trial, the background of the offender, and calls for mercy from jurors, employers, clergymen, and the public.[57]

While the exercise of mercy in South Africa generally followed the same predicable legal or moral patterns as elsewhere, the inherent discriminatory consequences were even starker. A deliberate and planned murder was the prototypical death penalty-eligible crime, but some deliberate murders were excused by other mitigating factors, such as the social rank or race of the murderer and victim. As Turrell writes, "[m]ercy could not, and did not, even out the racist biases embedded in the system."[58] In addition, many men (and they were almost always men) were executed for impulsive or unpremeditated murders, while many more were reprieved, suggesting arbitrariness in the application of clemency.[59] Over time, and especially after 1935 when the mandatory death penalty was replaced by a partially discretionary death penalty, the trend was toward punishing with death only

53 R. Douglas and K. Laster, *A Matter of Life and Death: The Victorian Executive and the Decision to Execute, 1842–1967*, 24 Aust. & N.Z. J. Criminology 144, 146, 152 (1991).

54 Caruso and Crawford, *supra* note 3 at 314.

55 Joseph Azize, *The Prerogative of Mercy in NSW*, 1(6) Pub. Space: J. L. & Soc. Just. 1, 3–4 (2007).

56 *Id.* at 5–6.

57 Plater and Milne, *supra* note 23 at 25–26.

58 Turrell, White Mercy, *supra note* 40 at 237.

59 Turrell, *"It's a Mystery," supra note* 38 at 99–100.

murders containing elements of deliberation and planning.[60] When South Africa became a Republic in 1961, the president inherited a pardon power that was coextensive with the one previously held by the British monarch prior to that date.[61] However, the abolition of the common law mandatory death penalty in 1935 does not completely account for the decline of clemency in South Africa over the twentieth century. Certainly, the clemency rate in the period from 1923 to 1934 (76 percent) fell to 61 percent between 1935 and 1946.[62] However, clemency rates continued to plunge after the apartheid system was installed in 1948, from 61 percent to only 21 percent between 1958 and 1966. The reasons for the plunge were murky: except for a stricter approach in the case of the rape of white women by non-white men, the government announced little in the way of policy.[63]

In South Africa, the prerogative of mercy resided in the monarch's representative, the governor-general. Unlike the British Home Secretary, the governor-general was required to consult with his executive council in each case, but the final decision was his alone. In cases of irreconcilable difference of opinion, cabinet members occasionally resigned or threatened to resign. South African Governor-General Herbert Gladstone, son of longtime British Prime Minister William Gladstone, exercised the prerogative of mercy frequently against the recommendations of his executive council largely because of his prior experience as Home Secretary in Britain. Subsequent governors-general found the prerogative of mercy slipping away from them toward a collective cabinet decision, based heavily on the law advisor's report and the Minister of Justice's recommendation except in cases of high policy.[64] Reports of counsel, the presiding judge, and the attorney general were sent to the Minister of Justice along with the full record of the case, allowing the Minister to make a recommendation. As van

60 In South Africa, the mandatory death penalty was replaced by the doctrine of extenuating circumstances in 1935, in which the death penalty was mandatory unless the defendant showed, beyond a fair preponderance of the evidence, that extenuating circumstances existed in his case that reduced his moral blameworthiness for the crime. If the judge found extenuating circumstances, the judge had total discretion to tailor an appropriate sentence. This system exacerbated sentencing inconsistencies because it involved two discretionary acts rather than only one. *See* Andrew Novak, *Capital Sentencing Discretion in Southern Africa: A Human Rights Perspective on the Doctrine of Extenuating Circumstances*, 14 Afr. Hum. Rts. L.J. 24, 30 (2014); Criminal Procedure and Evidence (Amendment) Act 46 of 1935 § 61.

61 Rolph, *supra* note 27 at 139, *citing* Republic of South Africa Act, No. 32 of 1961.

62 Ellison Kahn, *How Did We Get Our Lopsided Law on the Imposition of the Death Penalty for Common Law Crimes? And What Should We Do About It?* 2 S. Afr. J. Crim. Just. 137, 146 (1989).

63 B.v.D. van Niekerk, *...Hanged By the Neck Until You Are Dead*, 86 S. Afr. L.J. 457, 459–60 (1969).

64 Turrell, *supra* note 40 at 234.

Niekerk writes, however, "the Minister can at most devote little personal attention to each case," and the real decisions are probably made by Justice Department officials whose methods of investigation are unknown to the outside world. He cautioned that reprieves could "only contribute very marginally to exclude all risk of a judicial error" in the South African system.[65]

Canadian scholars have also struggled to find consistency among widely disparate patterns of executions and reprieves. In Canada, the process of executive clemency reflected broader societal conceptions about race and gender. Women sentenced to death, for instance, faced selective leniency due to the chivalrous attitudes that permeated the appeals to the clemency authority.[66] An examination of those put to death since the formation of the Confederation of Canada in 1867 showed that an individual's ethnic background, gender, and religion were correlated to some degree with his or her status as a capital defendant as well as the final disposition of such cases.[67] The pardon power was a site of contested control between London and the colonies. Until the 1830s, the provincial government of Upper Canada largely resisted the reforms then sweeping English criminal law, in part due to its lower crime rate.[68] The outbreak of the Upper Canada Rebellion in 1837 altered the exercise of the royal prerogative of mercy. With a mandatory death penalty for treason, the colonial government passed emergency legislation to allow conditional pardons for persons who pleaded guilty, allowing the colonial government to charge a large number of rebels with political offenses without bogging courts down with trials. Although provincial legislation was subject to imperial review, the fast-breaking events during the rebellion allowed Upper Canada considerable freedom.[69] The conditional pardons were a win–win: the government avoided being seen as weak by refraining from prosecution or by dropping charges, while the conditions allowed it to extract considerable concessions from the rebels, including transportation to a penal colony such as Australia.[70] The Colonial Office was not amused at Upper Canada's attempt to try a large number of people for treason, conditionally pardon them, and then saddle the Crown with the expense of transporting them to Australia.

65 van Niekerk, *supra* note 63 at 460–61.

66 Margaret Dudgeon, *The Death Penalty in Canada: Ethnicity, Abolition and the Current Debate, in* Capital Punishment: New Perspectives 275, 279 (Peter Hodgkinson ed., 2013). *See also* Lesley Erickson, Westward Bound: Sex, Violence, the Law, and the Making of a Settler Society 213 (2011).

67 Dudgeon, *supra* note 66 at 287.

68 Barry Wright, *"Harshness and Forbearance": The Politics of Pardons and the Upper Canada Rebellion, in* Qualities of Mercy: Justice, Punishment, and Discretion 77, 81 (Carolyn Strange ed., 1996).

69 *Id.* at 83–5.

70 *Id.* at 86–87.

The Colonial Office was also skeptical that pleading guilty to high treason was constitutional, and ultimately issued a general amnesty for the rebels.[71]

The secretive, standardless exercise of executive mercy discretion in Canada was closely guarded. The decision-makers insisted that it would defeat the point to define or disclose the mercy process or subject it to criteria.[72] In Canada, jury recommendations for mercy could be passed on to the executive even if the judge did not recommend mercy. All-male juries were often influenced by the same social influences as judges, including purported chivalrousness as to female defendants; women were frequently recommended for mercy.[73] Among indigenous populations, juries could give recommendations for mercy if they believed cultural factors explained the defendant's behavior, though judicial recommendations for mercy were often more influential. Cultural outsiders – judges, the colonial governor and his council, and later the minister of justice – were responsible for deciding when in the legal process Native culture mattered and whether it mattered enough to commute a death sentence.[74] Foreigners or recent immigrants also received reprieves, though not without consideration of their nationalities. Strange notes, however, that judges and justice ministers frequently congratulated themselves on the class- and color-blind qualities of Canadian justice compared to justice in the United States.[75] The reduction in the number of capital offenses and the construction of a modern penitentiary in Kingston, Ontario, marked the end of routine dependence on the mercy power. The prerogative became increasingly anachronistic for ordinary criminal offenses, although it retained potent symbolic significance in later political trials.[76] The most prominent example is that of Métis leader and Manitoba founder Louis Riel in 1885, who was convicted and executed for high treason for his role as organizer of the North-West Rebellion against the Canadian government. A posthumous pardon or reprieve for Riel is deeply controversial: Métis and Québécois leaders and Riel's family believe he did nothing wrong and instead deserves complete exoneration rather than simply the removal of the stigma of conviction.[77]

71 *Id.* at 90–1.

72 Carolyn Strange, *The Lottery of Death: Capital Punishment, 1867–1976*, 23 MAN. L.J. 594, 595 (1995). For more on the process of executive mercy in Canada before modern times, see Chapter 7 of this book or Kenneth L. Avio, *The Quality of Mercy: Exercise of the Royal Prerogative in Canada*, 13 CANADIAN PUB. POL'Y 366, 367–8 (1987).

73 F. Murray Greenwood and Beverly Boissery, UNCERTAIN JUSTICE: CANADIAN WOMEN AND CAPITAL PUNISHMENT, 1754–1953 at 123 (2000).

74 Tina Loo, *Savage Mercy: Native Culture and the Modification of Capital Punishment in Nineteenth-Century British Columbia*, *in* QUALITIES OF MERCY: JUSTICE, PUNISHMENT, AND DISCRETION 108–09 (Carolyn Strange ed. 1996).

75 Strange, *supra* note 44 at 148–50.

76 Wright, *supra* note 68 at 90–1, 97–8.

77 Jean Teillet, *Exoneration for Louis Riel: Mercy, Justice, or Political Expediency?*, 67 SASK. L. REV. 359, 362, 392 (2004).

The friction between the Colonial Office and colonial governors over the prerogative of mercy persisted as the Empire expanded. In 1920, the Governor of Kenya sought review by a legal advisor in London over concerns about the validity of a conviction in a rape case. The Colonial Office returned the case file, indicating that it would only become involved in a murder case, and then only if the prisoner appealed to the Judicial Committee of the Privy Council.[78] If a colonial prisoner lost an appeal to the Privy Council, he or she would ordinarily seek mercy from the colonial governor and not directly from the Secretary of State for the Colonies. The colonial regulations stipulated that when a sentence of death was commuted, the colonial governor was required to send a report to London, whereas death sentences actually carried out were only reported in annual returns. This was, in part, because commutation of sentence was a departure from law and the Colonial Office was more interested in these than in instances where the law was carried out. In 1907, the Secretary of State sent a personal letter that chided the Governor of Jamaica who followed a policy of commuting all death sentences apparently as a result of personal objections.[79] When there was no reprieve or mercy, the Colonial Office was only concerned with whether a hanging was carried out efficiently and humanely, requesting details about botched executions and providing guidelines for colonial prison authorities.[80]

In Kenya, the colonial use of the death penalty was highly contested: between London and Nairobi, between Nairobi and the provinces, and between the executive and judicial branches. While some officials believed that the death penalty was an effective tool for imposing order on African populations, others argued that capital punishment was unsuitable as a punishment given markedly different local views on homicide and other crimes. After sentencing and appeal, a capital conviction was sent to the governor sitting with his executive council for clemency consideration.[81] While some of the grants for clemency were no doubt arbitrary and others followed familiar British precedents, a number were unique to their colonial context, shaping British justice to fit the African context: interracial murderers or murderers of state officials, for instance, were treated harshly, as were Indian defendants, as they were perceived to be above the "savagery" of the African. By contrast, murders that resulted from attacks on suspected witches were more complicated; witchcraft was a challenge to the colonial legal order, but executing a witch could provoke a public outcry.[82] Murders that occurred as a result of a local cultural practice, such

78 N.J. Miners, *The Governor, the Secretary of State and the Prerogative of Mercy*, 17 Hong Kong L.J. 77, 79 (1987).

79 *Id.* at 80–81.

80 *Id.* at 81.

81 Stacey Hynd, *Murder and Mercy: Capital Punishment in Colonial Kenya, ca. 1909–1956*, 45 Int'l. J. Afr. Hist. Stud. 81, 83, 86 (2012).

82 *Id.* at 87–90.

as infanticide or retaliation for rape, also received mercy.[83] Political or African nationalist activities could fuel a cycle of violence. During the Kenyan state of emergency in the 1950s, Mau Mau rebels were treated especially harshly: nearly 1,100 Kikuyu men went to the gallows for often political capital offenses. More than 400 others were reprieved, including women and those under age 18 at the time of the offense, though many of those acquitted or released were subsequently arrested on lesser charges. Sir Evelyn Baring, then the colonial governor of Kenya, refused to spare some of the Mau Mau "terrorists" even when the trial judge recommended mercy.[84]

In India, where powers of mercy had long been exercised by Mughal emperors and previous rulers, the common law prerogative of mercy was first introduced to India with the acquisitions of Bombay and Madras by the British East India Company in the 1600s. The King's prerogative right was granted by royal charter to the Viceroy of India. Although this prerogative right continued to exist, the more frequently-used statutory clemency powers granted to the Home Department of India were included in the Indian Penal Code of 1860 and the Code of Criminal Procedure in 1861. The Viceroy rarely became involved in the clemency process.[85] The following cases were typically submitted by the Minister for Home Affairs to the Viceroy for consideration: cases of a political character, cases arousing public interest, cases in which the death sentence was imposed on appeal, or cases in which there was some doubt about the merits. After 1937, however, the Viceroy was to make final decisions in all mercy petitions (about 700 per year), though only after considering recommendations by the Ministers for Law and Home Affairs on the executive council. In the Constituent Assembly in 1947, the framers of the Indian constitution debated and ultimately recommended broad powers of mercy for the presidency, including equivalent mercy powers for state governors in a federal system. As part of a compromise, however, both the president and state governors were given concurrent mercy power over state-level death penalty cases.[86]

Arthur Creech Jones, Secretary of State for the Colonies between 1946 and 1950, explained the conventions concerning the colonial exercise of the royal prerogative of mercy in a statement to the House of Commons in 1947. In the statement, he explained that the Colonial Secretary (after 1968,

83 *See* Stacey Hynd, *Deadlier Than the Male? Women and the Death Penalty in Colonial Kenya and Nyasaland, c. 1920–57*, 12 Wiener Zeitschrift für kritische Afrikastudien 13, 19 (2007).

84 David Anderson, Histories of the Hanged: The Dirty War in Kenya and the End of Empire 7, 111 (2005).

85 Bikram Jeet Batra, *"Court" of Last Resort: A Study of Constitutional Clemency for Capital Crimes in India*, Jawaharlal Nehru University Center for the Study of Law and Governance Working Paper Series, CSLG/WP/11, at 6–8 (April 2009).

86 *Id.* at 8–16.

the Secretary of State for Foreign and Commonwealth Affairs, or the Foreign Secretary) could intervene in a colonial governor's decision when justice demanded:

> I am advised that the delegation by His Majesty to Colonial Governors of the power of pardon does not entirely empty the King of his own prerogative of mercy. If a petition is presented to His Majesty praying for mercy, it is my duty to advise him what, if any, action should be taken upon it. The normal practice of the Secretary of State for the Colonies is not himself to intervene in an individual case and not to advise His Majesty to intervene.... [T]he Governor, knowing all the circumstances, is in a better position to judge whether the prerogative of mercy should be exercised in any particular case.... I do not, however, say that, if some exceptional case were brought to the Secretary of State's notice in which there were an indication that a miscarriage of justice had occurred, he would shut his eyes to it.... It is inconceivable that, in order to prevent a miscarriage of justice in such a case, I should have to advise His Majesty to intervene, and in practice, therefore, it is highly improbable that intervention by His Majesty on the advice of the Secretary of State would ever take place.[87]

Based on these conventions, the Foreign Secretary's 1973 recommendation to the Queen to commute the death sentence of Tsoi Kwok-cheong in Hong Kong was highly unusual, the first time in many years that the Foreign Secretary intervened in the exercise of the royal prerogative of mercy by a colonial governor.[88] Despite observing a de facto moratorium on executions for many years and commuting all death sentences as a matter of course, the governor of Hong Kong, in the midst of an anti-crime campaign, feared the loss of public confidence if he spared Kwok-cheong, convicted of the murder of an off-duty police officer.[89] According to the Hong Kong Letters Patent, which chartered the colony in 1843, the Crown delegated the power of the pardon to the colonial governor subject to the review of the appropriate Secretary of State. In practice, however, the Colonial Office did not closely review every case and left colonial governors a wide berth. Only once, in a perjury case in 1931, did the Colonial Secretary intervene with the governor of Hong Kong after scrutinizing a case file and concluding that the conviction was unjust.[90] If a death sentence

87 441 House of Commons Debates, ser 5, col 232–3 (Aug 11, 1947), *quoted in* Miners, *supra* note 78 at 86.

88 Miners, *supra* note 78 at 77–78.

89 Daniel N. Abrahamson, *Capital Punishment in Post-Colonial Hong Kong: Issues, Answers, and Options*, 24 N.Y.U. J. INT'L L. & POL. 1219, 1225 n. 20 (1992).

90 Miners, *supra* note 78 at 78.

were upheld by the Supreme Court of Hong Kong, the executive council, composed of a dozen senior colonial officials and presided over by the governor, reviewed a report prepared by a trial judge. If the governor disagreed with the decision of a majority of the executive council, he was required to state on the record "at length" his reasons for doing so.[91] The governor and the executive council almost always followed the recommendation of the trial judge, although Sir William Peel as governor granted clemency in two cases where the Executive Council voted five to four to deny clemency.[92]

Although Kwok-cheong's death sentence was commuted in Hong Kong, the Foreign Secretary allowed an execution to proceed in Bermuda in 1977. There, the Foreign Secretary advised the Queen to reject a petition for reprieve on behalf of two condemned prisoners. The local prerogative of mercy committee had advised the governor of Bermuda to reject the petition.[93] Erskine Burrows was convicted of the murder of then-colonial governor David Eccles and his aide, an overt political attack on the Crown. Burrows was sentenced to death, as was Larry Tacklyn, an accomplice in a later murder. The executions of the two men took place on December 2, 1977, a day after their appeals were dismissed. Riots broke out in opposition to the hangings, and the governor of Bermuda requested British troops. The first detachment landed in Bermuda two days later and a state of emergency was only lifted a week after the executions.[94] These two executions in Bermuda were the last to occur on British soil anywhere in the world. Unlike Hong Kong, where the colonial governor and executive council were appointed by the Queen, Bermuda had a fully-elected legislature at this time and the prerogative of mercy committee had been appointed with the advice of the elected premier. Permitting the executions of Burrows and Tacklyn, but not of Kwok-cheong, might have been a deferential gesture to local responsible government.[95]

Rhodesia's constitutional relationship with Great Britain became more complicated than other colonies with the unilateral declaration of independence of its minority white settler community on November 11, 1965. Although the 1961 constitution delegated the royal prerogative of mercy to the governor-general of Rhodesia, the Queen remained the Rhodesian head of state until 1970. In 1968, she attempted to pardon three African nationalists who were to be put to death by the Rhodesian Front government,

91 Abrahamson, *supra* note 89 at 1224 n. 18.

92 Miners, *supra* note 78 at 80.

93 *Id.* at 87.

94 Robert T. Sigler and David King, *Affirmative Action in a Colonial Context: Bermudianization of the Bermuda Police*, 14 Police Stud. Int'l Rev. Police Dev. 127, 129–130 (1991).

95 Miners, *supra* note 78 at 88–89.

following the advice of the Commonwealth Secretary.[96] The Rhodesian cabinet and courts believed this was unconstitutional and that only the Rhodesian government had the right to pardon a condemned prisoner; consequently, the Queen was powerless to exercise a royal prerogative of mercy. The three men were executed to enormous international outrage, including a unanimous condemnation by the United Nations Security Council.[97] Once the white settler government established a republic and removed the Queen as head of state, the subsequent Rhodesian constitutions granted the mercy power to the president, though executive power rested with the prime minister as head of government. When he exercised the prerogative of mercy, the president did so based on the advice of an executive council comprising the prime minister and other ministers selected by the president. Usually, the Rhodesian minister of justice referred the matter to the executive council after first having discussed the case with the full cabinet. Presidential pardons in Rhodesia were exceptionally rare. One was granted in 1974 to a man serving a sentence for store-breaking after a fingerprint analysis showed that the man was in prison for a different crime at the time. An older brother with a number of criminal convictions falsely confessed to the crime to protect his younger brother, who had a clean record.[98]

Colonial subjects widely "used petitions as a means of self assertion and for challenging colonial authority," and petitions, including those for mercy, became a "form of public expression and protest," revealing a great deal about the attitudes of subject populations toward early colonial government.[99] One mercy petition from Calabar, Nigeria, in 1959, prayed for the governor to exercise his prerogative of mercy by pardoning a two-year sentence of imprisonment for manslaughter. The petition pleaded for mercy based on "extreme youthfulness at the time of the incident. I was barely eighteen years at the time and more or less impulsive by nature. I was at this time smarting under a sense of injustice and I confess I acted foolishly at a time when my reasoning was off its true balance."[100] Studies of colonial Africa show that the rate of mercy in British colonies was comparable with England and Wales in the same period; it was not unusual to commute half of all death sentences each year.[101]

96 South African Democracy Education Trust, 1 THE ROAD TO DEMOCRACY IN SOUTH AFRICA: 1960–1970 at 527 (2004).

97 *Amnesty International Briefing: Rhodesia/Zimbabwe*, 6 ISSUE: J. OPINION 34, 37 (1976); Andrew Novak, *Abuse of State Power: The Mandatory Death Penalty for Political Crimes in Southern Rhodesia, 1963–1970*, 19 FUNDAMINA 28, 45 (2013).

98 Rolph, *supra* note 27 at 137–138.

99 Chima J. Korieh, *"May It Please Your Honor": Letters of Petition as Historical Evidence in an African Colonial Context*, 37 HIST. IN AFR. 83, 87 (2010).

100 *Id.* at 88, *quoting* Petition from David Asuquo of Calbar, Nigeria, to the Governor of the Eastern Region, Aug. 21, 1959.

101 Stacey Hynd, *Killing the Condemned: The Practice and Process of Capital Punishment in British Africa, 1900–1950s*, 49 J. AFR. HIST. 403, 405–06 n. 7 (2008).

In death penalty cases, the usefulness of mercy as a pressure valve for newly-established legal systems in the colonies was especially important. In the furthest outposts of the Empire, the legal system was skeletal and openly acknowledged to be imperfect, more an administrative and political system than a professionally legal one. Writing about Nyasaland (colonial Malawi), Hynd notes that an accused was likely to face a bewildering formal justice process without defense counsel. If appeals failed, the prerogative of mercy as exercised by a colonial governor on the advice of his executive council was the only recourse to avoid the gallows – ultimately making the death penalty more political than other criminal punishments.[102] Mercy in Nyasaland served in part as a tool of racialized colonial justice that stereotyped African behavior. As mercy was decided on a case by case basis, it could be arbitrary: in 1935, for instance, the governor of Nyasaland pardoned a murderer of two children even though the case lacked typical mitigating factors and the judge had not recommended mercy.[103] For the most part, however, the exercise of mercy in colonial Nyasaland followed familiar patterns: the motive of the crime, the weapon used, the age of the offender, and the level of danger to the existing social order were all considerations. In the minds of colonial officials, "the death penalty was a British imposition, which required adaptation and moderation through mercy to function effectively and 'humanely' in an African environment."[104] So many sentences were commuted in colonial Nyasaland that in 1922 the colonial government proposed abolishing the mandatory death penalty and creating a discretionary regime in which a judge could consider mitigating factors in tailoring an appropriate sentence. The Colonial Office rejected the proposal.

Despite these similarities to British practice, certain local and culturally-contingent variations were discernible in colonial Nyasaland. For instance, spousal murders and gender-based violence were particularly high given the familial stress generated by rapid urbanization and labor migration.[105] The colonies used the same standard of insanity as in English law, but given assumptions about the differences between the "European" mind and the "African" mind, conceptions about what constituted insane or socially abnormal behavior differed between the metropole and the colonies. Witchcraft and superstitious killings triggered a kind of African cultural defense, punished strictly in the penal code but often subject to mercy. The flexibility in criminal sentencing as a result of executive mercy helped fill the gap between colonial and customary notions of murder and criminal liability, which had the consequence of helping to legitimate British

102 Stacey Hynd, *"The Extreme Penalty of the Law": Mercy and the Death Penalty as Aspects of State Power in Colonial Nyasaland, c. 1903–47*, 4 J. East Afr. Stud. 542, 544–5 (2010).
103 *Id.* at 546.
104 *Id.* at 548.
105 *Id.* at 549.

authority while allowing larger structural injustices in the colonial system to persist.[106]

At independence, new constitutions preserved the mercy power for the elected head of state or local monarchs. In the republics, this was not a sovereign prerogative but rather a specifically-enumerated constitutional power. In the Irish Free State, which became self-governing after 1922, the British monarch appears to have retained the prerogative of mercy until the creation of an Irish republic in 1936. Subsequent decisions by the Supreme Court of Ireland categorically established that the Irish head of state did not inherit the royal prerogatives from the King; rather executive power was enumerated in the constitution itself.[107] In most former colonies where independence constitutions were more recent, the constitutional authority for the mercy power is made explicit in the constitutional document itself.[108] The distinction between a constitutional clemency power and a sovereign prerogative may be more theoretical than real, but the exercise of the clemency power under a written and justiciable constitution has, since independence, opened some aspects of the exercise of the mercy power to judicial and legislative review. A mercy power governed by the constitutional mandates of equality and due process, for instance, may limit the scope of executive discretion. In most Commonwealth countries, the modern construction of the clemency power, now governed by administrative regulation, is no longer an "act of grace" by the sovereign, but a constitutionally-defined process.

The constitutional pardon power in the United States of America

As in its other colonies, the British Crown delegated a broad pardoning power in the American colonies to local British authorities. Although there was some variation among colonies, most governors could pardon offenders or remit fines as they saw fit. In the royal colonies, such as Maryland and North Carolina, the royal charters granted expansive pardon powers to the colonial governor, though he was subject to the King's instructions. The charter colonies of Connecticut, Rhode Island, and Massachusetts Bay (until 1691) had more freedom, as the colonial charter vested the pardon power in the governing joint-stock company, and the company delegated it to the legislature. In 1691, Massachusetts Bay received a royal charter, which did not contain a pardon provision; from that point, the governor appointed by the King exercised the prerogative of mercy as the direct representative of

106 *Id.* at 554.
107 Cox, *supra* note 48 at 25–35, *citing* Byrne v. Ireland, [1972] I.R. 241 (Sup. Ct. Ire.). *Byrne* related to the sovereign prerogative of immunity from civil suits at common law.
108 *Id.* at 25–35.

the monarch.[109] Under royal charters, colonial governors generally had the ability to conditionally pardon offenders, and governors of Virginia, for instance, granted pardons on conditions of banishment, military service, or indentured servitude in the West Indies.[110] In the era leading up to American independence, states became a laboratory of experiments, many limiting the pardon power they professed skepticism toward strong executives. The Georgia and New Hampshire legislatures vested the pardon power in themselves rather than the governor and the 1780 constitution of Massachusetts limited the ability of the governor to pardon prior to conviction.[111] Most state governments featured a clemency power shared between the governor and the legislature, or vested in the legislature alone. Only in New York, Delaware, Maryland, and the Carolinas did the governor possess the full mercy power. Similarly, the Articles of Confederation lacked a presidential mercy power.[112] Eventually, the clemency power returned to state governors. Connecticut's 1818 constitution, for instance, allowed the governor to issue temporary reprieves but not pardons; the earlier constitution vested clemency in the legislature alone.[113]

Unlike the encumbered clemency power at the state level, the framers of the US constitution vested an expansive pardoning power in the federal president. The framers were greatly influenced by political thinkers such as John Locke and Baron de Montesquieu, who believed that the clemency power provided a benefit in mitigating the law's severity. However, Montesquieu was skeptical of the pardon power in a democracy: if a pardon was a personal act of grace from a monarch, then there could be no executive pardon power where a crime was an offense against the people rather than the King.[114] The English jurist William Blackstone was sympathetic to this view, believing that the same government should not judge and pardon.[115] Influential American jurists, such as James Wilson and Joseph Story, disagreed, believing that the constitutional separation of powers sufficiently separated the judicial and executive mercy functions.[116] Federalists generally supported the presidential pardoning power as they tended to favor a stronger executive, while Anti-Federalists had deep reservations, many believing that the US Senate should be involved in pardon decisions.[117]

109 Norman D. Lattin, *The Pardoning Power in Massachusetts*, 11 B.U. L.Rev. 505, 507–08 (1931).

110 Harold J. Krent, *Conditioning the President's Conditional Pardon Power*, 89 Cal. L. Rev. 1665, 1672 (2001).

111 *Id.* at 1672; Lattin, *supra* note 109 at 508.

112 Jeffrey Crouch, The Presidential Pardon Power 14 (2009).

113 Meah Dell Rothman, *The Pardoning Power: Historical Perspective and Case Study of New York and Connecticut*, 12 Colum. J.L. & Soc. Probs. 149, 161–62 (1976).

114 Kathleen Dean Moore, Pardons: Justice, Mercy, and the Public Interest 25 (1989).

115 Krent, *supra* note 110 at 1672.

116 Crouch, *supra* note 112 at 12–13.

117 *Id.* at 15.

The president's "Power to grant Reprieves and Pardons for Offenses against the United States, except in Cases of Impeachment" in the US constitution is a direct lineal descendant of executive clemency provisions which had been exercised by the English Crown.[118] However, the framers dedicated only a minimal amount of time and debate to the clemency provision and failed to outline any terms for issuing a pardon. As a result, the boundaries of the pardon power were only clarified in subsequent judicial interpretations.[119] The US Supreme Court has made clear that the president's power to pardon is plenary, explaining in *Ex Parte Grossman* that "the executive can reprieve or pardon all offenses after their commission, either before trial, during trial or after trial, by individuals, or by classes, conditionally or absolutely, and this without modification or regulation by Congress."[120] This is a sweeping affirmation of the presidential pardon power in the United States, one that far exceeds the limits, legal or conventional, of most executives in the common law world.

Should the president's pardon power be construed as an "act of grace" to an individual supplicant or as a bureaucratic decision made for the public welfare? In two separate if contradictory decisions, the US Supreme Court has affirmed both views.[121] The first of these views, that clemency is an "act of grace" for the lucky chosen few, was first expressed in *United States v. Wilson* in 1833, which involved the right of a convicted robber to *refuse* a pardon. In that case, President Andrew Jackson pardoned the defendant's capital conviction, and in a later proceeding for a related charge, the defendant refused protection of the pardon by pleading not guilty.[122] The Supreme Court looked to the English prerogative of mercy to determine that a pardon was a kind of gift that could be refused, disregarding the framers' evident lack of enthusiasm for English pardoning practice.[123] According to Chief Justice John Marshall, "A pardon is an act of grace, proceeding from the power entrusted with the execution of the laws, which exempts the individual, on whom it is bestowed, from the punishment the law inflicts for a crime he has committed."[124] If the true nature of a pardon was an act of grace, the Court found that a recipient retained the power to decide whether to accept it; consequently, Wilson could refuse to plead the pardon in court.[125] In 1856, the Supreme Court confirmed Chief Justice Marshall's conception of a pardon as an "act of grace" in *Ex Parte*

118 US Const. art. II § 2 (1787).
119 Christopher C. Joyner, *Rethinking the President's Power of Executive Pardon*, 43 Fed. Probation 16, 16–17 (1979).
120 Ex Parte Grossman, 267 US 87, 120 (1925), *citing* Ex Parte Garland, 71 US 333, 380 (1866).
121 Crouch, *supra* note 112 at 29.
122 US v. Wilson, 32 US 150 (1833).
123 Moore, *supra* note 114 at 50–51.
124 *Wilson*, 32 US at 160.
125 *Id.* at 163. Also summarized in Crouch, *supra* note 112 at 30.

Wells, and an even stronger affirmation of the "act of grace" metaphor came in *Burdick v. United States* in 1915, where a newspaper editor refused to accept a pardon and answer questions about his sources without fear of self-incrimination.[126]

For the next hundred years after *Wilson*, presidents used pardons as they chose, having inherited the divinely-inspired pardoning power of the English monarch. In a "watershed" 1927 decision, *Biddle v. Perovich*, Justice Oliver Wendell Holmes "declined to extend the 'act of grace' reasoning of *Wilson*," providing a "different rationale for the pardon power" that conceived of the pardon power as being performed in the public interest.[127] According to the Court in *Biddle*, "[a] pardon in our days is not a private act of grace from an individual happening to possess power. It is a part of the Constitutional scheme."[128] Holmes continues: "Just as the original punishment would be imposed without regard to the prisoner's consent and in the teeth of his will, whether he liked it or not, the public welfare, not his consent, determines what shall be done" as to the pardon.[129] A pardoned person's consent was irrelevant. This position was reaffirmed in the 1974 decision *Schick v. Reed*, which likewise involved the constitutionality of a conditional pardon, finding that the conditions were valid even without the pardoned person's consent.[130] The "Holmes conception of a pardon better promotes the policy goals of the Constitution than does the Marshall conception," Buchanan writes, noting that the American constitutional scheme favors maximizing the president's unreviewable discretion over mercy.[131]

The nineteenth century saw many pardons, including Thomas Jefferson's pardon of deserters from the Continental Army and James Madison's pardon of deserters from the War of 1812. The Civil War, however, involved pardon on a far greater scale, as it was the first conflict in which a substantial portion of the army was conscripted. President Abraham Lincoln pardoned many deserters on the condition that they return to fight with their units, and many did, while President Andrew Johnson pardoned the leaders of the Confederacy.[132] The post-Civil War period saw a bruising constitutional battle between the president and Congress about the scope of the pardon power. Congress passed the Confiscation Acts allowing the president to grant "pardons and amnesties" to help dispose of Confederate property that had been seized during the war. In 1872, the Supreme Court

126 Ex Parte Wells, 59 US (18 How.) 307 (1856); Burdick v. US, 236 US 79 (1915). *See generally*, G. Sidney Buchanan, *The Nature of a Pardon Under the United States Constitution*, 39 Ohio St. L.J. 36, 40 (1978).
127 Crouch, *supra* note 112 at 31; Biddle v. Perovich, 274 US 480 (1927).
128 *Biddle*, 274 US at 486.
129 *Id.*
130 Schick v. Reed, 419 US 256 (1974).
131 Buchanan, *supra* note 126 at 65.
132 Moore, *supra* note 114 at 51.

affirmed the president's general amnesty in 1872, in effect recognizing the president's power to amnesty as part of the Article II power to grant "reprieves and pardons."[133]

The Supreme Court also wrestled with the boundary between the president and Congress in the exercise of the clemency power. In the case *Ex Parte Garland* in 1866, the Court found unconstitutional a Congressional law that required an attorney and public office holder in Arkansas to take an oath of loyalty to the United States even after the president issued a full pardon in 1865.[134] *Garland* described an extremely flexible clemency power, which "extends to every offence known to the law, and [which] may be exercised at any time after its commission, either before legal proceedings are taken, or during their pendency, or after conviction and judgment."[135] Justice Stephen Field wrote that the presidential pardon power "is not subject to legislative control," and Congress could not "limit the effect of his pardon, nor exclude from its exercise any class of offenders."[136] In subsequent post-Civil War decisions, the Supreme Court affirmed that Congress could not curb or limit the presidential amnesty to the former Confederate rebels by preventing restitution or recovery of property.[137]

As the Supreme Court has observed, even constitutional plenary powers may be subject to some limitations in the constitution itself.[138] Today, the US Constitution generally imposes several outer limits on the pardoning power beyond the impeachment exclusion at Article II.[139] First, a pardon likely "cannot interfere with the vested property rights of a third party in violation of the Takings Clause" of the Fifth Amendment. For instance, if a defendant forfeited property as a result of a criminal conviction and that property was lawfully returned to or acquired by another person, a pardon could not return that property to the defendant without just compensation.[140] Second, a pardon "cannot require the payment of funds from the US Treasury in violation of the Taxing and Spending Clause" of Article I, which delegates the power of the purse strings to Congress.[141] Third, a pardon

133 Armstrong v. United States, 80 US 154 (1872).

134 Ex Parte Garland, 71 US (4 Wall.) 333 (1866).

135 *Id.* at 334.

136 *Id.*

137 *See* US v. Padelford, 76 US 531 (1869); US v. Klein, 80 US 128 (1871); Carlisle v. US, 83 US 147 (1872); Osborne v. US, 92 US 474 (1876).

138 Schick v. Reed, 419 US 256, 267 (1974). *See also* Mark Strasser, *The Limits of the Clemency Power on Pardons, Retributivists, and the United States Constitution*, 41 BRANDEIS L.J. 85, 89 (2002).

139 Brian M. Hoffstadt, *Normalizing the Federal Clemency Power*, 79 TEX. L. REV. 561, 594–595 (2001); Strasser, *supra* note 138 at 115 *et seq.*

140 *Id.* at 594.

141 Knote v. US, 95 US 149 (1877); Hart v. US, 118 US 62 (1886). In these two Civil War cases, the claimants were unable to recover property seized during the war that had been deposited in the US Treasury, even though the president amnestied the claimants. These cases were distinguished from the line of Civil War cases mentioned above because the proceeds were already in the US Treasury. *Id.*

"cannot require a prisoner to forfeit his constitutional rights unreasonably," which may impose limits on the president's power to issue conditional pardons if those conditions violated constitutionally-protected rights.[142] Fourth, some authority indicates that a pardon cannot be granted in violation of the Fifth Amendment's Due Process Clause, including Justice Sandra Day O'Connor's concurrence in *Ohio Adult Parole Authority v. Woodard* in 1998.[143] The decision suggests some minimal procedural safeguards may be required and that a grant of clemency may not be wholly wanton or arbitrary. In addition, a conditional pardon likely cannot impose as a condition a cruel and unusual punishment in violation of the Eighth Amendment, such as, for instance, requiring a death row prisoner to undergo castration as a condition for removal from death row.[144] The Equal Protection Clause may impose additional constraints on an executive's pardon power if that power is exercised in a discriminatory fashion.[145]

The archives of the office of the US Pardon Attorney reveal interesting characteristics of the earliest presidential pardons. In the early republic, judges had only a limited opportunity to set aside jury verdicts or grant a new trial, and no right to appeal yet existed. It was often "easier for judges to take a sympathetic case to the president with a recommendation for clemency than to resort to the rigid machinery of justice."[146] Presidents sometimes found themselves providing a kind of appellate review of sentences in a process that was not strictly a legal one. Despite the early introduction of discretionary judicial sentencing with the Crimes Act of 1790, some offenses still had mandatory death sentences. In addition, mandatory minimum sentences were introduced in the early nineteenth century for trading in slaves, counterfeiting or fraud on the US Bank, theft of mail, and crime in the District of Columbia. In 1800 and 1807, Congress imposed mandatory criminal sanctions for engaging in the slave trade, including serving on board a slave ship traveling between foreign ports. Mandatory sentencing for these crimes, including early and harsh penalties for postal crimes, triggered a large number of pardon and clemency applications. Disparate sentences caused by the peculiar legal status of the

142 According to the D.C. Circuit in Hoffa v. Saxbe, 378 F.Supp. 1221 (1974), the Court found that a condition on a pardon was lawful so long as (1) it was directly related to the public interest; and (2) it did not "unreasonable infringe" on the individual commuttee's constitutional rights. In *Hoffa*, union leader James Hoffa received a conditional pardon for obstruction of justice, on the condition that he not engage in union activities until at least 1980. The court upheld the conditions. *Hoffa*, 378 F.Supp. at 1236.

143 Ohio Adult Parole Authority v. Woodard, 523 US 272, 289 (1998) (Connor, J., concurring).

144 This possibility is raised by Strasser, *supra* note 138 at 115, *citing* Schick v. Reed, 419 US 256, 266 (1974) (holding that the pardon power allows "the attachment of any condition which does not otherwise offend the Constitution").

145 *See* Strasser, *supra* note 138 at 116 *et seq.*

146 George Lardner and Margaret Colgate Love, *Mandatory Sentences and Presidential Mercy: The Role of Judges in Pardon Cases, 1790–1850*, 16(3) FED. SENT'G REP. 1, 6 (2004).

District of Columbia resulted in a number of early pardon applications because the comparatively harsh penal code of Virginia applied to one part of the District, while the less severe penal code of Maryland applied to the remainder. Offenses on one side of the Potomac River could receive the death penalty while elsewhere only a penalty of whipping a fine would apply. Judges did not hesitate to recommend clemency until a single comprehensive criminal code was established in the District in 1831.[147]

Although the presidential pardon power in the United States generally remains as broadly-defined and unreviewable as in the early republic, use of the power has declined in recent decades. The process of seeking a presidential pardon has become a lengthy and bureaucratic one, funneled through the Department of Justice. As federal crime escalated in the Prohibition Era, the pardon process became more burdensome and requests consumed an increasing amount of time. Eventually, as in the United Kingdom, it was limited by administrative regulation. The rise of modern probation and parole statutes replaced much of the need for conditional pardons, as parole boards had powers of investigation and enforcement that presidents did not have.[148] Certainly, controversial political pardons have continued to the present era outside of the bureaucratic process, and the most famous deserve mention: President Gerald Ford's pardon of Richard Nixon, President Jimmy Carter's pardon of the Vietnam draft dodgers, President George H.W. Bush's pardon of the officials implicated in the Iran-Contra scandal, and President Bill Clinton's pardon of large political donor Marc Rich. Nonetheless, the United States fits within a global trend toward the rationalization of the charismatic mercy power; one of the most deeply personal executive powers has been tamed.

Conclusion

The original conception of the royal prerogative of mercy at common law was a power personal to the King, who had the broad ability to reprieve or exonerate offenses against the sovereign. The expansiveness of the mercy prerogative waxed and waned over the centuries in battles with parliament and local officials, but by the early eighteenth century the mercy power was subject to bureaucratic control, exercised only on a recommendation by the Secretary of State for Home Affairs. The use of the pardon power became limited by convention and later by administrative regulation, and as the British Empire expanded, these conventions were delegated to the colonial governors as representatives of the monarch. In most colonies, the mercy power was exercised by the governor acting in consultation with an executive council or cabinet, though research from Australia, Canada,

147 *Id.* at 1–2.
148 Krent, *supra* note 110 at 1677–78.

and South Africa shows that the mercy decision was frequently subject to discriminatory or arbitrary application, erratic even by British standards. The mercy power could be a site of contested control between the Colonial Office and the governors, but the Colonial Secretary (and later the Commonwealth and then the Foreign Secretaries) rarely intervened in a mercy decision. Through the imperial process, the prerogative of mercy passed into the constitutions of independent countries, including the United States, where it was construed broadly as the presidential pardon power in Article II of the US constitution. In the United Kingdom and abroad, including the United States, the mercy power has transformed from a personal prerogative of the ruler exercising an individual "act of grace" to a broadly bureaucratic clemency power regulated by statute and exercised for the greater public good.

3 International law and the amnesty and pardon power

Public international law imposes outer boundaries on the exercise of the clemency power, though these limitations are fragmentary and drawn from separate and overlapping sources. In general, two major treaties, the International Covenant on Civil and Political Rights (ICCPR) and the American Convention on Human Rights, specifically require the existence of a clemency or pardon mechanism in all death penalty cases. Some human rights treaty bodies go further than this, requiring an effective mercy procedure that includes prescribed criteria, an application process, notification to the applicant, and some means of making representations to the committee. On the other hand, a consensus may be emerging that the use of the clemency and pardon power in order to shield perpetrators from serious human rights abuses violates state obligations to prosecute international crimes and provide victims with a genuine remedy, especially in the case of a general amnesty prior to investigation and prosecution. In this way, international law imposes both a ceiling and a floor on the clemency power. This chapter will also briefly analyze the extent to which international criminal tribunals provide for a pardon or clemency mechanism.

Although they have similar legal consequences and legal motivations, amnesties are analytically distinct from pardons from a juridical point of view, generally connoting an institution differentiated from pardon in that (a) it is general, in that it applies to categories of offenders and not to named individuals; (b) it negates the effects of the conviction and not merely of the sentences; and (c) it applies primarily, though not exclusively, to politically-motivated offenses. Many constitutions worldwide vest the amnesty power in the legislature rather than the head of state, such as Finland, the Netherlands, Jordan, and Panama. As Sebba writes, the English common law never developed the concept of an amnesty, and the US constitution is uncertain about which branch of government has an amnesty power. In practice, amnesty proclamations have been made by the US president, and sometimes supported by congressional action, though the constitutional basis for amnesties has typically been found within the pardon power of Article II.[1] In the United Kingdom, the historical use of a collective pardon, group pardon, or general pardon blurs the distinction more, as these serve in essence as a blanket amnesty prior to conviction for a category of offenders rather than individual offenders.[2] Unlike amnesties, pardons are frequently given after conviction, or at least after an individual perpetrator has been identified and potentially investigated, and therefore do not bar truth and accountability to the same degree.[3] Ahmed and Quayle agree pardons and amnesties are largely indistinct, though an amnesty often has the consequence of preventing a court from going through the process of discovering the truth about a crime through a trial at all, while a pardon typically only shields a person from criminal punishment or civil liability.[4]

The right to seek clemency in death penalty cases

International law requires countries that retain the death penalty to have a clemency mechanism available for death row inmates. While this does not impose a single structure or procedure on domestic constitutional systems, at a minimum it would presumably prevent arbitrary or discriminatory grants of clemency and necessitate a form of review distinct from a judicial appeal. Article 6(4) of the ICCPR states: "Anyone sentenced to death shall have the right to seek pardon or commutation of the sentence. Amnesty, pardon or commutation of the sentence may be granted in all cases."[5] Extrapolating from this, international law thus provides for a "right" to seek pardon or commutation of sentence. In order for this right to be meaningful, states are under an obligation to provide *effective* measures for the proper consideration of clemency in *every* case.[6] International human rights mechanisms and national courts have occasionally provided guidance about the boundaries of Article 6(4), including whether blanket denials of clemency are permissible.

1 Leslie Sebba, *The Pardoning Power: A World Survey*, 68 J. Crim. L. & Criminology 83, 118–119 (1977).

2 *Id.*

3 Ronald C. Slye, *The Legitimacy of Amnesties Under International Law and General Principles of Anglo-American Law: Is a Legitimate Amnesty Possible?*, 43 Va. J. Int'l L. 173, 238 (2002).

4 Anees Ahmed and Merryn Quayle, *Can Genocide, Crimes Against Humanity and War Crimes Be Pardoned or Amnestied?*, 79 Amicus Curiae 15, 16 (2009).

5 Art. 6(4), International Covenant on Civil and Political Rights, opened for signature Dec. 19, 1966, 999 U.N.T.S. 85 (entered into force March 23, 1976).

6 Saul Lehrfreund, *The Impact and Importance of International Human Rights Standards: Asia in World Perspective*, *in* Confronting Capital Punishment in Asia: Human Rights, Politics, and Public Opinion 23, 42 (Roger Hood and Surya Deva eds., 2013).

In a challenge to the mandatory death penalty, the UN Human Rights Committee in *Thompson v. St. Vincent and the Grenadines* ruled that the existence of a clemency and pardon mechanism did not sufficiently individualize sentencing in death penalty cases, ultimately holding that a mandatory death sentence violated Article 6 of the ICCPR, as it constituted cruel and degrading treatment.[7] A dissent by four members of the committee found that, if genuine, a clemency process *could* sufficiently individualize the sentence as Article 6(4) required a state party "to consider in good faith all personal circumstances and circumstances of the particular crime which the condemned person wishes to present." According to the dissent, clemency consideration under Article 6(4) "must be carried out in good faith and according to a fair procedure."[8] In a subsequent proceeding, *Kennedy v. Trinidad and Tobago*, the Committee ruled that the wording of Article 6(4) did not prescribe a particular procedure according to which the prerogative of mercy must be exercised, as states parties retained the discretion to establish their own procedures. The Committee upheld Trinidad and Tobago's clemency procedures even as it unanimously determined that the mandatory death penalty for felony murder violated the ICCPR, as petitioners for clemency receive a hearing and are informed of the date on which clemency would be considered.[9]

The UN Human Rights Committee has also considered whether an arbitrary or discriminatory grant of clemency violates Article 6(4) of the ICCPR. In *Teesdale v. Trinidad and Tobago*, the Committee turned away a challenge where the president of Trinidad and Tobago commuted a death sentence to 75 years life imprisonment with hard labor. In that case, the petitioner argued that 53 other prisoners that year had their sentences commuted to life imprisonment with the possibility of parole after 12 to 15 years. However, the Committee found that the petitioner had not provided enough information about the other cases commuted to life imprisonment with hard labor, and therefore it could not determine whether the commutation of the sentence was arbitrary.[10] The case included two dissents. The opinion of Committee members David Kretzmer and Ivan Shearer stated that while the Committee accepted that "the power to grant a pardon or commutation of sentence is by its very nature subject to wide discretion," like any other governmental power it "must be exercised in a non-discriminatory manner so as to ensure the right of all individuals to equality

7 Thompson v. St. Vincent, Comm. No. 806/1998, UN Doc. CCPR/C/70/D/806/1998 (U.N.H.R.C. 2000), ¶ 8.2.

8 *Id.* at ¶¶ 9, 11 (Kretzmer, D., Amor, A., Yalden, M., Zakhia, A., dissenting).

9 Kennedy v. Trin. & Tobago, Comm. No. 845/1998, UN Doc. CCPR/C/74/D/845/1998 (U.N.H.R.C. 2002) ¶ 7.4.

10 Teesdale v. Trin. & Tobago, Comm. No. 677/1996, UN Doc. CCPR/C/74/D/677/1996 (2002).

before the law."[11] A second dissenting opinion, by member Hipólito Solari Yrigoyen argued that mercy "discretion is not absolute and must be based on reasonable criteria."[12] While Article 6(4) of the ICCPR created a right in the defendant to seek clemency, according to these interpretations the decision-maker was *also* bound by the minimum due process standards of the ICCPR, including the equality provisions.

The Inter-American Human Rights System has imposed more robust procedural minimum standards in death penalty cases. Article 4(6) of the American Convention on Human Rights follows a similar pattern to the ICCPR: "Every person condemned to death shall have the right to apply for amnesty, pardon, or commutation of sentence, which may be granted in all cases."[13] As in the ICCPR, unpardonable capital crimes are prohibited. The Inter-American Commission on Human Rights has held that procedures for granting mercy or pardon must guarantee condemned prisoners an effective and adequate opportunity to participate in the process. According to the Commission in *McKenzie v. Jamaica*, the right to seek clemency "encompasses certain minimum procedural guarantees for condemned prisoners in order for the right to be effectively respected and enjoyed," including the right to be informed of when the deliberations will take place, to make representations personally or through counsel, and to receive a decision within a reasonable time prior to execution.[14] In *Lamey v. Jamaica*, the Commission considered the ruling by the Judicial Committee of the Privy Council in London, the highest court of appeal in Jamaica, that opened the prerogative of mercy to judicial review and laid down procedural due process protections for the first time, including the right to make presentations to the advisory mercy committee and to know the evidence on which the committee made its decision.[15] *Knights v. Grenada*, also issued on the same day, extended this holding throughout the Commonwealth Caribbean.[16]

In the Bahamas, which is not a state party to the American Convention on Human Rights, the Inter-American Commission extended its reasoning to apply to the American Declaration on the Rights and Duties of Man, which protects generally each individual's "right to life, liberty and the

11 *Id.* (Kretzmer, D. and Shearer, I., dissenting in part).

12 *Id.* (Yrigoyen, H., dissenting in part).

13 American Convention on Human Rights, Nov. 22, 1969, 1144 U.N.T.S. 143, O.A.S.T.S. No. 36, art. 6(4) (entered into force July 18, 1978).

14 McKenzie v. Jamaica, Inter-Am. Comm'n H.R., Case 12.023, Report No. 41/00 (April 13, 2000), ¶ 228. The Inter-American Commission on Human Rights again found Jamaica's clemency proceedings did not comply with the American Convention in Aitken v. Jamaica, Case 12.275, Report No. 58/02, Inter-Am. C.H.R., Doc. 5 rev. 1 at 763 (2002) at ¶¶ 118–20.

15 Lamey v. Jamaica, Case Nos. 11/826, 11/843, 11/846, 11/847, Report No. 49/01 (I.A.C.H.R. April 4, 2001).

16 Knights v. Grenada, Report No. 47/01 (I.A.C.H.R. April 4, 2001).

security of his person."[17] In *Edwards v. Bahamas*, the Commission found that although the Bahamas had a constitutional clemency mechanism, it was unguided by prescribed criteria and a petitioner had no right to apply to the mercy committee; to be informed of the time at which the petitioner's case would be heard; to make oral or written submissions to the mercy committee; or to present, receive, or challenge evidence considered by the committee.[18] As in its earlier holdings, the Commission ruled that consideration of a case by a clemency committee could not substitute for individualized sentencing discretion in a death penalty case. The Commission went further, laying down minimal due process standards in clemency cases:

> These protections include the right on the part of condemned prisoners to apply for amnesty, pardon or commutation of sentence, to be informed of when the competent authority will consider the offender's case, to make representations, in person or by counsel, to the competent authority, and to receive a decision from that authority within a reasonable period of time prior to his or her execution. It also entails the right not to have capital punishment imposed while such a petition is pending decision by the competent authority. In order to provide condemned persons with an effective opportunity to exercise this right, a procedure should be prescribed and made available by the State through which prisoners may file an application for amnesty, pardon or commutation of sentence, and submit representations in support of his or her application. In the absence of minimal protections and procedures of this nature, Article XXIV of the American Declaration is rendered meaningless, a right without a remedy. Such an interpretation cannot be sustained in light of the object and purpose of the American Declaration.[19]

Article 24 of the American Declaration protects the right to petition a competent authority for redress of grievances and the right to a prompt response, which the Commission applied to clemency procedures.[20] However, in case arising from Tennessee, the Commission found that the procedures of the Tennessee Board of Pardons and Paroles provided

17 Art. 1, American Declaration of the Rights and Duties of Man, adopted in 1948, O.A.S. Res. XXX, O.A.S. Off. Rec. OEA/Ser.L/V/I.4 Rev. (1965).

18 Edwards v. Bahamas, Case Nos. 12/067, 12/068, 12/086, Report No. 48/01, [2001] IACommHR 24 (I.A.C.H.R. Apr. 4, 2001) at ¶¶ 166–70.

19 *Id.* at ¶ 170.

20 Article 24 states in full, "Every person has the right to submit respectful petitions to any competent authority, for reasons of either general or private interest, and the right to obtain a prompt decision thereon." American Declaration of the Rights and Duties of Man, *supra* note 17 at art. 24.

sufficient minimal due process protections so as not to violate Article 24 of the Declaration.[21]

The European Court of Human Rights has gone further than other human rights treaty bodies in critiquing the sufficiency of clemency procedures. In *Kafkaris v. Cyprus*, the European Court of Human Rights found that a sentence of mandatory life imprisonment without the possibility of parole violated the European Convention on Human Rights, unless a prisoner had a meaningful opportunity for release.[22] The Court did not find a violation of the right to life, however, as Cyprus's clemency mechanism could sufficiently tailor a mandatory life sentence. Even though the Cypriot clemency procedure did not involve a hearing, public criteria, notification to the prisoner, or judicial review, the Court was satisfied that in practice the president routinely granted such clemency and considered a wide variety of factors in the decision-making process.[23] A partially dissenting opinion joined by five judges in that case emphasized that although a state party's choice of a specific criminal justice system was in principle outside the scope of the Convention, including the sentence review and release procedures that it has chosen, the state's power in the criminal justice realm is "not unlimited."[24] The opinion found that Cyprus's clemency procedure did not include sufficient checks against arbitrariness:

> In particular, there is no obligation to inform a prisoner of the Attorney-General's opinion on his application for early release or for the President to give reasons for refusing such an application. Nor is this the President's practice. In addition, there is no published procedure or criteria governing the operation of these provisions. Consequently, a life prisoner is not aware of the criteria applied or of the reasons for the refusal of his application. Lastly, a refusal to order a prisoner's early release is not amenable to judicial review. This lack of a fair, consistent and transparent procedure compounds the anguish and distress which are intrinsic in a life sentence and which, in the applicant's case, have been further aggravated by the uncertainty surrounding the practice relating to life imprisonment at the time.[25]

In 2013, the Grand Chamber of the European Court of Human Rights expanded *Kafkaris*'s logic in *Vinter v. United Kingdom*, ruling that a life-term prisoner was entitled to know, *at the outset of the life term*, when he

21 Workman v. United States, Case 12.261, Report No. 33/06, Inter-Am. C.H.R., OEA/Ser.L/V/II.127 Doc. 4 rev. 1 (2007).
22 Kafkaris v. Cyprus, App. No. 21906/04 (E.C.H.R. Feb. 12, 2008).
23 *Id.* at § 163.
24 *Id.* at § 3 (Tulkens, Cabral Barreto, Fura-Sandström, Spielmann, Jebens, JJ., dissenting in part).
25 *Id.*

or she would have a meaningful "prospect of release."[26] *Vinter* reversed a case decided after *Kafkaris* that a violation of Article 3 of the European Convention prohibiting cruel and degrading punishment only occurred after a prisoner, ineligible for parole or early release, had served a sufficiently long time in prison to be meaningfully considered for clemency.[27] Under the stricter rule of *Vinter*, a violation of Article 3 occurs at the time the sentence is passed if there is no meaningful opportunity for clemency within a finite amount of time. To that end, in 2012, the Court found a retroactive violation of Article 3 where Bulgaria's clemency mechanism did not permit such defined, meaningful review until a decision of the Bulgarian Constitutional Court in 2012 opened clemency to judicial review and required that the president follow public and pre-established criteria in making clemency decisions.[28]

In 2012, the European Court of Human Rights upheld the United Kingdom's extradition of two defendants facing mandatory life sentences for murder in Maryland and Florida, respectively, determining that both states provided a meaningful possibility of release.[29] The petitioner in the Florida case was facing a mandatory sentence of life without parole, but the Court noted that a number of first-degree murder sentences had been commuted by the governor with approval of two ministers, and the five-year waiting period was even waived in some cases.[30] In the Maryland case, the petitioner was facing only a discretionary sentence of life without parole, which was distinguishable from the irreducible life sentence in *Kafkaris*.[31] The Court was less gentle on US federal procedures, finding in 2014 that Belgium violated the European Convention on Human Rights when it extradited a prisoner eligible for life imprisonment without the possibility of parole to the United States.[32] In that case, the Court carefully reviewed the procedures of the US Pardon Attorney in the Department of

26 Vinter v. United Kingdom, App. Nos. 66069/09, 130/10, 3896/10 (E.C.H.R. July 9, 2013). According to the Court, "in determining whether a life sentence in a given case can be regarded as irreducible, the Court has sought to ascertain whether a life prisoner can be said to have any prospect of release. Where national law affords the possibility of review of a life sentence with a view to its commutation, remission, termination or the conditional release of the prisoner, this will be sufficient to satisfy Article 3." *Id.* at § 109.

27 *See* Iorgov v. Bulgaria, App. No. 36295/02 (E.C.H.R. Sept. 2, 2010). In *Iorgov*, the Court scrutinized Bulgaria's clemency procedures – solely within the discretion of the president – and noted that "the domestic law does not deprive the applicant of all hope of release or reduction of sentence," even though "this is a discretionary power rather than one exercised by a judicial body, and that refusal to exercise it is not open to appeal." *Id.* at §§ 52–53. According to the Court, the question was whether there was "any hope for the applicant of being released." *Id.*

28 Harakchiev v. Bulgaria, App. Nos. 15018/11, 61199/12 (E.C.H.R. July 8, 2014).

29 Harkins v. U.K., App. Nos. 9146/07, 32650/07 (E.C.H.R. Jan. 17, 2012).

30 *Id.* at §§ 139–40.

31 *Id.* at § 141.

32 Trabelsi v. Belgium, App. No. 140/10 (E.C.H.R. Sept. 4, 2014).

Justice, holding that no president in modern times had granted clemency for the federal crime of terrorism and the right to seek clemency was only theoretical in the defendant's case:

> [T]he Court needs simply note that while the said provisions point to the existence of a "prospect of release" within the meaning of the *Kafkaris* judgment – even if doubts might be expressed as to the reality of such a prospect in practice – none of the procedures provided for amounts to a review mechanism requiring the national authorities to ascertain, on the basis of objective, pre-established criteria of which the prisoner had precise cognisance at the time of imposition of the life sentence, whether, while serving his sentence, the prisoner has changed and progressed to such an extent that continued detention can no longer be justified on legitimate penological grounds.[33]

Countries that lack true clemency and pardon mechanisms or that exclude some capital crimes as unpardonable have been implicated in potential Article 6(4) violations. In 2014, the UN Assistance Mission for Iraq (UNAMI) and the UN High Commissioner for Human Rights issued a report on the death penalty in Iraq, which faulted the Iraqi constitution for prohibiting the granting of clemency or pardon for terrorism crimes in violation of the ICCPR.[34] Most crimes frequently leading to death sentences in Iraq fell under the Anti-Terrorism Law of 2005, but Article 73(1) of the Iraqi constitution prohibited granting of a special pardon by the president on recommendation of the prime minister, the constitutional clemency process established in Iraq. The provision also excluded a special pardon for international crimes and corruption, both of which would presumably also violate Article 6(4) of the ICCPR.[35]

Pressure is also increasing on countries that do not have true clemency or pardon mechanisms to establish such processes. Although China is not yet a state party to the ICCPR (though it is a signatory), the country does not have a formal clemency mechanism in death row cases.[36] China's Criminal Procedure Law states that the People's Court responsible for execution at a lower level shall cause the sentence to be executed within seven days, unless the case involves possible error, meritorious service on the part of the prisoner, previously unknown evidence, or pregnancy. In

33 *Id.* at ¶¶ 135–38.

34 United Nations Assistance Mission for Iraq and UN High Commissioner for Human Rights, *Report on the Death Penalty in Iraq*, Oct. 2014, www.ohchr.org/Documents/Countries/IQ/UNAMI_HRO_DP_1Oct2014.pdf.

35 *Id.* at 25; Iraq Const. art. 73(1) (2005).

36 Liu Renwen, *Recent Reforms and Prospects in China*, *in* Confronting Capital Punishment in Asia: Human Rights, Politics, and Public Opinion 107, 118–21 (Roger Hood and Surya Deva eds. 2013).

those cases, the lower court is to immediately submit a report to the Supreme People's Court for review, though this is purely a judicial procedure – the Supreme People's Court can only reverse for legal insufficiency – and not a mercy process. Renwen has recommended a clemency mechanism to either the Standing Committee of the National People's Congress or to the President to consider pardon or commutation of sentence to ensure China's compliance with Article 6(4) of the ICCPR.[37]

The International Court of Justice has also considered whether clemency review was effective under international law in a challenge based on the denial of consular notification and assistance to Mexican nationals on death row in the United States. In 2003, Mexico sued the United States over the denial of consular notification and visitation rights of Mexican nationals on death row.[38] The critique of the American clemency process was ancillary to the Court's review of the fair trial rights of capital proceedings as a general matter. Mexico argued that clemency was an ineffective remedy to satisfy the international obligations of the United States, as it was "standardless, secretive, and immune from judicial oversight," giving governors and parole boards virtually unfettered discretion.[39] The United States, by contrast, insisted that clemency procedures were "well suited to the task of providing review and reconsideration," noting that it was "more than a matter of grace; it was part of overall scheme for ensuring justice and fairness in the legal process."[40] Interestingly, the arguments by Mexico and the United States in this case closely reflected the "act of grace" and "public welfare" conceptions of clemency posed by Justices John Marshall and Oliver Wendall Holmes.[41]

The legality of amnesty for human rights violations

Amnesty is permissible under international law, and may even be encouraged by the United Nations and other multilateral and non-governmental organizations in a post-conflict setting or as part of a comprehensive peace agreement. Nonetheless, a trend is emerging to exclude from amnesty certain international crimes that could create impunity for serious human rights abuses, on the grounds that governments have obligations to prosecute certain crimes such as genocide, torture, and crimes against humanity. To grant amnesty or pardon to an offender accused of such

37 *Id.*

38 Avena and Other Mexican Nationals (Mexico v. United States of America), Judgment, I.C.J. Reports 2004, p. 12.

39 *Id.* at 64.

40 *Id.*

41 Austin Sarat, *At the Boundaries of the Law: Executive Clemency, Sovereign Prerogative, and the Dilemma of American Legality*, 57 AMERICAN Q. 611, 625–26 (2005).

crimes could leave victims without a remedy in the judicial system.[42] Amnesties have been widely used since ancient times to express public grace and forgiveness, bring the law into compliance with accepted reality, and, certainly, to prevent public scrutiny and accountability. Most uses of the amnesty – for instance, for delinquent tax payments or anti-corruption efforts – are relatively uncontroversial, and typically are legislative initiatives that do not implicate the pardon power.[43] Increasingly, international law imposes an absolute obligation on states to prosecute particular crimes, such as torture, genocide, war crimes, and terrorism, and amnesty for these crimes in order to prevent prosecution of the offender violates this obligation. This is true notwithstanding limited prosecutorial resources or the reconciliatory goals of a criminal justice system.[44]

Amnesties are encouraged in international law, with limitations. Article 6(5) of Protocol II of the Geneva Conventions, which deals with noninternational armed conflicts, provides that at the end of hostilities, "authorities in power shall endeavour to grant the broadest possible amnesty to persons who have participated in the armed conflict," including those who are imprisoned or detained for reasons related to the conflict.[45] When Article 6(5) of Protocol II was adopted, the Union of the Soviet Socialist Republics stated in its explanation of its vote, that the provision must not be construed to enable war criminals or those guilty of crimes against humanity to evade punishment. The International Committee of the Red Cross shares those views, as such amnesties are incompatible with the rule obliging states to investigate and prosecute persons suspected of having committed war crimes in non-international armed conflict.[46]

The majority of national courts that have applied Article 6(5) have used it as a legal basis to validate or uphold amnesties covering serious crimes. The South African Constitutional Court did so in the *AZAPO* case, in which it upheld the amnesty provisions of the 1995 Promotion of Unity and Reconciliation Act establishing the country's Truth and Reconciliation Commission as consistent with international law and the national constitution.[47] In that case, the Constitutional Court emphasized that in

42 *See generally*, Roman Boed, *The Effect of a Domestic Amnesty on the Ability of Foreign States to Prosecute Alleged Perpetrators of Serious Human Rights Violations*, 33 Cornell Int'l L.J. 297, 313–23 (2000).

43 Slye, *supra* note 3 at 174, 175.

44 *Id.* at 184–86.

45 Protocol Additional to the Geneva Conventions of 12 August 1949, and Relating to the Protection of Victims in Non-International Armed Conflict, 1125 U.N.T.S. 610, 614 (1979), at art. 6(5).

46 International Committee of the Red Cross (ICRC), *Customary International Humanitarian Law Rule 159: Amnesty*, www.icrc.org/customary-ihl/eng/docs/v1_rul_rule159 (last accessed March 16, 2015).

47 Azanian Peoples Organization (AZAPO) v. President of the Republic of South Africa, 1996 (4) S.A. 672. *See* Mark Freeman, Necessary Evils: Amnesties and the Search for Justice 34 (2009).

internal conflicts, former adversaries must live with each other in the same territory, and the state itself is best equipped to determine which measures are the most conducive to promoting reconciliation and development.[48] The United Nations has also encouraged post-conflict amnesties in Angola, Croatia, Afghanistan, and Sudan.[49] Increasingly it seems that an increasing number of amnesties are specifically *excluding* international crimes such as genocide, war crimes, and crimes against humanity, which may indicate recognition of an emerging norm of customary international law. From 1999 to 2007, 34 amnesty laws excluded at least some international crimes from the amnesty, though 28 others did not.[50]

If granting an amnesty runs the risk of offering impunity to human rights abusers, refusing an amnesty risks overzealous prosecution, helping to underscore the advantages of amnesty in a post-conflict setting. In Ethiopia, the transitional government that took power after the fall of the Derg junta in 1991 justified its rejection of amnesty with the international community's fight against impunity. Ethiopia opted for criminal prosecution of Derg leaders, establishing a Special Prosecutor's Office in 1992 and commencing the "Red Terror" trials in 1994, which were heard in courts all over the country.[51] However, the Ethiopian example looks like an exercise in retributive rather than restorative justice, especially contrasted with the South African one where an amnesty was used as leverage during the negotiation process and was combined with other reconciliatory mechanisms to minimize impunity. Derg and military officials were accused of repeated and systemic crimes that resulted in thousands of deaths, yet the trial and the resulting death sentences (some *in absentia*) raised troubling due process concerns that turned the verdicts into a kind of "victor's justice," with long delays, strained resources, and weak defense representation.[52] Leniency on human rights abusers can lead to impunity, but harshness can damage transitional justice processes.

48 *AZAPO*, 1996 (4) S.A. 672 at ¶ 31. According to the Court, "[t]he erstwhile adversaries of such a conflict inhabit the same sovereign territory. They have to live with each other and work with each other and the state concerned is best equipped to determine what measures may be most conducive for the facilitation of such reconciliation and reconstruction. That is a difficult exercise which the nation within such a state has to perform by having regard to its own peculiar history, its complexities, even its contradictions and its emotional and institutional traditions. What role punishment should play in respect of erstwhile acts of criminality in such a situation is part of the complexity." *Id.*

49 ICRC, *supra* note 46.

50 Freeman, *supra* note 47 at 53.

51 Kjetil Tronvoll, Charles Schaefer and Girmachew Alemu Aneme, *The "Red Terror" Trials: The Context of Transitional Justice in Ethiopia*, *in* THE ETHIOPIAN RED TERROR TRIALS: TRANSITIONAL JUSTICE CHALLENGED 1, 7–8 (Tronvoll, Schaefer and Aneme eds., 2009).

52 Andrew Novak, THE DEATH PENALTY IN AFRICA: FOUNDATIONS AND FUTURE PROSPECTS 64 (2014).

The strongest argument against the legality of amnesties in at least some cases is the international obligation to prosecute, or at least criminalize, certain conduct, including genocide, war crimes, torture, enforced disappearance, terrorism, and forced labor.[53] An additional legal argument is the obligation under international human rights law to ensure an effective remedy for a human rights violation. This does not necessarily require prosecution; rather, it simply requires that an avenue exist to carry out prosecution if warranted. Some human rights treaties create a right to compensation for the violation of specific rights, such as unlawful detention, and an amnesty that precludes compensation for these violations could conflict with a state's treaty obligations.[54] No single treaty discourages amnesty. This absence is notable in the Rome Statute of the International Criminal Court, which does not contain an explicit prohibition or a discouragement on the use of political amnesty. Indeed, the issue was deeply controversial at the Rome Conference and ultimately omitted from the final treaty altogether. A prohibition on amnesty was considered during the negotiations on the International Convention for the Protection of All Persons from Enforced Disappearance but likewise ultimately abandoned.[55]

Soft law documents more unambiguously discourage amnesty for human rights violations. The 1989 UN Principles on the Prevention of Extralegal, Arbitrary, and Summary Executions state that in no circumstances, including during wartime, shall blanket immunity from prosecution be granted to any person allegedly involved in extrajudicial executions.[56] Although the later Convention on Enforced Disappearances did not contain an amnesty exclusion, a 1993 General Assembly declaration on enforced disappearances did contain such a provision, noting at Article 18 that alleged perpetrators "shall not benefit from any special amnesty law or similar measures that might have the effect of exempting them from any criminal proceedings or sanction."[57] The provision has occasionally been invoked where an amnesty risked granting impunity for serious crimes. Timor-Leste has faced criticism for the amnesty provisions in its penal code, which state that a pardon (*indulto*) could be granted for any crime. The UN Human Rights Council's Working Group on Enforced Disappearances recommended that Timor-Leste exclude from the pardon power offenses that could amount to crimes against humanity. The Working Group also expressed concern that clemency and commutations of sentence were

53 Freeman, *supra* note 47 at 36–39.
54 *Id.* at 40.
55 *Id.* at 33.
56 Principles on the Effective Prevention and Investigation of Extra-Legal, Arbitrary and Summary Executions, E.S.C. res. 1989/65, annex, 1989 UN ESCOR Supp. (No. 1) at 52, UN Doc. E/1989/89 (1989).
57 UN Commission on Human Rights, *Question of Enforced Disappearances.*, 4 March 1994, E/CN.4/RES/1994/39, available at: www.refworld.org/docid/3b00f0c724.html.

"frequently granted," including for serious international crimes, without transparent processes, input from victims, or criteria issued in advance.[58]

Although not explicitly prohibited in international treaty sources as a general matter, the jurisprudence of international courts and tribunals has, in certain circumstances, found that amnesties violate international law. The Committee Against Torture has criticized or disregarded amnesties in its non-binding judgments on the obligations of states parties under the Torture Convention.[59] The UN Human Rights Committee has held that amnesties that prevent investigation, prosecution, and punishment of perpetrators of gross human rights violations are incompatible with a state's obligations under the ICCPR.[60] The Committee has stated that member states "may not relieve perpetrators from personal responsibility" for mass atrocity such as killings, torture, and enforced disappearances.[61] In *Rodriguez v. Uruguay*, the UN Human Rights Committee found that Uruguay's Law No. 15,848 (*Ley de Caducidad de la Pretensión Punitiva del Estado*) was incompatible with Uruguay's obligations under the ICCPR, as it effectively excluded in a number of cases the possibility of investigation into past human rights abuses and thereby prevented the state party from providing effective remedies to the victims of those abuses. The Committee also expressed "concern[...] that, in adopting this law, the State party has contributed to an atmosphere of impunity which may undermine the democratic order and give rise to further grave human rights violations."[62] International tribunals have also found that amnesties in certain cases may violate the fundamental rights of victims, potentially framed as the right to justice, the right to truth, the right to judicial protection, the right to an effective remedy, and the right to a fair trial or hearing.[63]

58 U.N. Human Rights Council, Report of the Working Group on Enforced or Involuntary Disappearances, Dec. 26, 2011, A/HRC/19/58/Add.1.

59 *See, e.g.*, Conclusions and Recommendations of the Committee Against Torture, Senegal, A/51/44, ¶ 112, 9 July 1996; Conclusions and Recommendations of the Committee Against Torture, Peru, Azerbaijan, Kyrgyzstan A/55/44, ¶¶ 59–61, 68, 74 (1999).

60 Human Rights Committee, Comments on Peru, UN Doc. CCPR/C/79/Add.67 (1996) at ¶ 9 ("Such an amnesty prevents appropriate investigation and punishment of perpetrators of past human rights violations, undermines efforts to establish respect for human rights, contributes to an atmosphere of impunity among perpetrators of human rights violations, and constitutes a very serious impediment to efforts undertaken to consolidate democracy and promote respect for human rights"). *See also* Concluding Observations of the Human Rights Committee, Chile, UN Doc. CCPR/C/79/Add.104 (1999) at ¶ 7; Concluding observations of the Human Rights Committee, Croatia, CCPR/CO/71/HRV (2000) at ¶ 11.

61 UN Human Rights Committee, General Comment No. 31, "Nature of the General Legal Obligation Imposed on State Parties to the Covenant," CCPR/C/21/Rev.1/Add.13 ¶ 18 (May 26, 2004).

62 Rodriguez v. Uruguay, Comm. No. 322/1988, UN Doc. CCPR/C/51/D/322/1988 (U.N.H.R.C. 1994) at ¶ 12.4.

63 Slye, *supra* note 3 at 191–92.

The jurisprudence of the Inter-American Human Rights System is more extensive, as the restoration of democratic rule in the Southern Cone in particular accompanied a number of political amnesties.[64] The Inter-American Commission has found that blanket amnesty laws that apply to crimes against humanity violate international law. In assessing the legality of El Salvador's 1987 Amnesty Decree, the Commission noted that "by foreclosing the possibility of judicial relief in cases of murder, inhumane treatment and absence of judicial guarantees, [the amnesty law] denies the fundamental nature of the most basic human rights."[65] In *Barrios Altos v. Peru*, the Inter-American Court of Human Rights likewise found that the blanket self-amnesty passed by a military regime was incompatible with human rights norms, but this case was not strictly a contested case as the state party did not defend the amnesty laws passed by the predecessor regime.[66] In *Barrios Altos*, the Court ruled that amnesty provisions were invalid where "they are intended to prevent the investigation and punishment of those responsible for serious human rights violations such as torture, extrajudicial, summary or arbitrary execution and forced disappearance," as these violate "non-derogable rights recognized by international human rights law."[67] The Court adopted similar views in *Almonacid-Arellano v. Chile*, ruling that the 1978 Chilean self-amnesty decree violated the American Convention on Human Rights to the extent that it shielded crimes against humanity from prosecution.[68]

The African Commission on Human and Peoples' Rights has twice ruled that specific amnesties violated international law: Mauritania's 1993 self-amnesty and Zimbabwe's 2000 self-amnesty. In Mauritania, the Commission noted that an amnesty law that aimed to nullify suits for compensation or seeking redress filed by victims or their beneficiaries could not shield the government from its obligations under the African Charter.[69] The government had passed an amnesty in 1993 primarily to members of the military when they surrendered power and allowed presidential and legislative elections to take place. The Commission's amnesty holding was primarily related to the admissibility of the case. Because the amnesty foreclosed

64 Freeman, *supra* note 47 at 49.

65 Masacre Las Hojas v. El Salvador, Case 10.287, Report No. 26/92, Inter-Am.C.H.R., OEA/Ser.L/V/II.83 Doc. 14 at 83 (1993). In a subsequent case, the Commission also found that El Salvador's 1993 General Amnesty Law violated the American Convention on Human Rights. Lucio Parada Cea v. El Salvador, Case 10.480, Report No. 1/99, Inter-Am. C.H.R., OEA/Ser.L/V/II.95 Doc. 7 rev. at 531 (1998).

66 Barrios Altos v. Peru, Ser. C, No. 75 [2001], IACHR 5 (Mar. 14, 2001).

67 *Id.* at sec. 41.

68 Almonacid-Arellano v. Chile, IACtHR Series C No 154 (Sept. 26, 2006).

69 Malawi African Association v. Mauritania, Comm. Nos. 54/91, 61/91, 98/93, 164/97, 196/97 and 210/98 at ¶¶ 81–85 (A.C.H.P.R. 2000).

redress in Mauritania's courts, internal remedies were exhausted and the Commission had jurisdiction to hear the underlying claims.[70]

In *Zimbabwe NGO Forum v. Zimbabwe*, the Commission reached the legality of an amnesty on the merits and not simply at the admissibility phase. In Zimbabwe, the government of President Robert Mugabe was alleged to have used the constitutional clemency and amnesty power to prevent the prosecution of members of the state security force and the ruling party for serious human rights violations.[71] Mugabe had previously used presidential clemency to prevent prosecution for human rights violations by state security forces or dissidents between 1982 and the end of 1987, as part of the unity accord between the two largest political parties.[72] The Clemency Order No. 1 of 2000 was a "troubling example of the use of the presidential power of pardon to prevent victims of political violence and human rights abuses from seeking to enforce their rights through the courts."[73] The Clemency Order granted a "free pardon" to "every person liable to criminal prosecution for any politically motivated crime committed during the period 1st January to 31st July, 2000."[74] The pardon also commuted the punishment of anyone already convicted and serving a criminal sentence, but excluded habitual criminals or sentences imposed by courts-martial. Finally, the order also excluded murder, rape, robbery, indecent assault, statutory rape, theft, possession of arms, and any offense involving fraud or dishonesty from the order, along with conspiracy to commit these crimes and accomplices thereto.[75] In 2006, the Zimbabwe High Court set aside a conviction where the defendants were members of the ruling party, who kidnapped and assaulted a victim, causing death, during the violence following parliamentary elections in 2000. Although the amnesty excluded murder, the defendants were charged with culpable homicide and kidnapping. Because the defendants proved that they committed a politically-motivated crime and because culpable homicide and kidnapping were not excluded from the amnesty, the convictions were reversed.[76] According to the Law Society of Zimbabwe, the pardon "will add credence to the perception of condonation and encouragement of violence

70 *Id.* at ¶ 80.

71 Human Rights Watch, PERPETUAL FEAR: IMPUNITY AND CYCLES OF VIOLENCE IN ZIMBABWE 24 (2011).

72 Richard Gamuchirai Banda and Tawanda Masuka, *An Analysis of the Marginalization of Women in Conflict Resolution Initiatives in Zimbabwe: The Case of the Global Political Agreement*, 2(1) SOUTH. PEACE REV. J. 56, 66 (2013), *citing* Clemency Order No. 1 of 1988.

73 *Use of the Presidential Pardon in Zimbabwe*, 45 J. AFR. L. 231, 231 (2001).

74 Clemency Order No. 1 of 2000 (General Notice 457A).

75 *Id.*

76 State v. Dube, [2006] ZWBHC 13 (March 2, 2006), *citing* Clemency Order No. 1 of 2000: General Amnesty for Politically Motivated Crimes (October 10, 2000) (Zimb.).

by the government" and "seriously undermine efforts by Zimbabweans to restore a climate of legality."[77]

The African Commission on Human and Peoples' Rights found that the Zimbabwean clemency order violated the African Charter. According to the Commission, the clemency power was to be used where the president believed the public welfare would be better served by it, with broad discretion to do what he or she deemed to be the right thing. However, in issuing a clemency order that prohibited prosecution and released perpetrators of politically-motivated crimes such as abduction, forced imprisonment, arson, and kidnapping, "the State did not only encourage impunity but effectively foreclosed any available avenue for the alleged abuses to be investigated, and prevented victims of crimes and alleged human rights violations from seeking effective remedy and compensation."[78] This case was notable because the Commission found a violation of the African Charter even though the most serious crimes were excluded from the amnesty.

Are international courts and tribunals bound by amnesties and pardons bestowed on perpetrators for serious international crimes? Conventional wisdom suggests that the morality and practicality of the "justice-for-peace" tradeoff is a sufficient argument in favor of amnesties, but that wisdom is increasingly suspect.[79] For an amnesty or pardon to be legitimate under international law, it must not contravene a state's obligation under any human rights treaty to which it is a party. Domestic amnesties, regardless of their legality, cannot immunize a perpetrator from prosecution under international law before international tribunals.[80] In *Prosecutor v. Furundžija*, the International Criminal Tribunal for the Former Yugoslavia ruled that because of the *jus cogens* nature of serious international crimes, domestic or customary rules that allow amnesties for these crimes are null and void.[81]

Only one international criminal tribunal has pronounced on the legality of a national amnesty thus far in a criminal prosecution: the Special Court for Sierra Leone. The Special Court considered whether the Lomé Agreement, a ceasefire agreement between the government of Sierra Leone and the main rebel faction, could prevent prosecution of heinous crimes committed during the war. The Agreement stated that an "absolute and free pardon" was given to all combatants and collaborators, though a note was added that the United Nations interprets that the amnesty shall not apply to

77 Statement by the Law Society of Zimbabwe, *quoted in Use of the Presidential Pardon in Zimbabwe, supra*, note 73 at 232.
78 Zimbabwe NGO Forum v. Zimbabwe, Comm. No. 245/2002 at ¶¶ 198, 211 (A.C.H.P.R. 2006).
79 Ahmed and Quayle, *supra* note 4 at 16.
80 *Id.* at 18.
81 *See* Prosecutor v. Furundžija, IT-95-17/1-T at ¶ 155 (I.C.T.Y. Dec. 10, 1998).

international crimes of genocide, crimes against humanity, or war crimes.[82] A similar challenge is brewing before the Extraordinary Chambers of the Courts of Cambodia, where Ieng Sary, a senior figure in the Khmer Rouge and former deputy prime minister and foreign minister from 1975 to 1979, argued that an amnesty and pardon given to him by the King of Cambodia in 1996 effectively immunized him from prosecution by the tribunal.[83] In Uganda, the Amnesty Act of 2000 has shielded members of the Lord's Resistance Army, a rebel group based in the north of the country, from prosecution before the country's new domestic International Crimes Division. Although the Ugandan Constitutional Court upheld the Amnesty Act, it violates Uganda's international obligations by providing near-blanket amnesty for war criminals.[84]

The Special Court for Sierra Leone in *Prosecutor v. Kallon* turned away an existential challenge to the Court's jurisdiction, finding that an amnesty for war crimes and crimes against humanity did not bar the Court's international criminal prosecutions.[85] The Court purportedly found a "crystallizing international norm that a government cannot grant amnesties for serious violations of crimes under international law," though it disputed the prosecutor's assertion that such a norm had crystallized.[86] In addition, the Court noted that it was "unrealistic to regard as universally effective the grant of amnesty by a State in regard to grave international crimes in which there exists universal jurisdiction."[87] Article 10 of the Court's own statute expressly provides that an amnesty falling within the Court's subject matter jurisdiction is not a bar to prosecution.[88] In subsequent decisions, the Special Court for Sierra Leone upheld *Kallon* and emphasized that "a norm of customary international law is developing towards the affirmation that granting amnesty for serious violations of human rights is in breach of international law."[89]

The European Court of Human Rights has also contributed to this amnesty jurisprudence, in accord with the emerging consensus that an amnesty for the purpose of granting immunity to human rights abusers violated international law. In *Abdülsamet Yaman v. Turkey*, the Court ruled,

82 Ahmed and Quayle, *supra* note 4 at 19.
83 *Id.* at 15.
84 Kirsty McNamara, *Seeking Justice in Ugandan Courts: Amnesty and the Case of Thomas Kwoyelo*, 12 Wash. U. Global Stud. L. Rev. 653, 659–60, 662–66 (2013), *citing* Kwoyelo v. Uganda, [2011] UGCC 10.
85 Prosecutor v. Kallon, [2004] SCSL 3.
86 *Id.* at ¶ 82.
87 *Id.* at ¶ 67.
88 UN Security Council, *Statute of the Special Court for Sierra Leone*, Jan. 16, 2002, available at: www.refworld.org/docid/3dda29f94.html (last accessed 20 March 2015).
89 Prosecutor v. Fofana, [2008] SCSL 44 at ¶ 86 (see footnote). *See also* Prosecutor v. Gbao, [2004] SCSL 11.

"where a State agent has been charged with crimes involving torture or ill-treatment, it is of the utmost importance for the purposes of an 'effective remedy' that criminal proceedings and sentencing are not time-barred and that the granting of an amnesty or pardon should not be permissible."[90] In a subsequent case, *Lexa v. Slovakia*, the Court considered the validity of a presidential amnesty for persons allegedly involved in the abduction and release of the son of the then-president of Slovakia, who was kidnapped, transported across the border to Austria, and found intoxicated in a car. The Court upheld the amnesty, finding that the government of Slovakia violated the European Convention on Human Rights when it subsequently prosecuted the petitioner, one of the beneficiaries of the amnesty.[91] In that case, the Court outlined the boundaries of international law, citing the UN declaration on enforced disappearances, the Inter-American Human Rights Commission's judgment in *Barrios Altos*, and the decisions of the Special Court of Sierra Leone. The Court ultimately determined that the amnesty law in question did not implicate the same principles of impunity for human rights abusers for an ordinary crime.[92]

Other international law considerations

In addition to the two primary limitations outlined above, international law touches on certain other aspects of the clemency and pardon power. The African Commission on Human and Peoples' Rights found that Nigeria was in violation of Article 6 of the African Charter, the prohibition on arbitrary detention, when it failed to release eleven soldiers who had received state pardons.[93] In 2009, Canada came in for criticism at the UN Human Rights Council's Universal Periodic Review for abandoning its long-held policy of seeking clemency for Canadian nationals on death row abroad.[94] Prime Minister Stephen Harper ended Canada's long-held policy advocating clemency for its nationals in 2007 in the case of Ronald Smith, a Canadian national on death row in Montana. The Canadian government had supported clemency for Smith on humanitarian grounds, and the state of Montana agreed in principle to transfer Smith to Canada. Harper's change of heart resulted in a statement by the Minister of Public Safety that the Canadian government would no longer pursue murderers tried in democratic countries that operated under the rule of law. In a parliamentary debate, the position of the government was to deal with clemency on a

90 Abdülsamet Yaman v. Turkey, App. No. 32446/96, § 55 (Nov. 2, 2004).
91 Lexa v. Slovakia, App. No. 54334/00 (E.C.H.R. Sept. 23, 2008).
92 *Id.* at §§ 96–99, 139.
93 Constitutional Rights Project v. Nigeria, (2000) A.H.R.L.R. 241 (ACHPR 1999).
94 Human Rights Council, Report of the Working Group on the Universal Peer Review, Oct. 6, 2009, A/HRC/11/17.

"case by case" basis.[95] In 2009, the Canadian Federal Court determined that the government's decision to withdraw support for Ronald Smith's clemency petition was unlawful.[96]

Pardon and commutation by international criminal tribunals is an additional area of growing research. The statutes of the International Criminal Tribunals for the Former Yugoslavia and Rwanda permitted pardon and commutation of sentence for convicted offenders. Under those statutes, if a prisoner sentenced by either tribunal was eligible for pardon or commutation of sentence in the state in which he or she was imprisoned, the president of the tribunal and judges would review the matter in accordance with the circumstances of the case and the interests of justice.[97] Similarly, the Special Tribunal for Lebanon in The Hague provides for a nearly identical process, whereby the president of the tribunal, in consultation with the judges, may issue pardon or clemency upon the request of the state of imprisonment.[98] The Special Court for Sierra Leone follows this same pattern, providing that pardons or commutations may be given by the president of the court in consultation with the judges.[99] By contrast, the Rome Statute of the International Criminal Court does not have a provision for pardon or commutation of sentence. Unlike the earlier tribunals, the Rome Statute does not allow the state of imprisonment to request a pardon or commutation, and the only revision or modification of sentences is left to the Court itself.[100]

Conclusion

Under the ICCPR and the American Convention on Human Rights, a clemency or pardon mechanism is required in all death penalty cases. International human rights bodies have construed this provision to include certain minimum due process standards to prevent arbitrariness or discrimination in the clemency process and to ensure genuine review. The European human rights system has gone further than this by extending the logic of this principle to life imprisonment without the possibility of parole,

95 Margaret Dudgeon, *The Death Penalty in Canada: Ethnicity, Abolition and the Current Debate*, *in* CAPITAL PUNISHMENT: NEW PERSPECTIVES 275, 290 (Peter Hodgkinson ed., 2013).

96 *Id.* at 290, *citing* Smith v. Canada, 2009 FC 228 (Can.).

97 Statute of the International Criminal Tribunal for the Former Yugoslavia, art. 28, 32 I.L.M. 1159 (1993); Statute of the International Criminal Tribunal for Rwanda, art. 27, UN Doc. S/RES/955 (1994). *See also* William A. Schabas, *Sentencing by International Tribunals: A Human Rights Approach*, 7 DUKE J. COMP. & INT'L L. 461, 509–512 (1997).

98 Statute of the Special Tribunal for Lebanon, art. 30, UN Doc. S/RES/1757 (2006).

99 Statute of the Special Court for Sierra Leone, art. 23, Jan. 6, 2002, available at: www.refworld.org/docid/3dda29f94.html.

100 Nidal Nabil Jurdi, THE INTERNATIONAL CRIMINAL COURT AND NATIONAL COURTS: A CONTENTIOUS RELATIONSHIP 108–09 (2013); Rome Statute of the International Criminal Court, art. 103, 105 (2002).

scrutinizing clemency mechanisms to ensure that a meaningful prospect of release exists. On the other hand, a consensus appears to be emerging that use of the clemency or amnesty power to give impunity for serious human rights abuses violates customary norms of international law since states have an obligation to prosecute serious crimes such as genocide and torture. One final question may be whether these two principles overlap: for instance, is a clemency mechanism required where a person is on death row for genocide? The answer appears to be yes, because clemency may be granted, even for the most serious crimes, for reasons other than impunity, such as concerns about the fairness of a trial. Finally, this chapter looked at other areas where international law touches the clemency power, including the pardon and clemency mechanisms at international criminal tribunals.

4 Comparative constitutional frameworks for the pardon power

Constitutions in the common law world vary considerably as to the structure and power of the clemency authority. In some countries, the clemency authority is an executive acting alone or a delegated authority appointed by the executive. Most constitutions, however, require that the executive consult with a clemency committee or advisory body, with the cabinet, or with a minister before making the ultimate decision, and a few require the executive to follow the recommendation of a committee or cabinet. In some states of the United States, the mercy power is wholly exercised by a committee with no executive involvement, though a governor may typically make appointments to the committee. In federal systems, such as India, Malaysia, and Nigeria, state and federal executives both possess the clemency power; this chapter will also compare these mechanisms.

The paradigmatic pardon power for a governor-general exercising the prerogative of mercy on behalf of the sovereign overseas generally includes five components that mirror the traditional power as exercised in Britain itself. Though there was no standard form in which a pardon was issued, it could be made for any offense under the law for which a person may be tried or convicted. It could also be either free or conditional. The prerogative included the power to grant a respite or delay in execution of a sentence, either indefinitely or for a defined period. In addition, the prerogative included the power to substitute a less severe form of punishment and allowed nullification of any sentence or penalty in whole or in part.[1] In essence, the purest form of the prerogative of mercy allowed a governor-general full discretion to replace a criminal sentence with one that was more lenient (though never more harsh), or with no sentence at all.

The clemency power is enshrined in nearly all written constitutions in the English-speaking world, descended from the King's prerogative of mercy at common law. Today, the clemency structure of these constitutions varies. In some jurisdictions, the executive continues to make the discretionary judgment alone. Article II of the United States constitution grants the

1 A.T.H. Smith, *The Prerogative of Mercy, the Power of Pardon and Criminal Justice*, [1983] Pub. L. 398, 417.

president alone the power to issue "reprieves and pardons," but this phrase has been interpreted to be coextensive with the common law prerogative and therefore to include the full spectrum of mercy powers.[2] Many newer constitutions provided that the executive may consult with another minister, the cabinet, or an advisory body and hear recommendations, a constitutionalization of the British colonial practice. These constitutions vary as to whether this consultation is discretionary or mandatory; in addition, some constitutions provide that the executive is either bound by the advice he or she receives or may only act based on a favorable recommendation. From a global perspective, the range of executive discretion possible under different constitutional regimes is extremely wide.

In addition to the basic structures of clemency authority in the common law world, this chapter looks at several other basic constitutional arrangements. The first are federal systems, such as the United States, India, and Nigeria, where clemency power is shared between federal and state or provincial governors. In addition, some countries bifurcate the clemency authority between multiple actors, such as delegating reprieves and remissions of sentence to the governor but pardons and commutations to a board. This chapter will also explore constitutional provisions specific to death penalty cases and to actual innocence claims. Finally, the chapter looks at two unique constitutional arrangements: Louisiana's constitutional provisions for an automatic pardon and Kenya's prohibition on pardons by lame-duck executives or interim presidents.

Structure of decision-making authority

Constitutions vary considerably as to the level of discretion exercised by the executive and the degree to which input from other actors is required or discretionary. First, some systems permit the executive to act alone, which most closely mirrors the traditional practice. Second, constitutional provisions may provide for input from another minister, often a minister of justice or attorney general; consultation with the full cabinet; or involvement of an advisory mercy committee. Finally, some constitutional regimes delegate the pardon power entirely to a board or an independent actor.

Executive acting alone

In a number of Commonwealth countries as well as the United States federal system, the constitutional clemency authority is an executive acting alone, with unfettered discretion to grant mercy or pardons, without the assistance of another minister or a committee. While the actual practice in

2 Jeffrey Crouch, The Presidential Pardon Power 20 (2009).

these countries may be delegated to other regulatory or bureaucratic actors, these delegated powers are not constitutionally required. The recent Constitution of Bhutan, for instance, gives the monarch (*Druk Gyalpo*) the unlimited power to grant amnesty, pardon, and reduction of sentences.[3] This power is wholly unchecked by legislative or judicial powers. The Hong Kong Special Administrative Region is another jurisdiction in which the Chief Executive has the unlimited constitutional power of pardon and commutation of sentence.[4] Some constitutions provide an executive with a pardon power, but specify no procedure or limitations on that power. The Comoros is an example, simply stating: "The President of the Union shall be vested with the power to grant pardons."[5] The constitutions of Bangladesh, Maldives, and Sudan have similar abstract provisions.[6] Where a collective body rather than a single person has executive authority, the mercy power is held by that body, though inevitably more actors are involved in this shared decision-making process than in one with a singular executive. Under Nepal's interim constitution, the Council of Ministers, which has executive authority, possesses the ability to grant pardons and suspend, commute, or reduce any sentence without limitation.[7] A number of modern constitutions, particularly of British overseas dependencies, have clemency provisions that hew closely to the traditional conception of the pardon power. In British overseas dependencies, the governor-general typically holds the four traditional aspects of the prerogative of mercy to be exercised on behalf of the Queen without the involvement of a minister, cabinet, or committee.[8] The constitution of the province of Queensland, Australia, permits the state governor to grant a pardon, commutation, or reprieve for any period that the governor deems appropriate, or the remission of a fine, penalty, or forfeiture, any of which may be unconditional or subject to lawful conditions.[9]

The most common constitutional clemency structure among states in the United States of America allows the executive, acting alone, the power to grant clemency, though many of these provisions are modified by statute to require additional input. This is the structure used by at least twenty-one

3 BHUTAN CONST. art. 2(16) (2008).
4 H.K. CONST. art. 48(12) (1990).
5 COMOROS CONST. art. 12 (1991).
6 SUDAN INTERIM CONST., art. 58(1)(i) (2005); BANGL. CONST. art. 49 (1972); MALDIVES CONST. art. 115 (2008).
7 NEPAL INTERIM CONST. art. 151 (2007).
8 *See, e.g.*, ANGUILLA CONST. art. 76 (1982); PITCAIRN CONST. art. 29 (2010). The constitution of the British Indian Ocean Territory is the same, except that the Territory is governed by a commissioner rather than a governor-general. BRIT. INDIAN OCEAN TERR. CONST. art. 11 (1981). In Nauru, the constitutional prerogative provision is virtually identical except that it is exercised by a republican president. NAURU CONST. art. 80 (1968).
9 QUEENSLAND CONST. art. 36 (2001).

US states and Puerto Rico.[10] In several of these states, the mercy power is limited in minor ways. In California, the governor ordinarily acts alone in granting clemency, but the constitution requires a recommendation from four state supreme court justices to grant a pardon or commutation to a person twice convicted of a felony.[11] This override is controversial because it intertwines the state judicial branch in clemency decisions and adds a cumbersome bureaucratic layer.[12] The most controversial aspect of a system in which the executive acts alone is that the executive may be influenced by political considerations. Former California Governor Pat Brown, for instance, refused to commute the death sentence of a man whom he believed had an undiagnosed mental illness. During the mercy decision-making process, Brown learned that a legislator with a swing vote on an important piece of unrelated legislation favored the execution.[13]

Executive acting with a designated minister

Some constitutions authorize the involvement of another individual, typically one who is accountable to the electorate as a member of the government. This is often the case in countries where the executive is a nonpolitical figure, such as a spiritual leader or traditional authority. Under the Constitution of Samoa, the indirectly-elected head of state, a paramount chief known as the *O le Ao o le Malo*, has the power to grant pardons, reprieves, and respites, and remit, suspend, or commute any sentence. The constitution states that the head of state shall act in his discretion after consultation of a minister appointed by the prime minister, which inserts a political and democratically-accountable actor in the decision-making process, though this may also open it to political pressures.[14] New Zealand has a similar process. Though New Zealand lacks a written constitution, the 1983 Letters Patent provide that the governor-general, an appointed representative of the Queen, may pardon a person before or after conviction, grant a respite for an indefinite or specified period, or remit the whole or

10 Alaska Const. art. 3 § 21 (1956); Ark. Const. art. 6 § 18 (1874); Cal. Const. art. 5 § 8 (1879); Colo. Const. art. 6 § 7 (1876); Haw. Const. art. 5 § 5 (1950); Ill. Const. art. 5 § 12 (1870); Miss. Const. art. 5 § 124 (1890); N.J. Const. art. 5 § 2 (1947); N.M. Const. art. 5 § 6 (1911); N.Y. Const. art. 4 § 4 (1777); N.C. Const. art. 3 § 5 (1971); Ohio Const. art. 3 § 11 (1851); Ore. Const. art. 5 § 14 (1859); S.D. Const. art. 4 § 3 (1889); Vt. Const. chap. II § 20 (1793); Va. Const. art. 5 § 12 (1971); Wash. Const. art. 3 § 9 (1889); W.Va. Const. art. 7 § 11 (1863); Wyo. Const. art. 4 § 5 (1889). *See also* P.R. Const. art. 4 § 4 (1952).

11 Cal. Const. art. 5 § 8 (1879).

12 California Commission on the Fair Administration of Justice, Clemency in Capital Cases 51 (2009).

13 David Tait, *Pardons in Perspective: The Role of Forgiveness in Criminal Justice*, 13 Fed. Sent'g Rep. 134, 135 (2000).

14 Samoa Const. art. 110 (1960).

a part of any sentence.[15] Former Governor-General Sir Denis Blundell explained that as governor-general he was required by royal instructions to seek the advice of at least one minister. If he declined the advice, he was to report the decision to the Queen. The obligation was to listen to the advice, not to accept it.[16] Today, the governor-general of New Zealand considers and acts on the advice of the minister of justice in exercising the prerogative of mercy.[17]

The constitution of Ireland allows another minister to exercise at least some forms of clemency in lieu of the president. Article 13.6 of the Irish constitution states that the president (*uachtarán*) has the right to pardon an offender or commute or remit any punishment, but the powers of commutation or remission may be conferred by law on other authorities except in capital cases.[18] With the abolition of the death penalty in Ireland, this provision was amended to remove the operative death penalty clause.[19] As a consequence, the commutation or remission power (but not the pardon power) may be vested entirely in another minister. The Criminal Justice Act of 1951 confers these powers on the minister of justice.[20] In Florida, the governor may grant reprieves up to 60 days and may suspend the collection of fines and forfeitures. However, to grant full or conditional pardons, commute sentences, or remit fines, the governor must receive the approval of two cabinet members.[21] In Sri Lanka, the constitution provides in death penalty cases that the attorney general, the government's chief legal advisor, is to provide a report on the case to the minister of justice, a political appointee, who in turn provides a recommendation to the president.[22] These provisions, from Samoa, New Zealand, Ireland, Florida, and Sri Lanka, are diverse and illustrate the differing roles that members of the cabinet or ministers of justice may play in the mercy decision. Some roles are purely advisory, as in Samoa and New Zealand, while others are binding on the executive, as in Florida. The motivation is to require the input of a democratically-accountable actor in the mercy process.

15 B.V. Harris, *The Irish President, the New Zealand Governor-General and the Head of State in a Future New Zealand Republic*, 2009 N.Z. L.Rev. 605, 644 (2009).

16 Denis Blundell, *Some Reflections Upon the Office of Governor-General in New Zealand*, 10 Victoria U. Wellington L.Rev. 197, 200 (1980).

17 Governor General of New Zealand, *The Prerogative of Mercy*, https://gg.govt.nz/role/royalprerogative.htm (last accessed March 5, 2015).

18 Ir. Const. art. 13(6) (1937).

19 Twenty-First Amendment to the Constitution Act of 2001, sched. 2, part 2 (Ir.). The amendment went into effect in 2002 after it was approved in a referendum and also included a constitutional prohibition on capital punishment. *See id.*

20 Harris, *supra* note 15 at 644.

21 Fla. Const. art. 4 § 8 (1968).

22 Sri Lanka Const. art. 34(1) (1978).

Executive acting with a cabinet

While some constitutional orders require the involvement of a government minister, others authorize a more robust mechanism involving the entire cabinet. Papua New Guinea spreads the ultimate decision-making power to the entire cabinet, known as the National Executive Council (NEC). Under the Papua New Guinean constitution, the governor-general as head of state must act "with, and in accordance with" the advice of the NEC in granting clemency. The prime minister is a member of the NEC. The constitution also creates an advisory committee on the prerogative of mercy, which is to provide a report to the NEC in every capital case.[23] The constitution explicitly renders these provisions non-justiciable.[24] While in Papua New Guinea the executive must follow the advice of the cabinet, in Marshall Islands the executive has no role; the clemency decision is one for the cabinet alone. The constitution of the Marshall Islands vests all executive authority in the cabinet, which is collectively responsible to the legislature (the *Nitijela*). The president, as head of state and government, is elected from among the members of the *Nitijela*. According to the constitution, the cabinet, not the president, has the power of reprieve and pardon.[25] In Kiribati, the traditional king (*Beretitenti*) must act "in accordance with the advice of the Cabinet" under the constitution, indicating that the cabinet has final say in mercy decisions.[26] In Tuvalu, the governor-general must also act in accordance with the advice of the cabinet.[27]

More common are those constitutions that require the governor-general to consult with or receive advice from the cabinet or executive council, while ultimately retaining the final decision-making power. The constitution of Saint Helena, a British dependency, states that in exercising the mercy power, the governor "shall act in his discretion but shall first consult the Executive Council."[28] The constitutions of Montserrat and the Turks and Caicos Islands include an identical provision as Saint Helena, but provide an exception where a situation is "too urgent to permit such consideration," in which case the governor may act alone without consulting the council.[29] Malta is similar, though the provision is limited to death penalty cases, making it an inoperative provision now that Malta has abolished capital

23 Papua N.G. Const. arts. 151(1), 152 (1975).

24 *Id.* at art. 153(3).

25 Marsh. Is. Const. art. 5 §§ 1(1), 3(f) (1979).

26 Kiribati Const. art. 50 (1979).

27 Tuvalu Const. art. 80(1) (1986).

28 St. Helena Const. art. 52(2) (1988).

29 Montserrat Const. art. 7(2) (1989); Turks & Caicos Const. art. 84 (1988). Montserrat, Turks and Caicos Islands, and Anguilla are the only constitutions in the Caribbean that do not create an advisory committee on the prerogative of mercy. While Montserrat and Turks and Caicos Islands authorize the involvement of the cabinet instead, Anguilla delegates the decision to the governor alone. Anguilla Const. art. 76 (1982).

punishment. In that provision, the minister of justice is to share the written report of the trial judge in capital cases with the cabinet, and the cabinet is to advise the president on whether a pardon or respite should be granted.[30] The constitution of Singapore provides that the cabinet, composed of the prime minister and other members of parliament, is to perform the advisory role as to the pardon and clemency power.[31] Zimbabwe's 1979 and 2013 constitutions require that the president consult with the cabinet in making mercy decisions.[32] This is in contrast to Botswana, where the constitution specifically exempts the prerogative of mercy from the general requirement that the president consult the cabinet on matters of policy "so far as practicable."[33]

The constitution of India has a more complex structure. Articles 72 and 161 of the constitution of India provide that the president and state governors alone grant pardons, reprieves, remissions, or commutations of sentence. Courts have generally refrained from laying down any additional parameters of these provisions.[34] In practice, however, the mercy power is delegated to the council of ministers of the Union of India or of the councils of state governments. Article 74 of the constitution of India provides that a council of ministers is to aid and advise the president in the exercise of his duties.[35] In *Maru Ram v. Union of India*, the Supreme Court of India has ruled that the constitutional requirement that the governor and the president act on the aid and advice of the council of ministers extends to the clemency and pardon power.[36] Some observers have suggested that this delegation of the mercy power to the council of ministers may violate the constitutional separation of powers.[37]

Although article 74 simply provides that the president is required to consult with the council of ministers, a 1979 amendment to this provision establishes that the president is permitted to send the advice back to the council of ministers once for reconsideration. If the council returns the

30 Malta Const. art. 93(2) (1964).

31 Sing. Const. arts. 22P(1)-(2) (1965).

32 Zim. Const. sched. 8, art. 20.1.3(g) (1979) ("on the advice of Cabinet); Zim. Const. art. 112(1) (2013) ("after consultation with the Cabinet").

33 Bots. Const. art. 50(2)-(3) (1966).

34 Article 72(1) reads, "the President shall have the power to grant pardons, reprieves, respites or remissions of punishment or to suspend, remit or commute the sentence of any persons convicted of any offense." Article 161(1) gives state governors a mirror right as to "any law relating to a matter to which the executive power of a state extends." India Const. arts. 72(1), 161(1) (1950).

35 India Const. art. 74 (1950). This provision originally stated in full: "There shall be a Council of Ministers with the Prime Minister at the head to aid and advise the President in the exercise of his functions." *Id.*

36 Maru Ram v. Union of India, (1981) 1 S.C.C. 107.

37 Poornima Sampath and Pryadarshini Narayanan, *Mercy Petitions: Inadequacies in Practice*, 12 Student Advoc. 72, 77 (2000).

same advice, the president is *required* to accept it.[38] As a result, the power of the president with respect to mercy petitions is limited. Although addressed to the president, such petitions are first examined by the Ministry of Home Affairs, which makes a recommendation on the mercy petition and sends it to the president for signing. The president must either accept the recommendation, or return the file once for reconsideration. If it is re-sent with the same recommendation, the president must approve the decision.[39] The Ministry of Home Affairs makes the final "recommendation" on behalf of the council of ministers.[40] This procedure has come in for significant criticism based on concerns about the quality of the investigation put forward by the Ministry of Home Affairs. According to the Asian Centre for Human Rights, the ministry has recommended to the president that he or she reject petitions for mercy without considering the requisite records of the trial courts; in addition, the ministry has concealed evidence of prisoner mental health from the president and granted recommendations that appear to violate judicial precedent.[41]

Despite the requirement that the president follow the advice of the council of ministers, in reality presidents have exercised significant agency over the disposition of mercy petitions. Because no time limit exists for signing or rejecting clemency petitions, President Kocheril Raman Narayanan (1997–2002) took the unprecedented step of keeping eight petitions pending, possibly because of concern about the verdicts or the appropriateness of the death sentences.[42] Narayanan's successor, A.P.J. Abdul Kalam (2002–2007) inherited Narayanan's eight pending petitions and received five more of his own with recommendations from the Home Minister to reject the petitions. Although it was widely reported that President Kalam personally opposed the death penalty, it appears that he did not reject the recommendation of the Home Minister in one case, resulting in the

38 India Const. art. 74(1) (1950). The amended provision reads: "There shall be a Council of Ministers with the Prime Minister at the head to aid and advise the President who shall, in the exercise of his functions, act in accordance with such advice: Provided that the President may require the Council of Ministers to reconsider such advice, either generally or otherwise, and the President shall act in accordance with the advice tendered after such reconsideration." *Id., as amended in* 1976. The original provision stated, "there shall be a Council of Ministers with the Prime Minister at the head to aid and advise the President in the exercise of his functions," but it did not require that the president follow the advice of the council. *Id.*

39 Bikramjeet Batra, *A Knotty Tale: Understanding the Death Penalty in India, in* Capital Punishment: A Hazard to a Sustainable Criminal Justice System? 213, 221 (Lill Scherdin ed., 2014).

40 Bikram Jeet Batra, *"Court" of Last Resort: A Study of Constitutional Clemency for Capital Crimes in India*, Center for the Study of Law and Governance, Jawaharlal Nehru University Working Paper Series, CSLG/WP/11 (2009).

41 Asian Centre for Human Rights, Arbitrary on All Counts: Consideration of Mercy Pleas By the President of India 12–24 (2014).

42 Batra, *supra* note 39 at 221.

execution of Dhananjoy Chatterjee in August 2004. However, by the end of September 2005, 20 files had accumulated with President Kalam, all of which carried the recommendation to reject the petition. Apart from Chatterjee, the only petition signed by Kalam was a rare one in which the Home Minister recommended commutation. By the time he left office the list of pending petitions had grown to 23, and his successor, President Pratibha Patil (2007–2012), received four more. President Patil returned twenty of the mercy petitions to the Minister of Home Affairs with recommendations to commute the sentences. Although she accepted the Home Minister's recommendation to reject in three cases, no executions took place during her presidency. As a result, three successive Indian presidents ensured that only one execution took place during a period of fifteen years.[43]

Singapore has a strong presidential structure that provides that the president "may, on the advice of the Cabinet" grant clemency, which has triggered a constitutional challenge over whether this provision required the president to consult with the cabinet, and, if so, whether he was bound by the cabinet's advice.[44] In *Yong Vui Kong v. Attorney General*, the Court of Appeal ruled that the president was required to follow the recommendation put forth by the cabinet.[45] The court cited Article 21(1) of Singapore's constitution, which states, "[e]xcept as provided by this Constitution, the President shall, in the exercise of his functions under this Constitution or any other written law, act in accordance with the advice of the Cabinet or of a Minister acting under the general authority of the Cabinet."[46] However, this provision is structured differently from the pardon clause, which simply stated that the president *may*, on the advice of his cabinet, grant a pardon. Academic scholarship has been critical of the Court's holding that the president was bound by the cabinet's advice, especially because Singapore's constitutional structure has changed dramatically since independence when it had a Westminster parliamentary model with a powerful head of government. After 1991, Singapore has a strong presidential model, in which the head of state is directly elected and possesses constitutionally-guaranteed powers. Reading the president's mercy power as constrained by the cabinet's advice may be incongruent with this constitutional structure.[47]

Executive acting with a general advisory body

Most constitutions require that executives consult with the cabinet in exercising the mercy power, or provide that the executive is to consult with a

43 *Id.* at 222–4.
44 *See* SING. CONST. art. 22P(1) (1965).
45 Yong Vui Kong v. A.G., [2011] SGCA 9.
46 SING. CONST. art. 21(1) (1965).
47 Shubhankar Dam, *Presidential Pardon in Singapore: A Comment on* Yong Vui Kong v. Attorney General, 42 COMM. L. WORLD REV. 48, 52 (2013).

specially-created advisory mercy committee or pardons board. However, a handful of constitutions have a slightly different requirement, providing that the executive is to consult with a body that advises him or her on many different executive functions and not simply the mercy power. These general advisory bodies differ as to whether they are purely appointed (Brunei Darussalam), a mixture of *ex officio* and appointed (Nigeria), or democratically accountable (Massachusetts). However, they all have in common the characteristic that they advise not only on the prerogative of mercy, but on other discretionary powers of the executive as well. The constitution of Brunei Darussalam establishes a pardons board to advise the Sultan on the prerogative of mercy; however, these provisions are currently suspended.[48] Instead, the 2006 suspension order confers on the Privy Council of Brunei the advisory mercy function, though the Sultan retains "absolute discretion" in making the ultimate decision.[49] The Brunei Privy Council is composed of members of the royal family and other senior government officials appointed to the position, and it advises on amendments to the constitution and other powers in addition to the prerogative of mercy.[50] Similarly, in Tonga, a Privy Council advises the king on matters of mercy and various other executive, legislative, and judicial functions.[51] The Privy Council includes the Lord Chancellor, the president of the supreme court, and the attorney general, and is chaired by the king himself, who has authority to appoint additional members.[52]

Ghana's constitution requires the President to act in consultation with the Council of State in exercising the mercy prerogative.[53] The Council of State, akin to a traditional council of elders, is a large body that advises the president on executive powers. Some members are elected, one from each region; some are prominent citizens appointed by the president; and a handful are *ex officio* positions, including the chief of defense staff, the inspector-general of police, and the president of the House of Chiefs, the upper house of parliament. Currently with 24 members, it is one of the largest advisory bodies to pronounce on the prerogative of mercy anywhere in the Commonwealth, and the interesting hybrid of elected, appointed, and *ex officio* members is able to provide public input to the decision-making process and retain institutional memory.[54] Nigeria's constitution is similar to Ghana's, creating an advisory committee also called the

48 BRUNEI CONST. arts. 8A, 9 (1959).

49 *See id.* at art. 9(1); Constitution of Brunei Darussalam (Suspension) Order, 2006 (S 15/06).

50 *New Members of the Privy Council*, BRUNEI TIMES, Apr. 7, 2011, www.bt.com.bn/news-national/2011/04/07/new-members-privy-council.

51 TONGA CONST. art. 37 (1885).

52 Jennifer Corrin and Don Paterson, INTRODUCTION TO SOUTH PACIFIC LAW 378 (2013).

53 GHANA CONST. art 72(1) (1992).

54 Government of Ghana, *Council of State*, www.ghana.gov.gh/index.php/2012-02-08-08-18-09/council-of-state (last accessed November 28, 2014).

Council of State. As in Ghana, the Nigerian equivalent advises the president on a number of policy issues, including population censuses and record-keeping; awards of national honors; appointments of members of the Independent National Electoral Commission, the National Judicial Council, and the National Population Commission; and any matter relating to the maintenance of public order when requested to do so.[55] Nigeria's Council of State is a massive body, even larger than Ghana's, composed of the president, vice president, president of the Senate, speaker of the House of Representatives, attorney general, all former heads of state, all state governors, and all former chief justices.[56]

Similarly to Ghana and Nigeria, the governor of Massachusetts is required to consult with a general advisory body known as the Governor's Council, composed of 8 members elected from specially-drawn districts (generally, each spanning five contiguous state senate districts). The Governor's Council provides advice to the governor on judicial nominations and appointment and removal of notaries public and justices of the peace, among other matters.[57] Unlike the Councils of State in Ghana and Nigeria, the Governor's Council in Massachusetts is not purely advisory with respect to the clemency power. The governor requires a recommendation from the Council in order to grant pardons and commutations of sentence.[58] New Hampshire has a similar structure. The governor of New Hampshire is required to follow the advice of the Executive Council, a general advisory body elected from five specially-created districts, before granting a pardon or commutation. Like the Governor's Council in Massachusetts, the Executive Council has effective veto over the governor's pardon decisions.[59]

Executive acting with an advisory clemency committee

By far the most common structure in the common law world is a constitutional framework in which the governor possesses plenary clemency authority but consults with or receives advice from a specially-appointed advisory mercy committee. The comparative structures of these committees are explored further in Chapter 6. Zambia's constitution is illustrative. The president must issue a death warrant if clemency is denied, an order for the sentence to be commuted, or a pardon under his hand and seal.[60] The

55 Nigeria Const. arts. 175(3), 235(a)-(b) (1999).
56 *Id.* at sched. 3 part 1(b)(5)-(6).
57 State of Massachusetts, *Governor's Council*, www.mass.gov/portal/government-taxes-public-service/about-state-government/govs-council.html (last accessed March 6, 2015).
58 *See* Mass. Const. ch. 2 art. 8 (1780); Mass. Gen. Laws, ch. 127 § 152.
59 N.H. Const. pt. 2 art. 52 (1783); N.H. Rev. Stat. Ann. §§ 4:21–4:26.
60 Bako Chipola, *Capital Punishment in Zambia and the Presidential Prerogative of Mercy*, LL.B. Thesis, University of Zambia 44 (2004), *citing* Zam. Const. art. 59 (1991).

president creates an Advisory Committee on the Prerogative of Mercy, whose members he appoints and who serve at his pleasure; he alone determines the terms of reference for the committee members.[61] The committee reviews the record of the case and the recommendations of the trial judge. Churches and non-governmental organizations have successfully called upon the president to exercise mercy for death row inmates, though the ultimate process of consideration is secretive. However, at a recent death penalty conference, the advisory committee was revealed to meet at secret locations and to base its decisions on moral grounds, the specific facts of a case, and public interest.[62]

Although the specific provisions vary, most countries in the Commonwealth Caribbean and common law Africa have similar structures, as do countries such as Malaysia, Papua New Guinea, Solomon Islands, and several US states.[63] These constitutions differ as to whether the executive must consult with the committee prior to deciding clemency, or whether the governor calls on the committee at his or her own pleasure. Malawi's constitution creates an Advisory Committee on the Granting of Pardon, the makeup of which the constitution leaves to an act of parliament.[64] The constitution of Belize has a lengthy provision establishing and regulating the procedure for the Belize Advisory Council, which advises the governor-general in mercy decisions. The constitution provides for appointment and removal of members, the terms of conditions of office, provision for a quorum, and reporting and transparency requirements.[65] In Trinidad and Tobago, the structure is two-tiered: a minister designated by the president consults with the advisory committee. The minister is not bound by the advice of the committee, nor is the president bound by the advice of the minister.[66] In Sierra Leone, the cabinet appoints the advisory mercy committee with the vice-president presiding.[67] In The Gambia, the committee on the exercise of the prerogative of mercy consists of the attorney general and three other persons appointed by the president and confirmed by the legislature. The president is required to consult with the committee, but is not bound by the body's recommendation.[68]

In several US states, the governor possesses the clemency and pardon power but may seek recourse to a specially-appointed advisory mercy board. In Wisconsin, the governor has absolute discretion in the granting

61 *Id., citing* Zam. Const. art. 60 (1991).
62 Chipola, *supra* note 60 at 47.
63 *See, e.g.*, Ant. & Barb. Const. art. 85 (1981); Bots. Const. art. 54 (1966); Gren. Const. art. 73 (1973); Guy. Const. art. 189 (1980); Malawi Const. art. 89(2)(a) (1994); Malay. Const. art. 42 (1957); Papua N.G. Const. art. 152 (1975); Solomon Is. Const. art. 45(2) (1978).
64 Malawi Const. art. 89(2)(a) (1994).
65 Belize Const. art. 54 (1981).
66 Trin. & Tobago Const. arts. 87–88 (1976).
67 Sierra Leone Const. art. 63(1).
68 Gambia Const. arts. 82(1)-(2) (1996).

of clemency, but appoints a non-statutory pardon advisory board that includes members from the departments of justice and corrections, four public members, and the governor's legal counsel.[69] By statute, the governor of Iowa must first obtain the advice of the Board of Parole in clemency petitions, though the board's recommendations are not binding and the governor may reject a recommendation.[70] Similarly, Kentucky's constitution grants the governor alone the power of mercy, but by statute he or she must seek the advice of the Parole Board before acting. As in Iowa, the governor is not bound by this advice.[71] In Maine, the governor acts alone in considering and granting clemency, but the parole board may, at the governor's request, advise him concerning applications for pardons, reprieves, and commutations in addition to its parole functions.[72] In addition, the Maine governor's Board on Executive Clemency holds hearings involving petitioners and makes recommendations to the governor. He is free to reject the recommendations.[73]

Similar structures exist in Michigan and Missouri, where the governor retains the authority to grant clemency. In both states, by statute, the parole board is required to review all clemency petitions and make non-binding recommendations.[74] New Jersey's constitution authorizes the creation of an advisory body to aid in the exercise of the governor's clemency power, but no such commission has yet been established.[75] In South Dakota, statutory authority allows the governor to delegate authority over clemency to the Board of Pardons and Parole to hold hearings and issue non-binding recommendations.[76] Similarly, in Tennessee, regulation provides that the parole board may, upon request of the governor, consider and make nonbinding recommendations concerning all requests for commutations or pardons. Petitioners are entitled to a hearing before the parole board.[77] By executive order in 2007, the governor of Colorado established a 7-member Executive Clemency Advisory Board to make advisory recommendations on mercy at the governor's request.[78] The governor of Maryland makes pardons "upon the recommendation of the Parole Commission," which may

69 Wis. Const. art. 5, § 6 (1848); Kathleen M. Ridolfi and Seth Gordon, *Gubernatorial Clemency Powers: Justice or Mercy?*, Crim. Just. 40 (Fall 2009).

70 Iowa Const. art. 4, § 16 (1857); Iowa Code secs. 914.3–914.4.

71 Ky. Const. § 77 (1891); Ky. Rev. Stat. Ann. § 439.450.

72 Me. Const. art. 5, § 11 (1820); Me. Rev. Stat. tit. 34A, § 5210(4). This provision was added in 1983.

73 State of Maine Department of Corrections, *Executive Clemency: Pardons and Commutations*, www.maine.gov/corrections/adult/pardon/ (last accessed Feb. 17, 2015).

74 Mich. Const. art. 5, § 14 (1963); Mich. Comp. Laws § 791.243; Mo. Const. art. 4, § 7; Mo. Rev. Stat. § 217.800.

75 N.J. Const. art. 5, § 2(1) (1947).

76 S.D. Codified Laws § 24-14-1.

77 Tenn. Comp. R. & Regs. § 1100-1-1-15.

78 Colorado Executive Order B-008 of 2007.

investigate and advise on pardon applications.[79] In Alaska, every governor since statehood has appointed some type of advisory panel to assist in making clemency evaluations, typically called executive clemency commissions or clemency advisory committees. Such ad hoc panels have comprised varying numbers of members, appointed by the governor. The extent to which the governors made use of the panels has varied, but they were not constitutionally or statutorily mandated until 2007.[80]

Executive requires recommendation by a clemency committee

Several jurisdictions in the common law world grant the clemency power to the governor, but only on the recommendation of a pardon board or committee, which is a hybrid structure. This structure is primarily used in several US states, though versions of it appear elsewhere. In Chuuk (Micronesia), the governor may grant clemency "after receipt of a favorable recommendation by a board prescribed by statute."[81] Under Cyprus's 1960 constitution, in non-death penalty cases the president and vice-president require the unanimous recommendation of the attorney-general and deputy attorney-general in order to exercise the clemency power.[82] In the Solomon Islands, the Committee on the Prerogative of Mercy is not advisory; the governor-general is bound by the advice of the committee.[83] In addition to these, in eight US states, including Arizona, Delaware, Indiana, Louisiana, Montana, Oklahoma, Pennsylvania, and Texas, the clemency power is held by the governor, but he only may grant clemency upon the favorable recommendation of a clemency board.[84] Pennsylvania heightens the requirement in death penalty cases: the board must vote unanimously, and not simply by majority, to commute a death sentence to life imprisonment.[85] On the other hand, Montana lowers the requirement in death penalty cases, allowing the governor to grant clemency in capital cases even where the board does not recommend clemency.[86] In January 2015, the Montana House of Representatives overwhelmingly passed legislation returning the

79 Md. Const. art. 2, § 20 (1867); Md. Regs. Code. tit. 12, § 18.01.16.
80 Ronald S. Everett and Deborah Periman, *"The Governor's Court of Last Resort:" An Introduction to Executive Clemency in Alaska*, 28 Alaska L.Rev. 57, 84 (2011).
81 Chuuk Const. (Micr.) art. 6 § 2 (1989).
82 Cyprus Const. art. 53(4) (1960). The original constitution provided that the attorney general and deputy attorney general must each represent either the Greek Orthodox and Turkish Muslim communities. *Id.* at art. 112(1).
83 Solomon Is. Const. art. 45(5) (1978).
84 Ariz. Const. art. 5 § 5 (1912); Ariz. Rev. Stat. § 31–401; Del. Const. art. 7 § 1 (1897); Ind. Const. art. 5 § 17; Ind. Code § 11-9-2-1; La. Const. art. 4 § 5(E)(1) (1974); Mont. Const. art. 6 § 12 (1972); Mont. Code Ann. § 46–23-301; Okla. Const. art. 6 § 10 (1907); Penn. Const. art. 4 § 9 (1968); Tex. Const. art. 4 § 11(b) (1876).
85 Penn. Const. art. 4 § 9 (1968).
86 Mont. Const. art. 6 § 12 (1972); Mont. Code Ann. § 46-23-301.

clemency power to the governor after a prominent case in which the board declined to recommend a grant of clemency despite the governor's support.[87]

A board or committee acting alone

In nine US states, the clemency power is vested exclusively in an executive board: Alabama, Connecticut, Georgia, Idaho, Minnesota, Nebraska, Nevada, South Carolina, and Utah. In three of these states, the governor sits as a member of the board. Nevada is illustrative: the Board of Pardons is composed of the governor, justices of the state supreme court, and the attorney general.[88] In Minnesota, the Board of Pardons is composed of the governor, attorney general, and chief justice of the state supreme court.[89] In Nebraska, the Board of Pardons is composed of the governor, attorney general, and secretary of state.[90] Although the constitution of Alabama originally created a three-member advisory board composed of the attorney-general, secretary of state, and state auditor, a constitutional amendment in 1939 granted the clemency power to the legislature, which has delegated it to a three-member Board of Pardons and Parole.[91] Under earlier constitutions, though not under its current one, Florida likewise had such a system. Although Florida originally vested the pardon power in the governor alone after statehood, subsequent constitutions provided for a five-member Board of Pardons. Under the 1885 constitution, the board comprised the governor, the attorney general, and three state supreme court justices, later replaced in 1896 by the secretary of state, the comptroller, and the state commissioner of agriculture in order to relieve the overburdened state supreme court of these additional duties. The governor was required to confirm pardons and commutations.[92] Florida's 1968 constitution returned the clemency power to the governor.[93]

As in Alabama, the other five states have boards appointed by the governor, though several require legislative confirmation of board members. Idaho has a five-member Commission of Pardons and Parole with plenary

87 H.B. 43 (Mont. 2015); *House Passes Bill to Allow Governor Clemency Powers*, Great Falls Tribune, Jan. 30, 2015, www.greatfallstribune.com/story/news/local/2015/01/30/house-passes-bill-allow-governor-clemency-powers/22620777 (last accessed May 13, 2015).

88 Ridolfi and Gordon, *supra* note 69 at 31.

89 Minn. Const. art. 5 §7 (1857).

90 Neb. Const. art. 4 § 3 (1875).

91 Ala. Const. art. 5 § 124 (1901, as amended to 1939). *See also* Pinkerton v. State, 29 Ala. App. 472 (Ala. Crim. App. 1940) (discussing the legislative delegation of the pardon power to the State Board of Pardons and Parole and the retroactive consequences for prisoners).

92 Vivien M.L. Miller, Crime, Sexual Violence, and Clemency: Florida's Pardon Board and Penal System in the Progressive Era 2–3 (2000).

93 Fla. Const. art. 4 § 8 (1968).

clemency authority. The governor appoints members and they are confirmed by the legislature for three-year terms, though only three may be from the same political party.[94] In South Carolina by statute, the governor appoints a seven-member Probation, Parole, and Pardon Board, which holds the primary clemency power.[95] Utah's Board of Pardons and Parole is appointed by the governor with the consent of the state senate. In Utah, the governor is only empowered to grant temporary respites or reprieves; the board has the power to pardon, commute sentences, and remit fines and forfeitures.[96] The governor of Georgia appoints the five members of that state's Board of Pardons and Paroles for seven-year terms.[97] Finally, although Connecticut's constitution does not provide for the clemency power (only the governor's power of reprieve), a statutory pardon scheme establishes a Board of Pardons with plenary clemency authority appointed by the governor.[98]

A board may help provide consistency and institutional memory in the exercise of the mercy power, and it may be resistant to political influence. However, boards tend to be more conservative on systematic or policy-driven grants of clemency and some of the creative opportunity for drawing attention to systemic failures in the criminal justice system is lost, as with, for instance, Illinois Governor George Ryan's mass commutation of death sentences in 2003. Mass commutations by committees or boards are extremely rare. One exception is when the Georgia Board of Pardons provided mass clemency to mitigate the harshness of federal immigration law changes in 1996, which removed exceptions from deportation for undocumented aliens who were accused of misdemeanors. Over a 15-month period ending in June 2001, the Georgia Board of Pardons granted 138 pardons to permanent resident aliens who suddenly found themselves subject to deportation, including those who had lived in the United States for many years or who had US citizen children. A misdemeanant – and even an occasional felon – with an otherwise clean record became eligible for a pardon to avert deportation. Discretionary mercy authority allowed the Board to correct manifest injustice not otherwise subject to redress.[99]

Executive acting with the legislature

In a handful of jurisdictions, the clemency and pardon power may be exercised only with the involvement of legislative actors. The most common

94 Idaho Const. art. 4 § 7; Idaho Code Ann. § 20-210.
95 S.C. Code Ann. § 24-21-920.
96 Utah Const. art. 7 § 12 (1895).
97 Ga. Const. art. 4 § 2 para. 1 (1983).
98 Conn. Const. art. 4 § 13 (1965); Conn. Gen. Stat. § 54-124a.
99 Elizabeth Rapaport, *The Georgia Immigration Pardons: A Case Study in Mass Clemency*, 13 Fed. Sent'g Rep., 184, 184–185 (2001).

mechanism is through a legislative pardon for the crime of treason, explored in Chapter 5. In one common law jurisdiction, the executive requires approval of the legislature to grant all forms of clemency. This is Rhode Island, where the governor requires the advice and consent of the state senate to grant pardons and exercise other clemency powers.[100] Given this structure, clemency is granted extremely rarely.

The clemency power in federal systems

In federal constitutional systems, the mercy power is often shared by the national executive and state or provincial ones. Under the US federal constitution, the president may only excuse or pardon federal crimes, while state governors are limited to the laws of their state jurisdictions.[101] The US Supreme Court has made clear that states are not constitutionally required under the federal constitution to provide any clemency mechanism, and each state is free to adopt its own clemency scheme.[102] Nor does a federal pardon automatically restore an offender's civil rights, such as the right to carry a firearm, serve on a jury, or vote, at least in the United States; this must be done according to state law.[103] Micronesia similarly has a federal constitution that provides only minimal constraints on state clemency powers. The constitution of Micronesia states that the president may grant pardons and reprieves, "except that the chief executive of each state shall have this power concurrently with respect to persons convicted under state law."[104] Tanzania's constitution also has a federalism clause, indicating that the president of Tanzania may exercise clemency for persons convicted and punished in mainland Tanzania as well as those convicted and punished in Zanzibar if the law was passed by the Tanzanian parliament and applied to Zanzibar. The sultan of Zanzibar retains the pardon power over that island's criminal offenses.[105]

In other jurisdictions, the federal constitution provides either a minimum procedure for state governments to follow or sets jurisdictional boundaries to which each sovereign – federal or state – must adhere. Nigeria's

100 R.I. CONST. art. 9, § 13 (1842).

101 US Department of Justice, *Pardon Information and Instructions*, Jan. 13, 2015, www.justice.gov/pardon/pardon-information-and-instructions. There are some minor exceptions. For instance, before Alaska statehood, the governor only had the power to reprieve; the president retained the power to review and confirm or annul reprieves granted by the governor. Ronald S. Everett and Deborah Periman, *"The Governor's Court of Last Resort:" An Introduction to Executive Clemency in Alaska*, 28 ALASKA L.REV. 57, 73 (2011).

102 Herrera v. Collins, 506 US 390, 414 (1993).

103 Christopher C. Joyner, *Rethinking the President's Power of Executive Pardon*, 43 FED. PROBATION 16, 20 (1979).

104 MICR. CONST. art. 10 § 2(c) (1981).

105 TANZ. CONST. art. 45(3) (1977).

constitution provides for a pardon power by state governors that is substantively similar to the federal power, except that the state governor is limited to pardons under the law of his or her respective state. However, the constitution does not specifically create a structure or process for those governors to follow, only requiring that state governors consult "with such advisory council of the State on prerogative of mercy as may be established by the Law of the State."[106] In other words, if a state establishes an advisory mercy council, the state governor must seek its advice in exercising the mercy power. Sri Lanka's constitution is even more robust, providing that the president can pardon both federal *and* state offenses, while state governors may only pardon state offenses. Unlike the president, provincial governors must consult with their provincial boards of ministers, though it appears the governor retains the ultimate decision. If a provincial governor does not agree with the advice of the board, under the constitution he has the discretion to refer the case to the president for orders.[107] In Sri Lanka's federal system, the president has a considerably broader prerogative of mercy than provincial governors do.

India's constitution generally lays out mirror mercy prerogatives for the president of the Union and to state governors that allows each sovereign to pardon offenses falling under the laws of their respective jurisdictions. However, article 72 provides several additional powers of the Union president, including that he or she may issue pardons for punishments passed by courts-martial and may pardon or commute all death sentences in the country, even when they fall under state rather than Union law.[108] Article 161 authorizing state governors to grant pardon or clemency is narrower in scope than the counterpart power of the President, as it is limited to state law and does not extend to courts martial or Union law.[109] The drafters of the constitution intended for overlap of state and Union pardon powers for death sentences. The constitution does not bar a prisoner from seeking clemency from the Union president once the state governor has denied the mercy petition, and in fact deliberately creates this opportunity. In essence, the constitution recognizes the special finality and severity of death sentences and places the Union president at the very top of the constitutional pardon scheme.[110]

Malaysia's federal constitution generally provides the same prerogative of mercy power to the federal executive (an elected monarch, the *Yang di-Pertuan Agong*) and to state-level executives (either hereditary state

106 Nigeria Const. art. 212(2) (1999).
107 Sri Lanka Const. art. 154B(9) (1978).
108 India Const. art. 72 (1950).
109 *Id.* at art. 161.
110 Parul Kumar, *The Executive Power to Pardon: Dilemmas of the Constitutional Discourse*, 2 N.U.J.S. L. Rev. 9, 13–15 (2009).

monarchs or secular state governors, depending on the jurisdiction).[111] The federal elective monarch has a more extensive power to pardon offenses tried by court-martial or offenses committed in the federal territories of Kuala Lumpur, Labuan, and Putrajaya, while the state governors or traditional monarchs only pardon offenses arising under the laws of that state. Each state possesses a pardons board, which consists of the federal attorney general, the chief minister of that state, and not more than three other members appointed by the state governor or traditional monarch. The federal attorney general is permitted to delegate his functions to another person.[112] The pardons boards are presided over by the state governors or traditional monarchs. Before tendering any advice, they must consider any written opinion from the federal attorney general. The constitution also creates a single pardons board for the federal territories of Kuala Lumpur, Putrajaya, and Labuan, with the federal elective monarch presiding.[113]

Additional comparative constitutional mercy provisions

The common law world is a site of significant experimentation in the delegation of the mercy power. Some constitutional orders devise unique schemes either apportioning the mercy power among different actors or triggering alternative processes for certain crimes. Finally, novel provisions on automatic pardons and late-term or transitional pardons may be of comparative interest in other jurisdictions.

Bifurcated clemency powers

In some jurisdictions, the clemency power is bifurcated among two or more actors. Most frequently, these allow the executive the ability to grant a temporary reprieve or to remit fines or forfeitures, while granting plenary clemency power (including power over pardons and commutations of sentence) to a board or committee. Of the six US state constitutions that divide their clemency power in this manner, five of them have explicit or implicit time limits for the duration of the governor's temporary grant of clemency. In Delaware, the governor may grant a reprieve for up to six months; all other exercises of the clemency power require a recommendation in writing by a majority of a constitutionally-created Board of

111 Nine of the Malaysian states are ruled by a hereditary monarch, seven of them sultans. The other four states (the colonial enclaves of Penang and Malacca and the Borneo territories of Sabah and Sarawak) are governed by secular ceremonial governors, called *Yang di-Pertua Negeri*. All thirteen form the Conference of Rulers, but only the nine hereditary monarchs can be elected King of Malaysia. Wan Arfah Hamzah, A First Look At the Malaysian Legal System 4–5 (2008).

112 Malay. Const. arts. 42(4)-(11) (1957).

113 *Id.* at arts. 42(4)-(11).

Pardons.[114] Pennsylvania has a similar structure, but the governor's power to reprieve does not contain a time limit and may be indefinite. However, granting pardons or commutations requires a recommendation by the Board of Pardons.[115] In Florida the governor may grant reprieves of up to 60 days, but may only exercise the power to pardon or grant commutations with the approval of two members of the cabinet.[116] In Nevada, the governor may reprieve a sentence for 60 days, but the pardon board (on which the governor sits) has plenary pardon authority.[117] Similarly, Utah and Idaho also allow the governor to reprieve a sentence until it can be considered at the next session of the pardons board.[118] In Texas, where the governor may only grant clemency upon the recommendation of the Board of Pardons and Paroles, the provision is even narrower: the governor is only empowered to grant a single 30-day reprieve in any death penalty case without the board's approval.[119] As noted earlier, the constitution of Ireland allows the Minister of Justice to exercise the powers of commutation or remission of sentence, but preserves the right of pardon for the president.[120]

The challenge with a bifurcated clemency power is the risk of a conflict of authority between the governor and the board. This occurred in February 2015 in Pennsylvania, when newly-elected Democratic Governor Tom Wolf granted a reprieve to inmate Terrance Williams, who was to be executed on March 4, 2015, as Wolf commissioned a task force to inquire into Pennsylvania's death penalty regime.[121] Wolf's predecessor in office, a Republican supporter of capital punishment, signed four death warrants in the waning days of his term on the expectation that Wolf would not be able to halt the executions.[122] Citing to recent exonerations and questioning the death penalty's fundamental fairness, Wolf noted that Pennsylvania had the fifth-largest death row in the United States, but had only executed three inmates since 1976 – all death row "volunteers" who gave up their appeals.[123] Because pardons or commutations of a death sentence require a

114 Del. Const. art. 7 § 1 (1897).

115 Penn. Const. art. 4 § 9(a) (1968).

116 Fla. Const. art. 4 § 8a (1968).

117 Nev. Const. art. 5 § 3 (1864).

118 Idaho Const. art. 4 § 7 (1890); Utah Const. art. 7 § 12 (1895). An interesting counterexample is Georgia, which does not bifurcate the clemency power: the chairman of the State Board of Pardons and Paroles may suspend the execution of a death sentence until the full board can meet. Ga. Const. art. 4 § 2 para. 2(c)(d).

119 Tex. Const. art. 4, § 11(b) (1876).

120 Ire. Const. art. 13.6 (1937, *as amended in* 2002).

121 Wallace McKelvey, *Gov. Tom Wolf Declares Moratorium on Death Penalty in Pa.*, PennLive.com, Feb. 13, 2015, www.pennlive.com/politics/index.ssf/2015/02/gov_tom_wolf_declares_moratori.html (including full text of Wolf's press release).

122 Christina Kauffman, *Corbett Signs 11th-Hour Death Warrants for Prisoners Including Man Convicted of York City Shooting*, York Dispatch, Jan. 14, 2015, www.yorkdispatch.com/breaking/ci_27318779/corbett-signs-11th-hour-death-warrants-prisoners-including.

123 McKelvey, *supra* note 121 (see full press release).

unanimous recommendation from the board of pardons, the Philadelphia District Attorney and others sued Wolf, arguing that an indefinite reprieve was not constitutional.[124] In 1994, the Pennsylvania Commonwealth Court, an intermediate appellate court, ruled in *Morganelli v. Casey* that the governor does not have a "silent" power of reprieve; he must affirmatively grant a reprieve after a death warrant has been issued.[125] In that case, former Governor Robert Casey, an opponent of the death penalty, failed to act on death warrants for a period of four years.[126] A dissent argued that the Pennsylvania constitution imposed no limits on the governor's power to reprieve.[127] The decision suggests that Wolf's reprieve is constitutional. Wolf affirmatively reprieved the death warrant for Williams, which seems to distinguish it from the death sentences in *Morganelli.* In addition, the permissible length of a reprieve is undefined in Pennsylvania's constitution or statutory law, and the *Morganelli* court indicated that a reprieve is granted "normally for a defined purpose or period."[128] Wolf's reprieve likely satisfies this standard, as it had a defined purpose. As this situation reveals, however, the constitution of Pennsylvania constrains the clemency power too tightly. By requiring unanimous recommendation of the pardons board in death penalty cases, the constitution closes an important safety valve and thereby contributes to an unusually bloated death row.

Death penalty-specific provisions

A handful of constitutions in the English-speaking world create alternative powers with respect to death penalty or capital cases. In Swaziland, the King's prerogative of mercy is specifically limited in the constitution solely to death penalty and life imprisonment sentences.[129] However, the constitution authorizes the legislature to enact a parole system under which sentences of imprisonment may be reduced for good behavior.[130] Similarly, in the constitution of South Carolina, the governor's clemency power is limited only to granting reprieves and to commuting a sentence of death to life imprisonment.[131] South Carolina's constitution indicates that all other forms of clemency "shall be regulated and provided for by law," which has allowed

124 Brief for Petitioner, Penn. v. Williams, E.D. Misc. Dkt. No. 14 (S.C. Feb. 18, 2015). In this filing, the Philadelphia District Attorney argues that Wolf is, in essence, using the reprieve power to grant an indefinite "moratorium" on the death penalty.

125 Morganelli v. Casey, 66 Pa.Commw. 574, 581 (1994).

126 *Id.* at 577.

127 *Id.* at 582–83 (Kelley, J., dissenting).

128 *Id.* at 581. The Court also noted that "the constitutional power of reprieve has no meaning or relevance until after the issuance of the death warrant, from the completion of which the reprieve provides a delay." *Id.*

129 Swaz. Const. art. 78(1) (2005).

130 *Id.* at art. 78(7).

131 S.C. Const. art. 4 § 14 (1895).

the legislature to establish by statute the Probation, Parole, and Pardon Board, appointed by the governor, which possesses plenary clemency authority in all other cases.[132] Alabama's constitution creates a bifurcated clemency power: the governor may grant reprieves and may commute death sentences, but all other clemency decisions must be made upon the advice of a pardons board.[133] According to Zambia's constitution, the president has the discretion to consult with the Advisory Committee on the Prerogative of Mercy as to granting clemency as a general matter. However, he is *required* to consult with the advisory committee where a petitioner has been sentenced to death.[134] The 1937 constitution of Ireland required the president to exercise the clemency power in capital cases, but permitted delegation of the clemency power to another minister in non-capital cases (today, exercised by the minister of justice).[135] In 2002, an amendment of the Irish constitution was approved, constitutionally entrenching death penalty abolition and removing the capital case distinction.[136]

The constitution of Cyprus also creates a somewhat novel death penalty-specific procedure. The structure of the clemency authority is a product of the power-sharing constitution of 1960 that attempted to bring together an autonomous Turkish minority and a Greek-speaking majority. The constitution is strongly "bi-communal," guaranteeing majority rule with minority representation through an intricate system of constitutional devices. These novel provisions include fixed numerical ratios between members of the Greek and Turkish communities in the legislature, cabinet, public service, army, and police. The constitution "recognizes the Turks and Greeks of Cyprus primarily as members of their respective communities with political and constitutional rights, that is, not as citizens of Cyprus but as members of one or the other community."[137] The constitution provides that the president must be Greek and the vice president must be Turkish, each elected separately from among their respective communities. The mercy power

132 *See* S.C. CODE ANN. § 24-21-920.

133 ALA. CONST. art. 5 § 124 (1901), *as amended by* AMEND. 38 (1939). This amended provision "provides the basis for a more bureaucratically and professionally oriented system of pardons and paroles than the ex officio board stipulated in the Constitution originally." WILLIAM H. STEWART, THE ALABAMA STATE CONSTITUTION 89 (2011). Although Alabama's constitution originally provided that the governor had the power to grant reprieves, paroles, commutations, and pardons, this provision was amended in 1939 to grant the legislature the power to provide for and regulate the administration of clemency and to allow courts to suspend sentences and order probation. The former system created a board of pardons composed of the state attorney general, the secretary of state, and the state auditor, who were to meet at the governor's request and issue recommendations in writing to the governor. The amendment was a major restriction on the governor's mercy power. ALA. CONST. art. 5 § 124 (1901), *as amended by* AMEND. 38 (1939).

134 ZAM. CONST. art. 60 § 4 ("shall"), 5 ("may").

135 IRE. CONST. art. 13.6 (1937).

136 Twenty-First Amendment of the Constitution Act of 2001, sched. 2, part 2 (Ire.).

137 Stanley Kyriakides, CYPRUS: CONSTITUTIONALISM AND CRISIS GOVERNMENT 57 (1968).

reflects these limitations. According to Article 53 of the Constitution of Cyprus, both the (Greek) president and the (Turkish) vice president have the right to exercise the prerogative of mercy with regard to persons belonging to their respective community who are condemned to death. The provision is limited to capital cases and only permits reduction of sentence to life imprisonment. Where the victim and the offender are members of different communities, the prerogative of mercy is exercised by agreement between the president and vice president. In the event of a disagreement, the vote for clemency prevails. In non-capital cases, the president and vice-president require the unanimous recommendation of the attorney general and deputy attorney general, though this power is apparently limited to remission, suspension, or commutation of sentence and not to full or absolute pardons.[138]

Actual innocence claims

Some jurisdictions have carved out a special clemency or pardon procedure for claims based on actual innocence, usually exempting such claims from waiting periods and other barriers to the exercise of mercy and often restoring a petitioner's full rights upon the grant of this special form of clemency.[139] The constitution of Georgia exempts claims of actual innocence from restrictions on the pardon power. According to the Georgia constitution, the legislature may prohibit the State Board of Pardons and Paroles from granting pardons for 25 years of a life sentence after a sentence of death has been commuted to life imprisonment; for mandatory minimum sentences or sentences without the possibility of parole; for sentences of persons with prior convictions for the same crime; or for consecutive life sentences.[140] However, the constitution exempts claims of actual innocence from these restrictions.[141] In Alabama, by statute, claims based on actual innocence are excluded from the three-year waiting requirement for seeking clemency, though this process requires approval from the sentencing court or prosecuting attorney.[142] Similarly, in Louisiana, applicants with a life sentence may avoid the 15-year waiting period in serving their sentence if they have sufficient new evidence to show that they would not have been found guilty at trial.[143]

Additionally, some states provide for an innocence-specific clemency mechanism. In Montana, by regulation, the pardons board specifically

138 Cyprus Const. art. 53 (1960).

139 Sarah Lucy Cooper and Daniel Gough, *The Controversy of Clemency and Innocence in America*, 51 Cal. W. L. Rev. 55, 93–94 (2014).

140 Ga. Const. art. 4, para. II(b)-(c) (1983).

141 *Id.* at para II(e). *See also* Ga. Code Ann. § 42-9-39(d).

142 Ala. Code §15-22-36(c).

143 La. Rev. Stat. Ann. § 15:572. For an overview of these provisions see Cooper and Gough, *supra* note 139 at 92–95.

permits pardon or commutation of sentence for claims based on actual innocence, and may present new evidence to the pardon authority.[144] North Carolina provides for a specific "pardon of innocence," in which the governor may pardon offenders based on claims of actual innocence.[145] The "Wilmington Ten," convicted of arson and conspiracy during a period of racial tension in Wilmington, North Carolina, had their convictions overturned in 1980 due to prosecutorial misconduct, race-based jury selection, and procedural irregularities; they received a pardon of innocence in 2012.[146] In Tennessee, the governor has an additional mercy power known as an exoneration, in which the governor may "exonerate" an applicant who has shown by clear and convincing evidence that he or she is actually innocent of the crime for which he or she was convicted.[147] Like the North Carolina "pardon of innocence," Tennessee's exoneration mechanism leads to an expunction of all criminal records and restores all rights of citizenship.[148] Upon recommendation of Tennessee's Board of Pardons and Parole, Tennessee Governor Phil Bredesen granted an exoneration in 2011.[149] The Texas Board of Pardons and Parole may also grant a "pardon of innocence" upon either evidence of actual innocence from the trial judge, prosecutor, or sheriff, or a decision from a state judge in a habeas corpus hearing finding actual innocence.[150] While undoubtedly an important part of post-conviction relief in claims of actual innocence, scholars have noted that the clemency and pardon power is likely an insufficient safeguard, on its own, to adequately protect the rights of the innocent.[151]

144 Mont. Admin. R. 20.25.901A(1)(a).

145 N.C. Gen. Stat. Ann. § 15A-149.

146 Joy-Ann Reid, *North Carolina Governor Pardons "Wilmington 10,"* TheGrio.com, Dec. 12, 2012, http://thegrio.com/2012/12/31/north-carolina-governor-pardons-wilmington-ten/2.

147 Tenn. Code Ann. § 40-27-109.

148 *Id.* at § 40-27-109(b). *See also* Dwight Aarons, *Adjudicating Claims of Innocence for the Capitally Condemned in Tennessee*, 76 Tenn. L. Rev. 511, 550–51 (2009). Aarons argues the exoneration statute is "unnecessary" because exoneration for actual innocence is already subsumed into the clemency power. *Id.* at 551. However, because a pardon does not expunge a criminal record and restore a person to innocence, an exoneration reaches beyond the constitutional clemency power. '[W]hile a full pardon restores one's civil rights and remits all punishment associated with the conviction, it does not obliterate the fact of the commission of the crime and the conviction thereof; nor does it wash out the moral stain. In other words, it involves forgiveness and not forgetfulness." State v. Blanchard, 100 S.W.3d 226 (Tenn.Crim.App. 2002), *quoting* Randall v. Florida Dept. of Law Enforcement, 791 So.2d 1238, 1245 (Fla.App. 1 Dist.2001).

149 *Bredesen Grants 22 Pardons, 4 Commutations, 1 Exoneration*, The Chattanoogan, Jan. 11, 2011, www.chattanoogan.com/2011/1/11/192110/Bredesen-Grants-22-Pardons-4.aspx.

150 *Pardon for Innocence*, Tex. Dept. Crim. Just., www.tdcj.state.tx.us/bpp/forms/PFI%20App.pdf (last accessed March 5, 2015).

151 Cooper and Gough, *supra* note 139 at 94–95, *citing* Alyson Dinsmore, *Clemency in Capital Cases: The Need to Ensure Meaningful Review*, 49 U.C.L.A. L. Rev. 1825, 1857 (2002).

Automatic pardons

Given the rapidly increasing number of clemency petitions and cumbersome administrative process for review, some scholars have suggested a mechanism by which previous convictions would automatically disappear after a period of time.[152] The constitution of Louisiana provides for such an automatic pardon. According to that provision, a first offender convicted of a crime "shall be pardoned automatically upon completion of his sentence, without a recommendation of the Board of Pardons and without action by the governor."[153] In 1999, the constitutional provision authorizing automatic pardon for all first-time offenders was amended to its current form, restricting the automatic pardon to non-violent offenses or other specified, less serious offenses, including aggravated assault and battery, aggravated damage to property, purse snatching, and illegal use of weapons. This excluded murder, robbery, and rape from the automatic pardon; after the amendment, these offenses require application to the governor.[154] A second constitutional amendment in 1999 required the governor to receive a favorable recommendation by the pardon board before granting clemency. A number of alternative amendments to remove the clemency power altogether in favor of the board were introduced over the years but have never been approved. The structure of the pardons board has also come in for scrutiny after an indictment of the chairman on bribery charges in 1987.[155]

According to Berrigan, Louisiana's 1974 constitution "embodied the legislature's hope that criminal offenders had potential to change and live productive lives" by automatically restoring a convicted person's full citizenship rights upon completion of a sentence for first-time offenders. The new constitution also created a pardons board for the first time to consider requests by repeat offenders.[156] In Louisiana, a gubernatorial pardon restored a person to a "status of innocence of crime," and does not count as a prior conviction in the event that the person is subsequently convicted of another crime. The Louisiana constitution makes no distinction between

152 B.C. Naudé, *The Pardoning Power As a Duty of Justice*, 15 S. Afr. J. Crim. Just. 159, 171 (2002).

153 La. Const. art. 4 § 5(E) (1974). The list of petty violent crimes includes aggravated battery, second degree battery, aggravated assault, mingling harmful substances, aggravated criminal damage to property, purse snatching, extortion, or illegal use of weapons or dangerous instrumentalities. The criminal must never have been convicted of a felony. *Id.*

154 Helen Ginger Berrigan, *Executive Clemency, First-Offender Pardons; Automatic Restoration of Rights*, 62 La. L. Rev. 49, 54 (2001).

155 *Id.* at 53–54.

156 *Id.* at 49. She notes that a provision for an automatic pardon was first passed by constitutional amendment under the previous constitution in 1968. The amendment was passed due to controversy over the governor's use of the pardon power; the proposal defeated a competing amendment to restrain the governor's clemency power. *Id.* at 49–50. Louisiana's constitutional convention adopted the amendment as art. 4, § 5(E) of the new constitution. *Id.* at 50.

a gubernatorial pardon and a first-offender automatic pardon, but the Louisiana Supreme Court has found that a first-offender automatic pardon does not restore a person to a status of full innocence as with a gubernatorial pardon.[157] This means that the prior conviction may be used against the offender in a subsequent criminal prosecution and is subject to disqualifications from certain occupations, from serving on a jury, and from receiving a license for a firearm.[158] The distinction may be defensible because an automatic pardon is not based on innocence or the facts of an individual case. Each citizen may have their initial punishment cancelled once, but they must face the consequences of the prior conviction in the event of a subsequent conviction.[159] Hargrave criticizes the decision, believing that it frustrates the constitutional convention's policy of eliminating the need for first-time offenders to hire lawyers and endure a cumbersome clemency consideration process. While it is true that the pardons board has not individually considered each case, it is just as rational to assume that screening is not as necessary for first-time offenders and gubernatorial pardons are reserved for repeat offenders.[160]

Interim or transitional pardons

One of the most controversial uses of the pardon power is the propensity of a lame-duck executive to make clemency decisions on the eve of leaving office. As Tuckness and Parrish write of the United States, "presidents and governors typically issue pardons and commutations shortly before they leave office so that the decisions' inevitable unpopularity will not siphon off needed political capital."[161] In 1979, Tennessee Governor Lamar Alexander was secretly sworn in three days early to block outgoing Governor Ray Blanton from granting executive clemency to more convicted criminals in the waning hours of his term. Blanton was then under federal investigation for selling pardons and had previously freed 52 prison inmates in a late-night signing session.[162] US President Bill Clinton granted nearly 200 pardons on his last day in office, including to his brother for a prior cocaine conviction and to several major political donors.[163] Such acts routinely trigger populist calls for reform to restrict or suspend the pardon power during a lame-duck period in an executive term.

157 State v. Adams, 355 So.2d 917 (La. 1978).
158 Berrigan, *supra* note 154 at 51–53.
159 Cheney C. Joseph, *Procedure: Criminal Trial Procedure and Postconviction Procedure*, 39 La. L. Rev. 933, 948–49 (1979).
160 Lee Hargrave, *Public Law: Louisiana Constitutional Law*, 39 La. L. Rev. 807, 820–21 (1979).
161 Alex Tuckness and John M. Parrish, The Decline of Mercy in Public Life 1 (2014).
162 Gregory C. Sisk, *Suspending the Pardon Power During the Twilight of a Presidential Term*, 67 Mo. L. Rev. 13, 13 (2002).
163 *Id.* at 14.

One country in the Commonwealth has a prohibition on the exercise of the mercy power during periods of presidential transition: Kenya. In Kenya, a president is not entitled to exercise the clemency power beginning on the first day of the vote in a presidential election and continuing through the remainder of the term until a newly-elected president assumes office. The provision also prohibits exercise of the clemency power while the president is absent or incapacitated.[164] The consequence of this clause is that a president cannot make last-minute pardons. Nor is this provision limited to the prerogative of mercy: it extends to all discretionary appointment powers of the president, including the nomination and appointment of judges, public officers, cabinet secretaries, and diplomatic representatives, and the prerogative right to confer national honors.[165]

Conclusion

This chapter provided an overview of constitutional clemency mechanisms in the common law world. The structure of mercy ranges from an executive acting alone in the decision-making process to a board acting alone without an executive role, with many constitutions requiring some hybrid of both, including that an executive consult or receive a recommendation for clemency from an outside actor. The scope of executive authority varies widely across constitutions. In addition, a number of federal constitutions provide for complementary and often overlapping clemency powers by national executives and state or provincial executives. Finally, this chapter looked at a range of more unusual constitutional devices: the bifurcated structure, dividing clemency powers among different actors; special provisions pertaining to capital cases or claims based on actual innocence; and finally mechanisms providing for the automatic pardon and prohibiting pardons by outgoing or transitional executives.

164 Kenya Const. art. 134(1) (2010).
165 *Id.* at art. 134(2).

5 Scope of the pardon power

The mercy power is pockmarked with exceptions. This chapter explores constitutional limitations on the power of the pardon, including provisions for unpardonable crimes. This chapter compares provisions pertaining to posthumous pardons, secret pardons, self-pardons (or the pardon of close family members), and conditional pardons. The most common exclusion is pardon for impeachment, which was limited in Great Britain by the Act of Settlement in 1701 and prohibited by the United States constitution of 1787. Among US states, a treason exception is common, while a few other constitutions exclude pardons for courts-martial or offenses under Islamic law. While the King was traditionally permitted to issue pardons before conviction, and therefore able to halt investigations or prosecutions, this right became limited by convention in the United Kingdom only to cases where a person had already been convicted of a crime. Today, most executives in the common law world may only pardon after conviction; this includes most US state governors, though the United States president is a notable exception.

The King's power to pardon was virtually unlimited at common law, though over the centuries the mercy power became limited by convention. These conventions, to a greater or lesser degree, were inherited by many common law jurisdictions, including the United States and postcolonial Commonwealth nations. The King's pardon could traditionally extend to persons convicted of virtually any criminal offense of a public nature where the Crown was the prosecutor and had some vested interest in a prosecution. Civil damages in tort or other private remedies, for instance, were generally not included, but a number of "quasi-criminal" actions with penal consequences such as impeachment or criminal contempt of court created a gray area.[1] After King Charles II pardoned the Earl of Danby in 1678 after

1 A.T.H. Smith, *The Prerogative of Mercy, the Power of Pardon and Criminal Justice*, 1983 Pub. L. 398, 409–411 (including public nuisance as a "quasi-criminal" action). In the United States, scholars have debated the extent to which the president may pardon immigration violations, civil infractions, in order to prevent deportation. This is another "gray area." *See generally*, Samuel T. Morison, *Presidential Pardons and Immigration Law*, 6 Stan. J. Civ. Rts. & Civ. Liberties 253, 326 *et seq.* (2010) (also considering the constitutionality of pardons for the underlying criminal offenses that trigger removal proceedings).

articles of impeachment for treason were presented, the Act of Settlement of 1701 stated that no pardon could be pleaded as a bar to impeachment by the House of Commons, though this did not prevent a pardon subsequent to impeachment.[2] Throughout the common law world, these conventional constraints on the mercy power still exist in many modern constitutions, limiting the power well short of the traditional royal prerogative. In addition, exclusions from the pardon power reflect the unique political and cultural circumstances of postcolonial constitutional orders, such as limitations on the pardon of Islamic or other religious offenses or exclusions of corruption and economic crimes. Similarly, military offenses and self-pardons are excluded in some systems, while a majority limit the common law mercy prerogative to where an individual has already been convicted of an offense. Many US states prohibit pardons for treason, while a handful also restrict an executive's ability to commute sentences of death or life imprisonment without the possibility of parole. While these mercy exclusions often follow the conventions that developed over the centuries, many are also specific to their local constitutional contexts.

Posthumous pardons

No constitution in the common law world specifically makes provision for posthumous pardons, but such pardons existed under the Crown's prerogative of mercy in England. Often, posthumous pardons served important political ends. After a 1690 battle in Ireland between Catholic and Protestant partisans, the King granted a posthumous pardon to a soldier who fought against the Crown and was killed in battle because the soldier's brother and heir was a celebrated soldier of the Holy Roman Empire, a major ally.[3] Posthumous pardons were also used to right wrongful convictions. In 1966 the British government granted a posthumous pardon for Timothy Evans, who was wrongly executed in 1950 for the murder of his daughter and wife. Three years later, one of the prosecution witnesses in the case confessed to these and other murders and was hanged in 1953.[4] In 1993, a posthumous conditional pardon was issued to Derek Bentley, who was wrongly convicted of murder at age 19 and executed in 1953. His conviction was finally quashed by the Court of Appeal in 1998.[5]

Even though precedent exists for posthumous pardons, they are unusual. They nonetheless carry important symbolism, especially in the case of

2 Smith, *supra* note 1 at 408–409.

3 J.G. Simms, *County Sligo in the Eighteenth Century*, 91 J. Royal Soc. of Antiquaries of Ireland 153, 154 (1961).

4 Bernie Matthews, *Australian Miscarriages of Justice*, 10(1) Nat'l Legal Eagle 15, 15 (2004).

5 Adam Sage, *Appeals Court Opens Way to Pardon for Derek Bentley*, The Independent, July 8, 1993, www.independent.co.uk/news/appeal-court-opens-way-to-pardon-for-derek-bentley-1483493.html.

wrongful convictions or those tainted by prejudice. In 2010, the first posthumous pardon in Canadian history was given to Viola Desmond, a black woman jailed for defrauding the government by one penny when she sat in the section of a movie theater reserved for whites in protest of the informal segregation policy. One penny represented the cost difference between a ticket on the floor, reserved for whites, and a ticket in the balcony where she was asked to sit.[6] In Canada, a controversial campaign is underway for a posthumous pardon for Louis Riel, the Métis rebel leader who was hanged for treason in 1885. Métis leaders and the Riel family oppose the granting of a posthumous pardon, however, because they do not believe he should be "pardoned" for a crime that he did not commit. Instead, they prefer a bill in Parliament reversing his conviction. Such a posthumous pardon impacts Canada's relationship with Quebec and with First Nations leaders, including the Métis.[7] In 2013, after a multiyear campaign, the Queen granted a royal pardon to Alan Turing, the World War Two codebreaker who committed suicide after his 1952 conviction for "gross indecency" and homosexual acts.[8] Following the Turing pardon, gay rights advocates have called for the posthumous pardon of all 49,000 men convicted under Britain's anti-sodomy laws.[9]

The United States has historically not granted posthumous pardons at the federal level. In February 1999, President Bill Clinton granted the first posthumous presidential pardon in American history, to Lt. Henry Ossian Flipper, who was dismissed from the Army in 1881 after a court-martial for conduct unbecoming an officer and gentleman. Lt. Flipper was the only African-American in the commissioned officer corps until his discharge.[10] Lt. Flipper's descendants criticized the then-prevailing policy of the US Pardon Attorney not to grant posthumous pardons, arguing that they could promote public welfare. In 2008, President George W. Bush posthumously pardoned Charles Winters, who served 18 months in prison after he provided three military aircraft to Israel in the late 1940s, which helped

6 *In Rare Posthumous Pardon, Nova Scotia Apologizes for Black Woman's 1946 Arrest*, GLOBE & MAIL (Halifax), Apr. 15, 2010, www.theglobeandmail.com/news/national/in-rare-posthumous-pardon-nova-scotia-apologizes-for-black-womans-1946-arrest/article4315080; Nova Scotia Premier's Office, *Late Viola Desmond Granted Apology, Free Pardon*, Apr. 15, 2010, http://novascotia.ca/news/smr/2010-04-15-pardon.asp.

7 Jean Teillet, *Exoneration for Louis Riel: Mercy, Justice, or Political Expediency?*, 67 SASK. L. REV. 359, 359–60 (2004).

8 *UK Grants Posthumous Pardon to World War II Code-Breaker Alan Turing*, INDIAN EXPRESS, Dec. 25, 2013, http://archive.indianexpress.com/news/uk-grants-posthumous-pardon-to-world-war-ii-codebreaker-alan-turing/1211378.

9 Emma Margolin, *Petition Calls for Pardon of 49,000 Men Prosecuted Under UK Anti-Sodomy Law*, MSNBC.com, Feb. 23, 2015, www.msnbc.com/msnbc/petition-calls-pardon-49000-men-prosecuted-under-anti-sodomy-law.

10 Darryl W. Jackson, Jeffery H. Smith, Edward H. Sisson and Helene T. Krasnoff, *Bending Toward Justice: The Posthumous Pardon of Lieutenant Henry Ossian Flipper*, 75 IND. L.J. 1251, 1251–1253 (1999).

ensure the newly independent country's survival in the wars that followed. Winters's co-conspirator, the mastermind of the crime, did not receive any jail time. Though possessing some similarities, the 1975 Congressional resolution to restore full citizenship for Confederate General Robert E. Lee, who died in 1870, was not strictly a presidential pardon. Lee had been paroled and amnestied during his life and was never convicted of a crime, but due to administrative oversight his citizenship was never fully restored.[11]

American states have had a longer history than the federal government of granting posthumous pardons – though they are still rare. One of the earliest was the posthumous pardon by the governor of Illinois in 1893 for five people suspected of inciting the 1886 Haymarket Square riot, which started as a demonstration for an eight-hour workday and resulted in violent confrontation with police. The accused persons were never tied to the crime.[12] Most state-level posthumous pardons are more recent. In 1977, Massachusetts Governor Michael Dukakis pardoned Nicola Sacco and Bartolomeo Vanzetti, Italian immigrants who were infamously executed after an unfair trial.[13] In 1979, the governor of Pennsylvania granted a posthumous pardon to an Irish immigrant, who was executed in 1878 for the murder of a mine foreman after a trial with religious and ethnic implications. In 1996, Oklahoma Governor Frank Keating gave a posthumous pardon to J.B. Stradford, who was convicted of inciting a race riot that he was in fact trying to diffuse. In these three states, Massachusetts, Pennsylvania, and Oklahoma, the governor requires a favorable recommendation from a board of pardons, which was received in each case.[14]

Governors have also issued posthumous pardons on their own accord without the involvement of a pardons board. In 1990, the governor of Arizona pardoned four prison inmates who were killed serving as inmate labor on a firefighting detail, in recognition of their sacrifice in fighting the fire. The governor of Maryland posthumously pardoned a prominent civic activist and philanthropist in 1994 who had been convicted of stealing money from a bank of which he was the co-owner eight years earlier. In 1996, California Governor Pete Wilson posthumously pardoned Jack Ryan, who served 25 years in prison after being wrongly convicted of murder by a corrupt district attorney; the error was only discovered when one of his accusers confessed to committing perjury to help convict him. Additional posthumous pardons have been granted in states where the pardon power is solely tasked to a board of pardons: in Nebraska and Nevada (where the

11 Stephen Greenspan, *Posthumous Pardons Granted in American History* (March 2011), http://64.130.25.182/documents/PosthumousPardons.pdf (last accessed May 13, 2015).

12 *Id.* at 6.

13 Dukakis was not sure that he had the power to issue posthumous pardons under Massachusetts's constitution. His statement explicitly assumes that he has the power and he asked for the pardons to be treated as such. Greenspan calls these "quasi-pardons." *Id.* at 7.

14 *Id.* at 7–10.

governor is a member of the board) and Georgia (where the governor is not a member of the board).[15]

In modern times, posthumous pardons are issued more frequently than in prior decades. Recent examples come from Colorado, Florida, Georgia, Maryland, Montana, South Carolina, Texas, and Alabama, for crimes ranging from obscenity convictions for entertainers to wartime sedition and cases with racial overtones.[16] A number of these were affected by advances in forensic technology and, in particular, DNA evidence. In 2010, Texas Governor Rick Perry issued a posthumous pardon for Tim Cole, who was wrongfully convicted of rape in 1985 and imprisoned until his death in 1999. DNA evidence shows that Cole was wrongfully convicted.[17] In 2013, Alabama's parole board granted a posthumous pardon to the Scottsboro boys, nine African-American teenagers falsely accused and convicted of raping two white women on a train.[18] The Alabama Legislature unanimously passed the Scottsboro Boys Act earlier that year to allow the State Board of Pardons and Parole to issue posthumous pardons for felony convictions at least 80 years old where the crimes were tainted by racial discrimination. The Act exempts posthumous pardons from the notification, waiting, and publication requirements defined in Alabama law, such as providing notice to victims and their families.[19]

15 Jackson *et al.*, *supra* note 10 at 1277–1289. In 1986, the Nebraska Pardons Board unanimously voted to issue a posthumous pardon to William Jackson Marion, hanged in 1887 for murder, as the victim was later seen alive after Marion's execution. In 1987, the Nevada Board of Pardons and Paroles granted posthumous pardons to two union leaders convicted of murder in 1907 based on false testimony at trial, likely from mining interests trying to discredit the labor movement. In Georgia, the Board of Pardons and Paroles has granted three posthumous pardons, for a Jewish prisoner who was lynched by a mob in 1915 and for two Christian missionaries imprisoned for protesting the state's seizure of Cherokee territory. *Id.*

16 For instance, in 2011, the governor of Colorado granted a posthumous pardon to an immigrant with mental retardation who was wrongly convicted of a rape-murder and executed in 1939. Florida Governor Charlie Crist and New York Governor George Pataki granted posthumous pardons to two entertainers who were convicted of obscenity and lewd behavior. In 2005, Georgia issued a posthumous pardon for Lena Baker, an African-American woman who was executed in 1945 for killing a white man after he enslaved her and threatened her life. In 2001, Maryland Governor Parris Glendening issued a posthumous pardon for an African-American ice merchant who was hanged in 1919 for the rape and murder of the wife of a prominent businessman, despite two witnesses recanting their testimony and several jurors pleading for commutation of the sentence. In 2006, Montana Governor Brian Schweitzer granted posthumous pardons to 75 men and 3 women, mostly of German descent, who were convicted under a state sedition statute during World War One. In 2009, the South Carolina Parole and Pardons Board granted a posthumous pardon to two African-American brothers executed in 1915 for a murder of an elderly Confederate war veteran, a crime of which they were likely innocent. *Id.* at 3–10.

17 *Id.*

18 Alan Blinder, *Alabama Pardons 3 "Scottsboro Boys" After 80 Years*, N.Y. Times, Nov. 22, 2013, at A14.

19 Scottsboro Boys Act, SB97 (2013), https://legiscan.com/AL/bill/SB97/2013 (last accessed May 13, 2015).

Posthumous pardons have also been granted in Nigeria and Australia. In 2013, President Goodluck Jonathan pardoned several coup plotters, including former vice president Shehu Musa Yar'Adua, who died in prison in 1997, and Abdulkareem Adisa, former military governor of Oyo State, who died in a car accident in 2005. Yar'Adua and his accomplices had been convicted by a special military tribunal of treason and were sentenced to death by the military regime of General Sani Abacha before the country's return to civilian rule in 1998.[20] Newspaper reports indicate that as a result of the pardons, Yar'Adua and Adisa posthumously received their pensions for their rank in the Nigerian armed forces.[21] In what is believed to be Australia's first posthumous pardon, the Governor of Victoria pardoned Colin Campbell Ross, the owner of a wine bar who was executed in 1922 at age 29 for the sensational "gun alley murder" in Melbourne, Australia, in which a woman had been raped and strangled. Modern forensic evidence strongly shows that Ross was innocent of the crime.[22]

One of the most famous posthumous exercises of clemency was the 2006 mass pardon for 306 soldiers in the British Army during World War One, who were "shot at dawn" for cowardice or desertion. Between August 1914 and October 1918, about 240,000 courts-martial tried offenses on the battlefield such as cowardice, mutiny, and desertion. Of these, about 3,080 resulted in a death sentence and only 306 were carried out. Among these was Private Henry Farr, shot at dawn for cowardice on October 16, 1916, after he refused to go to the front line, exhibiting symptoms of shell shock or what would later be termed posttraumatic stress disorder.[23] Even during World War One, members of Parliament debated the fairness of the military's justice administration, with Labour MPs calling for a pardon as early as the 1920s. The executions themselves appeared class biased, with many of those put to death unfairly tried and sentenced, unable to offer mitigating evidence and without access to a psychiatric evaluation. Historical and academic inquiries fed a public campaign that garnered press attention and spawned letter-writing campaigns. Eventually, Britain's "shot at dawn campaign" spread to Ireland, Canada, Scotland, and New Zealand where activists had successfully achieved pardons or recognition for the executed. Farr was the first soldier pardoned, in August 2006; the other 305 soldiers

20 Festus Owete, *Nigerians Condemn Pardons for Alamieyesegha, Bulama*, Premium Times, March 13, 2013, www.premiumtimesng.com/news/124411-nigerians-condemn-pardon-for-alamieyesegha-bulama.html; *How Pardon was Granted to Alamieyeseigha, Others*, This Day, March 14, 2013, www.thisdaylive.com/articles/how-pardon-was-granted-to-alamieyeseigha-others/142114.

21 Bayo Oladeji, *State Pardon: Yar-Adua, Diya, Others Get N1.01 Billion as Benefits*, Leadership, March 18, 2013, http://allafrica.com/stories/201303180345.html.

22 John Silvester, *Ross Cleared of Murder Nearly 90 Years Ago*, The Age, May 27, 2008, www.theage.com.au/articles/2008/05/26/1211653938453.html.

23 Simon Wessely, *The Life and Death of Henry Farr*, 99 J. Royal Soc. of Med. 440, 440 (2006).

were pardoned in November that year.[24] A blanket pardon for the men was controversial because it implied censure of those attempting to administer military justice on the front lines; in addition, it is certain from the extant records that not all of those shot at dawn suffered from shell shock, and likely that only a small proportion of them did.[25] Nonetheless, it is equally undeniable that some injustice was done, and today the shot at dawn soldiers are treated as war victims rather than as convicted criminals.

Advance and accomplice pardons

Under most constitutions in the English-speaking world, an offender must be convicted before a pardon may be granted, as the purpose of a pardon is to cancel or reduce the consequences of a sentence or remove the disabilities of a conviction. This limitation follows constitutional traditions in Great Britain, where pardons prior to conviction declined over time. Prior to the formation of a modern police force, the pardon could be used as a tool of prosecutorial discretion by rewarding informants or accomplices, often made conditional on the conviction of the principal offender. However, after the creation of the Department of Public Prosecutions in 1879, the Attorney General was able to make decisions about when to initiate or terminate criminal proceedings without resort to the pardon power.[26] Although the most famous pardon in modern history, US President Gerald Ford's pardon of Richard Nixon, occurred before prosecution or conviction, most constitutional systems in the common law world (including most US states) do not permit exercise of mercy prior to conviction. Several constitutional systems go further and require appeals to be exhausted before an executive can initiate a pardon. In the United States, "after conviction" language was debated at the Constitutional Convention in 1787, but delegates rejected the provision because a "pardon before conviction might be necessary in order to obtain the testimony of accomplices."[27]

The constitution of Barbados is representative of the majority rule: the governor-general may "grant to any person *convicted* of any offence against the law of Barbados a pardon, either free or subject to lawful conditions."[28] Other common law countries with the "convicted" language include Belize, Jamaica, Fiji, Ghana, Sierra Leone, Tanzania, Kenya, and India, to name a

24 Douglas C. Peifer, *The Past in the Present: Passion, Politics, and the Historical Profession in the German and British Pardon Campaigns*, 71 J. Military Hist. 1107, 1111–1119 (2007).

25 David Sharp, *Shocked, Shot, and Pardoned*, 368 Lancet 975, 975–76 (2006).

26 Smith, *supra* note 1 at 413–415.

27 This proposal was made by Maryland delegate Luther Martin, and the objection made by Pennsylvania delegate James Wilson. Martin withdrew the proposal. Jeffrey Crouch, The Presidential Pardon Power 15–16 (2009).

28 Barb. Const., art. 78(1)(a) (1966).

few.[29] Thirty-one US state constitutions have a restriction limiting the clemency and pardon power to "after conviction" for an offense.[30] In addition, a host of American-influenced constitutions also contain an "after conviction" clause, including the constitutions of American Samoa, Liberia, some state constitutions of Micronesia, and the Northern Mariana Islands.[31] Even outside the common law world, pardons are typically limited to persons who have been convicted, but exceptions exist. In the former Czechoslovakia and Liechtenstein, criminal proceedings could be suspended or cancelled as part of the clemency power, while in Iceland and Sweden the head of state may order the withdrawal of a prosecution.[32]

Some constitutions are even more restrictive than the common law majority rule limiting the pardon power to "after conviction." In the Maldives, the president alone possesses the power of the pardon, but only for persons "convicted of a criminal offence who have no further right of appeal."[33] The constitution does not appear to provide for the pardon power before conviction or while a conviction is still on appeal. The constitution of Seychelles has another explicit restriction: unless otherwise provided in law, "the exercise of the power [of mercy] shall not be held out, offered or promised in advance of conviction," which is more restrictive than the majority common law "after conviction" rule.[34] In addition, though their wording varies, constitutions that restrict the clemency power only to reprieves, reduction of sentences, or capital cases, for instance, rather than

29 Belize Const. art. 52(1)(a) (1981); Jam. Const. art. 90(1)(a) (1962); Fiji Const. art. 115(1)(a) (1997); Ghana Const. art. 72(1)(a) (1992); Sierra Leone Const. art. 63(1)(a) (1991); Kenya Const. art. 133(1)(a) (2010); Tanz. Const. art. 45(1)(a) (1977); India Const. art. 72(1) (1950).

30 Ala. Const. art. 5, § 124 (1901); Ariz. Const. art. 5 § 5 (1912); Ark. Const. art.6, § 18 (1874); Colo. Const. art. 4 § 7 (1876); Ga. Const. art. 4 ¶ I(a) (1983); Haw. Const. art. 5 § 5 (1950); Idaho Const. art. 4 § 7 (1890); Ill. Const. art. 5 § 12 (1870); Ind. Const. art. 5, § 17 (1851); Iowa Const. art. 4 § 16 (1857); Maine Const. art. 5 § 11 (1820); Mich. Const. art. 5 § 14 (1963); Minn. Const. art. 5 § 7 (1857); Miss. Const. § 124 (1890); Mo. Const. art. 4 § 7 (1945); Neb. Const. art. 4 § 13 (1875); Nev. Const. art. 5 § 14 (1864); N.M. Const. art. 5 § 6 (1911); N.Y. Const. art. 4 § 4 (1777); N.C. Const. art. 3 § 5 (1971); Ohio Const. art. 3 § 11 (1851); Okla. Const. art. 6 § 10 (1907); Ore. Const. art. 5 § 14 (1859); Tenn. Const. art. 3 § 6 (1870); Tex. Const. art. 4, § 11(b) (1876); Wyo. Const. art. 3 § 53 (1889); Utah Const. art. 7 § 12(2)(a) (1895); Va. Const. art. 5 § 12 (1971); W.V. Const. art. 7 § 11 (1863); Wis. Const. art. 5 § 6 (1848). The Constitution of Massachusetts states that "no charter of pardon, granted by the governor, with advice of the council before conviction, shall avail the party pleading the same," which is an "after conviction" clause. Mass. Const. ch. 2 art. 8 (1780).

31 Am. Samoa Const. art. 4 § 9 (1967); Chuuk Const. (Micr.) art. 6 § 2(a) (1989); Kosrae Const. (Micr.) art. 5 § 10 (1983); N. Mar. I. Const. art. 3 § 9(c) (1978); Yap Const. (Micr.) art. 6 § 6 (1982); Liberia Const. art. 59 (1986).

32 Leslie Sebba, *The Pardoning Power: A World Survey*, 68 J. Crim. L. & Criminology 83, 117 (1977).

33 Maldives Const. art. 115(s) (2008).

34 Sey. Const. art. 60 (1993).

the full common law mercy prerogative, would require conviction to trigger the pardon power. Swaziland's constitution contains a pardon provision in which the King may only grant mercy to persons sentenced to death or life imprisonment.[35] Logically, such a limited provision would require conviction.

Some systems allow a pardon prior to conviction in order to give law enforcement and prosecution added flexibility. This is particularly true in two circumstances: first, where a criminal defendant is already incarcerated for another crime; and second, where a criminal defendant may possess information that could assist the prosecution of an accomplice or a principal offender. The constitution of Papua New Guinea contains both types of clauses. The pardon for all incarcerated persons, even prior to conviction, is expressly included. The pardon and clemency power is held by the governor-general "acting with, and in accordance with," the advice of his cabinet including the prime minister, who may provide clemency "to a person convicted of an offence or held in penal detention." The "penal detention" clause implies that a pardon could extend to a person in detention awaiting trial or during trial or perhaps awaiting deportation. In addition, the constitution allows a free or conditional pardon to an accomplice who provides evidence leading to the conviction of a principal offender.[36]

Like Papua New Guinea, a handful of other countries have an exception for accomplices who, prior to conviction, provide information leading to the arrest and conviction of the principal. The constitutions of Singapore and Sri Lanka have such a provision.[37] According to Sebba, a conditional pardon for an accomplice to provide information leading to the conviction of the principal offender reflects a common practice in the English criminal justice system during the late eighteenth and early nineteenth centuries, on the theory that only by making such an offer could the principal be apprehended and convicted. This manner of pardon fell into disuse in Great Britain but formally survived in some former colonial jurisdictions.[38] Smith writes that the last recorded use of the accomplice pardon was in 1861, where a reluctant witness received a pardon under the Great Seal after he declined to answer questions for fear of self-incrimination. Though not recorded, however, accomplice pardons likely persisted long after that date and even into the twentieth century.[39] This form of pardon is unique because it is designed specifically for suspects who have not yet been convicted, making it an exception to the majority common law rule that

35 SWAZ. CONST. art. 78(1) (2005).

36 PAPUA N.G. CONST. art. 151(3) (1975).

37 SING. CONST. art. 22P(1)(a) (1965, *as amended to* 2008); SRI LANKA CONST. art. 34(3) (1978).

38 Leslie Sebba, *The Pardoning Power: A World Survey*, 68 J. CRIM. L. & CRIMINOLOGY 83, 117 (1977).

39 Smith, *supra* note 1 at 414.

pardons may only attach after conviction. In New Zealand, for instance, it is the only permissible form of pardon before conviction.[40]

Prior to 2010, the constitution of Tonga stated that the "King with the consent of the Privy Council," an appointed general advisory body, could pardon "any person who has been convicted of a breach of law." A 2010 amendment changed this provision to read that the King in Privy Council may grant a royal pardon "to any person for a breach of law (including any person who has been convicted of a breach of law)," which implies that the King may now grant pardons before conviction.[41] Like Tonga's new constitution, a minority of countries in the common law world explicitly permit pardons prior to conviction. In a number of British overseas dependencies, the Governor-General may pardon "any person *concerned in* or convicted of" an offense. This provision exists in Anguilla, Cayman Islands, Falkland Islands, Montserrat, British Indian Ocean Territory, St. Helena, and the British Virgin Islands each retain the traditional scope of the royal prerogative of mercy.[42] A handful of former British colonies likewise have clauses that include both "concerned in" and "convicted of" language, including Guyana, Malta, Nigeria, and Zimbabwe.[43] These constitutions specifically grant the executive a pre-conviction power to pardon.

More common are constitutions that contain no "after conviction" language at all, suggesting that pre-conviction pardons may be permissible. The constitution of Bangladesh simply states that the President "shall have the power to grant pardons."[44] The constitution of Samoa is similar.[45] A literal interpretation of South Africa's constitution grants the president the right to pardon "offenders," which would not necessarily require a conviction.[46] By far the most famous mercy clause that does not contain "after conviction" language is the United States federal constitution, as made famous through President Ford's pardon of former President Nixon, which

40 Sebba, *supra* note 38 at 117.

41 TONGA CONST. art. 37 (1885); Act of Constitution of Tonga (Amendment) Act, Second Amend., Act No. 20 of 2010, § 9. Note that Tonga's Privy Council is an executive body that advises the King on a broad range of powers. It differs from the Privy Councils of Jamaica and Barbados, which advise the executive only on the mercy and pardon power, and thus are simply another name for an advisory committee on the prerogative of mercy.

42 ANGUILLA CONST. art. 76(a) (1982); FALKLAND IS. CONST. art. 71(a) (2009); MONTSERRAT CONST. art. 7(1)(a) (1989); CAYMAN IS. CONST. art. 39(1)(a) (2009); VIRGIN IS. CONST. art. 43(1)(a) (2007); ST. HELENA CONST. art. 52(1)(a) (1988); BRITISH INDIAN OCEAN TERR. CONST. art. 11(a) (1981).

43 MALTA CONST. art. 93(1)(a) (1964); GUY. CONST. art. 188(1)(a) (1980); NIGERIA CONST. art. 175(1)(a) (1999); ZIM. CONST. art. 112(1)(a) (2013). Zimbabwe also had such a clause in its previous constitution: ZIM. CONST. art. 31(I)(1)(a) (1979).

44 BANGL. CONST. art. 49 (1972).

45 SAMOA CONST. art. 110 (1960).

46 S. AFR. CONST. art. 84(2)(j) (1996).

occurred prior to prosecution or conviction.[47] This is different from the wording of most US state constitutions. Although the US President may pardon offenses before conviction takes place, he may not pardon them before an offense has been committed, which makes logical sense considering the purpose and nature of a pardon.[48] The Framers of the US constitution conceived of the pardon power expansively, believing that it was an integral component of the president's duty to ensure that laws were faithfully executed – not simply a grant of forgiveness or mercy. During the Constitutional Convention, Pennsylvania delegate James Wilson opposed limiting the pardon power solely to cases "after conviction," as this would limit the pardon's effectiveness as an instrument of law enforcement or as an aid to prosecution, akin to the modern-day practice of granting immunity from prosecution to an offender in order to obtain his or her testimony at trial. Similarly, Alexander Hamilton argued in *The Federalist Papers* that the value of the pardon power rested in its ability to quash civil uprisings and insurrections in order to restore tranquility.[49]

Impeachment

For historical reasons, many constitutions in the English-speaking world exempt impeachment of an elected official from the scope of the pardon power. By the Act of Settlement of 1701, a pardon was not a defense to impeachment, stating that "no pardon under the great seal of England [shall] be pleadable to an impeachment by the commons in parliament."[50] This legislation was passed after Charles II attempted to pardon Thomas Osborne, the Earl of Danby and Lord High Treasurer of England, in 1678 after articles of impeachment for treason had been introduced. Eventually, the two sides compromised: "Osborne was not impeached, but he did spend five years incarcerated in the Tower of London. More importantly, Parliament used the crisis as a springboard to pass legislation to rein in the king's clemency powers."[51] Today, this "exception" limiting use of a prior pardon as a defense to charges of impeachment is residual, having not been invoked in more than 200 years, but pardons *after* a conviction for impeachment appear to have been permissible.[52]

47 Mark J. Rozell, *President Ford's Pardon of Richard Nixon: Constitutional and Political Considerations*, 24 PRESIDENTIAL STUD. Q. 121, 126–127 (1994).

48 Harold J. Krent, *Conditioning the President's Conditional Pardon Power*, 89 CAL. L. REV. 1665, 1673 (2001).

49 H. Abbie Erler, *Executive Clemency or Bureaucratic Discretion? Two Models of the Pardons Process*, 37 PRESIDENTIAL STUD. Q. 427, 429 (2007).

50 Act of Settlement (1701), *reprinted in* ENGLISH HISTORICAL DOCUMENTS, 1660–1714, at 129 (Andrew Browning ed., 1953).

51 Jeffrey Crouch, THE PRESIDENTIAL PARDON POWER 12 (2009).

52 Smith, *supra* note 1 at 409.

The United States constitution has the most famous example of an explicit impeachment exception. Despite its otherwise expansive wording, the constitution provides that the President shall "have power to grant reprieves and pardons for offenses against the United States, except in cases of impeachment."[53] As a result, the stigma of disqualification from future office rendered by an impeachment conviction is unpardonable.[54] In the United States, forty state constitutions, like the federal constitution, specifically exclude impeachment from the pardon power.[55] Connecticut's constitution only includes a governor's power to reprieve, not to pardon, but excludes cases of impeachment; however, a board of pardons appointed by the governor has been created by statute and does not include an impeachment exception.[56] Most of these state constitutions do not provide for an impeachment pardon at all, but several of them provide for a legislative pardon. Vermont's constitution explicitly states that the governor cannot grant reprieves or pardons for impeachment and is unable to remit a sentence or mitigate punishment except through an act of legislation.[57] Hawaii's constitution specifically allows the legislature to authorize the governor to grant pardons before conviction and to grant pardons for impeachment, but this provision is not self-executing.[58] The wording of the constitutions of Virginia and West Virginia varies slightly, prohibiting reprieves and pardons after conviction when prosecution was carried out by the legislature, in essence an impeachment exclusion.[59] The remaining ten states do not include a provision prohibiting an impeachment pardon, and thus the inference is that such pardons are permitted, though some of

53 US Const. art. II § 2 (1787).

54 Ronald D. Rotunda, *An Essay on the Constitutional Parameters of Federal Impeachment*, 76 Ky. L.J. 707, 715 (1987). Note that an impeachment "conviction" only occurs in the United States upon a two-thirds vote of the US Senate. *Id.* at 714.

55 Ala. Const. § 124 (1901); Alaska Const. art. 3 § 21 (1956); Ariz. Const. art. 5 § 5 (1912); Ark. Const. art. 6, § 18 (1874); Cal. Const. art. 5 § 8 (1879); Colo. Const. art. 4 § 7 (1876); Conn. Const. art. 4 § 13 (1965); Del. Const. art. 7 § 1 (1897); Fla. Const. art. 4 §8 (1968); Haw. Const. art. 5, § 5 (1950); Idaho Const. art. 4 § 7 (1890); Ind.Const. art. 5, § 17 (1851); Iowa Const. art. 4 § 16 (1857); Ky. Const. § 77 (1891); Me. Const. art. 5 § 11 (1820); Md. Const. art. 2 § 20 (1867); Mass. Const. Ch. 2, arts. 8, 88 (1780); Mich. Const. art. 5 § 14 (1963); Minn. Const. art. 5 § 7 (1857); Miss. Const. § 124 (1890); Mo. Const. art. 4 § 7 (1945); Neb. Const. art. 4 § 13 (1875); Nev. Const. art. 5 § 13 (1864); N.H. Const. Part II, art. 52 (1783); N.J. Const. art. 5 §2(1) (1947); N.M. Const. art. 5 § 6 (1911); N.Y. Const. art. 4 § 4 (1777); N.C. Const. art. 3 § 5 (1971); Ohio Const. art. 3 § 11 (1851); Okla. Const. art. 6 § 10 (1907); R.I. Const. § 13 (1842); S.D. Const. art. 6 § 3 (1889); Tenn. Const. art. 3 § 6 (1870); Tex. Const., art. 4 § 11 (1876); Utah Const. art. 7 § 12(2)(a) (1895); Vt. Const. ch. 2 § 20 (1793); Va. Const. art. 5 § 12 (1971); W.V. Const. art. 7 § 11 (1863); Wis. Const. art. 5 § 6 (1848); Wyo. Const. art. 4 § 5 (1889). The Constitution of Puerto Rico also prohibits the pardon power for impeachment. P.R. Const. art. 4 § 4 (1952).

56 Conn. Const. art. 4 § 13 (1965); Conn. Gen. Stat. § 54–124a.

57 Vt. Const. ch. 2 § 20 (1793).

58 Haw. Const. art. 5 § 5 (1950).

59 Va. Const. art. 5 § 12 (1971); W.V. Const. art. 7 § 11 (1863).

the provisions contemplate implementing legislation or allow the legislature to set limits on the executive clemency power.[60] The constitution of Oregon contains no impeachment mechanism for elected officials at all.[61]

Most of the other constitutions in the English-speaking world that specifically include an impeachment exception were influenced by the United States constitution. These include the constitutions of the Micronesian states Chuuk, Kosrae, and Yap, though not Micronesia's federal constitution, as Micronesia was a former US trust territory after World War II.[62] Similarly, the constitutions of Palau, another former US trust territory, and of the Northern Mariana Islands, a US commonwealth, also include impeachment exceptions.[63] The constitution of the Northern Mariana Islands is illustrative, stating that the governor has the power to grant post-conviction reprieves, commutations, and pardons after consultation with a Board of Parole. As the provision states, however, "[t]his power shall not apply to impeachment."[64] Finally, the constitution of Liberia, a country founded by freed American slaves, likewise contains an impeachment exception.[65] The influence of the United States constitution in Liberia and in the Pacific trust territories is particularly strong because of the role of American lawyers in the drafting process and historical links through formal or informal colonialism.[66]

Besides these strongly American-influenced constitutional systems, in the common law world only the constitutions of Tonga and Malawi specifically exclude impeachment cases from the pardon power.[67] Under Tonga's constitution, the king, acting on consultation with the Privy Council, an executive advisory body, may grant any person a royal pardon "except in cases of impeachment." This provision, adopted in 2010, was amended to replace the word "maladministration" with "impeachment." The amendment also altered

60 Ga. Const. art. 4, § 2 (1983); Ill. Const. art. 5 § 12 (1870); Kan. Const. art. 1 § 7 (1859); La. Const. art. 1 § 16 (1974); Mont. Const. art. 6 § 12 (1972); N.D. Const. art. 5 § 7 (1889); Ore. Const. art. 5 § 14 (1859); Penn. Const. art. 4 § 9 (1968); Wash. Const. art. 3 § 9 (1889). South Carolina's constitution only allows the Governor to grant reprieves and to commute death sentences; the Governor does not have specific authorization to pardon (this is delegated to the Board of Probation, Parole, and Pardon by statute). As South Carolina's constitution does not contain an impeachment exception, one might assume that the Governor can reprieve impeachment cases but cannot pardon it. S.C. Const. art. 4 § 14 (1895); S.C. Code Ann. § 24-21-920.

61 Maurice Taylor Van Hecke, *Pardons in Impeachment Cases*, 24 Mich. L. Rev. 657, 659 (1926).

62 Chuuk Const. (Micr.) art. 6 § 2(a) (1989); Kosrae Const. (Micr.), art. 5 § 10 (1983); Yap Const. (Micr.) art. 6 § 6 (1982).

63 Palau Const. art. 8 § 7 (1979); N. Mar. I. Const. art. 3 § 9(c) (1978).

64 N. Mar. I. Const. art.3 § 9(c) (1978).

65 Liber. Const. art. 59 (1986).

66 Albert P. Blaustein, *The Influence of the United States Constitution Abroad*, 12 Okla. City U. L. Rev. 435, 457, 459–60 (1987).

67 Tonga Const. art. 37 (1885); Malawi Const. art. 89(2)(b) (1994).

the procedure for impeachment.[68] Malawi's constitution only holds that impeachment of the president or vice-president may not be pardoned by the president, a limited self-pardon exclusion.[69] While not strictly an impeachment exception, Sri Lanka's constitution provides for a special procedure for removing the disabilities of criminal convictions for elected officials. The constitution of Sri Lanka provides for a period of disqualification from elective office any person who has been convicted of a criminal offense, with the length of the disqualification varying by offense between three and seven years. The constitution specifically permits the president to pardon or reduce this period of disqualification for an elector or candidate for legislature who has been convicted of a criminal offense, including for bribery or corruption.[70]

Although not specifically involving impeachment, a recent case in Vanuatu highlights the specific difficulties created when a public officeholder is forced to leave office due to a criminal conviction and is subsequently pardoned. In *Sope v. Speaker of Parliament of Vanuatu*, the Court of Appeal considered a case where a member of parliament (and former prime minister) was convicted of two counts of forgery and sentenced to three years imprisonment.[71] Under Vanuatu law, if a member of parliament is convicted of an offense, and was sentenced for a term greater than two years, his or her seat becomes vacant thirty days after the conviction. The member, forced to vacate his seat, shortly thereafter received a pardon and sought to resume his seat in parliament, contending that the pardon had the effect of removing the disqualification retrospectively from the date of conviction. The Court of Appeal found, however, that although a pardon removed all disqualifications from a conviction, it did not retroactively undo events that happened or remove rights that vested in a third party. The member was free to run again for the seat but not to have it restored to him.[72]

Corruption

In corruption-endemic Nigeria, the constitution contains a provision exempting from the scope of executive mercy any punishment handed down for corruption or economic crimes by a special tribunal known as the Code of Conduct Tribunal.[73] Those punishments may include removal from

68 Act of Constitution of Tonga (Amendment) Act, Second Amend., No. 20 of 2010, § 9.

69 MALAWI CONST. art. 89(2)(b) (1994).

70 SRI LANKA CONST. arts. 34(2), 89(d)-(e), 91(a) (1978).

71 Miranda Forsyth, *The Legal Limits of a Presidential Pardon: Case Note on* Sope v. the Speaker of Parliament of Vanuatu, 7 J. S. PACIFIC L. (2003), www.paclii.org/journals/fJSPL/vol07no1/16.shtml (last accessed May 13, 2015), *citing* Barak Tame Sope Maautamate v. Speaker of Parliament, *unrep.*, CAC 04/03 (Vanuatu, May 2003).

72 *Id.*

73 NIGERIA CONST. sched. 5, art. 18(7) (1999).

elective office, disqualification from future public office, or seizure and forfeiture of any property acquired in the course of the corruption of office.[74] Such punishments do not prejudice any criminal prosecution, but the Tribunal cannot issue custodial sentences. In addition, the offender is provided a right of appeal to the Court of Appeal.[75] This provision is not a prohibition on pardoning corruption as such, and Nigerian presidents have frequently used the mercy power for corrupt officials. In 2013, President Goodluck Jonathan controversially pardoned the former governor of Bayelsa State, Diepreye Alamieyeseigha, who was convicted of stealing millions of dollars, because he was "remorseful." Alamieyeseigha was free to run again in subsequent elections.[76]

The 1979 Nigerian Code of Conduct, incorporated by reference into Nigeria's 1999 constitution, has a troubled history. The Code requires public officials to report all assets, and prohibits even high-level officials from receiving remuneration for two offices, accepting gifts, engaging in private business in a public job, holding foreign bank accounts, and any other acts that represent the abuse of office or conflicts of interest.[77] A Code of Conduct Bureau was intended to investigate and prosecute violations, while the Code of Conduct Tribunal was to adjudicate them. However, because the legislature did not pass implementing legislation, the Bureau was understaffed and the Tribunal never came into existence. Rampant corruption at all levels of the Nigerian state led to a 1983 military coup.[78] Under the subsequent military regime, special tribunals were authorized to sentence corrupt officials to long prison terms, but in practice most of these officials served only a short term in prison and were later rehabilitated with public appointments.[79] Not until 2000 did Nigeria finally pass a comprehensive anti-corruption law, the Corrupt Practices and Other Related Offenses Act of 2000.[80] The purpose of the Code of Conduct Tribunal is to investigate any large and unexplained increases in wealth by public officials, conducting prosecutions for failing to declare assets or for filing a false declaration of assets.[81] The Code of Conduct Bureau, at present, is

74 *Id.* at 18(2).

75 *Id.* at 18(3)-(5).

76 Daniel Egiegba Agbiboa, *Protectors or Predators? The Embedded Problem of Police Corruption and Deviance in Nigeria*, ADMIN. & SOC., Dec. 10, 2013, http://aas.sagepub.com/content/early/2013/12/08/0095399713513142.

77 Okechukwu Oko, *Subverting the Scourge of Corruption in Nigeria: A Reform Prospectus*, 34 N.Y.U. J. INT'L L. & POL. 397, 429 (2002).

78 Andreas Schedler, *Conceptualizing Accountability*, *in* THE SELF-RESTRAINING STATE: POWER AND ACCOUNTABILITY IN NEW DEMOCRACIES (Andreas Schedler, Larry Diamond and Marc F. Plattner, eds.) 13, 16 (1999).

79 Oko, *supra* note 77 at 402 n. 18.

80 *Id.* at 440.

81 *Id.* at 430.

underresourced and functions poorly, manipulated as it is by the executive and torn by ethnic and political divisions.[82]

Hong Kong provides an interesting counterexample to the Nigerian case, as targeted amnesties for police corruption in the late 1970s helped conserve prosecutorial resources, reduced ethnic tension in the police department, and formed part of a package of reforms that changed institutional culture. The creation of the Independent Commission Against Corruption (ICAC) in 1974 ultimately resulted in the establishment of clean government in Hong Kong, but ICAC faced early resistance in the police force from heavy-handed tactics that were insensitive to internal organizational dynamics and failed to break up cells of corrupt behavior within the force. Although the police units failed to win complete pardons, the strategic use of a blanket amnesty resulted in an increased number of officers willing to assist ICAC's work, ultimately improving the anti-corruption bureau's near-legendary success.[83] The relationship between mercy and corruption is also evident outside the common law world. In Indonesia, corruption charges were brought against former President Suharto in August 2000, though he was assured of a presidential pardon in the event of a conviction. The charges were dropped the next month when he became too ill to stand trial. Suharto's son was convicted of corruption, however, and unsuccessfully sought clemency from the new president.[84]

Self-pardons

A small number of constitutions prohibit or provide an alternative procedure for self-pardons by sitting officeholders, their close associates, or their families. Generally speaking, most constitutions do not apparently exclude self-pardon by the officeholder. The constitution of India, for instance, contains no such exception.[85] Prohibitions on self-pardon may be superfluous with constitutions that require executive consultation with other officials or a favorable recommendation from a board, and certainly so where the pardon power is exercised by a board acting alone. In any event, the self-pardon is rarely exercised. Self-pardons were unknown under English common law before the development of written constitutional orders in British colonies. The King by definition could not commit a crime against the Crown, because he could not commit a crime against himself, though this logic does not extend to modern republics where the

82 *Id.* at 431.

83 Roman David, *Transitions to Clean Government: Amnesty as an Anticorruption Measure*, 45 AUST. J. POL. SCI. 391, 396–99 (2010).

84 Natasha Hamilton-Hart, *Anti-Corruption Strategies in Indonesia*, 37 BULL. INDONESIAN ECON. STUD. 65, 75 (2001).

85 Parul Kumar, *The Executive Power to Pardon: Dilemmas of the Constitutional Discourse*, 2 N.U.J.S. L. REV. 9, 24–25 (2009).

officeholder and the sovereign are distinct. The only remedy for a criminal act by the sovereign was for Parliament to remove the King from office; similarly, in most constitutional systems impeachment continues to serve as the only check against self-pardon.[86]

Although the US Constitution only contains a single textual exclusion from the pardon power (impeachment), some scholars have suggested that the provision would also exclude self-pardon.[87] These arguments rest on structural arguments that the US Constitution does not permit self-dealing or that self-pardon otherwise violates the separation of powers, but the simplest reading of the text confirms that impeachment of the officeholder is the only constitutional remedy in the event of a self-pardon. Objections to the self-pardon may be based in natural law, which proclaims that one may not judge oneself. At periods in American history, the ability to self-pardon has become controversial, as it is apparently not prohibited under the US constitution. This may be objectionable because a presidential pardon before indictment, trial, and conviction could immunize a president from criminal prosecution after he or she leaves office.[88] No US state constitution specifically addresses self-pardons. In December 2014, the outgoing governor of Arkansas pardoned his son for a previous conviction for a felony marijuana conviction. The state's parole board, composed solely of appointees of the governor, had previously recommended the pardon, though the Arkansas constitution grants the ultimate decision-making power to the governor alone.[89]

In American history, no US president has pardoned himself. However, in a congressional hearing, US President Gerald Ford described how Nixon's chief of staff presented as an option to President Nixon that he self-pardon for the Watergate scandal prior to resigning. Before leaving office, President George H.W. Bush issued pardons to senior officials that formed a constructive self-pardon for the Iran-Contra scandal, effectively shutting down subsequent investigations and trials. Though Bush doubted that he could pardon himself, most legal scholars and presidential lawyers disagreed, and some have even suggested that he could have given the presidential powers to the Vice-President to issue him a pardon before leaving office, which would have removed any doubt.[90] He decided to risk prosecution. Apart from the constitutional question, a self-pardon would undoubtedly cause a political backlash.

86 *Id.* at 203.

87 *See, e.g.*, Brian C. Kalt, *Pardon Me: The Constitutional Case Against Presidential Self-Pardons*, 106 YALE L.J. 779 (1996).

88 Robert Nida and Rebecca L. Spiro, *The President As His Own Judge and Jury: A Legal Analysis of the Presidential Self-Pardon Power*, 52 OKLA. L. REV. 197, 199–200 (1999).

89 Andrew DeMillo, *Outgoing Ark. Governor Formally Announces Intent to Pardon Son*, WASH. TIMES, Dec. 5, 2014, www.washingtontimes.com/news/2014/dec/5/beebe-formally-announces-intent-to-pardon-son.

90 Nida and Spiro, *supra* note 88 at 212–216.

Unlike the United States and other major constitutions in the English-speaking world, some constitutions do prohibit the self-pardon altogether. The constitutions of Chuuk, Kosrae, and Yap, three self-governing jurisdictions in the Federation of Micronesia, contain such a provision. Chuuk's constitution excludes pardons for the current governor, lieutenant governor, justice of the Supreme Court, or member of the legislature.[91] The constitutions of Kosrae and Yap exclude only the governor and lieutenant governor.[92] Another set of constitutions combine the prohibition on self-pardon with another pardon exception, such as impeachment or treason. As noted, the constitution of Malawi contains a narrow provision stating that the president may not pardon either the president or the vice-president in cases of impeachment.[93] Vanuatu's constitution does not contain a self-pardon limitation. However, in 2004, Alfred Maseng Nalo was elected president of Vanuatu without disclosing that he was serving a suspended criminal sentence. Once the sentence was disclosed, he announced that he would not pardon himself. He was removed from the presidency about one month after his election.[94]

Malaysia's constitution contains a complex provision that limits self-pardon and pardon of close family members by the federal head of state and by state executives. Four Malaysian states are governed by secular ceremonial governors known as the *Yang di-Pertua Negeri*, including the island coastal enclaves of Penang and Malacca and the districts of Sabah and Sarawak on the island of Borneo. The remaining nine Malay states are governed by traditional hereditary monarchs. For the four jurisdictions governed by the ceremonial governors, the pardon power is exercised by Malaysia's federal head of state, an elective monarch known as the *Yang di-Pertuan Agong*, where the pardon concerns the ceremonial governor himself, his wife, or his children.[95] In pardoning a secular ceremonial governor or his family members, the federal elective monarch acts on the advice of the relevant state's pardon board. Where a pardon concerns the federal head of state, the *Yang di-Pertuan Agong*, or his spouse, the pardon power is exercised by the Conference of Rulers, which is the executive council composed of the state-level monarchs and governors that elects the federal monarch. The Conference of Rulers in this circumstance is obligated to consider any written opinion on the matter produced by the federal attorney general.[96] Where a pardon concerns a state hereditary monarch (but not

91 Chuuk Const. (Micr.) art. 6 § 2(a) (1989).

92 Kosrae Const. (Micr.) art. 5 § 10 (1983); Yap Const. (Micr.) art. 6 § 6 (1982).

93 Malawi Const. art. 89(2)(b) (1994).

94 *Vanuatu's President Won't Pardon Himself of Own Convictions*, Radio N.Z., May 1, 2004, www.radionz.co.nz/international/pacific-news/148389/vanuatu-president-won't-pardon-himself-of-own-convictions.

95 Malay. Const. art. 42(12)(a) (1957).

96 *Id.* at art. 42(12)(b).

the secular ceremonial governors) or where it concerns the son or daughter of the federal elective monarch, the Conference of Rulers will appoint another state-level hereditary monarch to exercise the pardon power in accordance with the advice of the pardons board for that state.[97] The state monarch appointed under this latter provision may not also be a member of the Conference of Rulers.[98] This system provides a series of checks designed to prevent the self-dealing inherent in a self-pardon.

Treason

At common law, the King had the power to pardon treason as early as the fourteenth century, though not without parliamentary challenges.[99] Today, the treason exclusion exists in the constitutions of twenty-two US states.[100] However, it does not exist in the United States federal constitution or in any other national constitution in the English-speaking world. The ability of the president to pardon treason was discussed at the Constitutional Convention, though the Framers ultimately opted to adopt the same unlimited power of the King of England with only the impeachment exception. Virginia delegates Edmund Randolph and George Mason sought to exclude the ability to pardon treason on the fear that the president could pardon himself or his accomplices.[101] The objection in this case was to the potential for self-dealing, and the US constitutional drafters were aware of the impeachment episode involving the King's pardon of the Earl of Danby, where a treasonous monarch pardoned his treasonous co-conspirators. Delegate James Wilson spoke against Randolph's proposal, believing that the power to pardon treason was best placed with the president and the potential for self-dealing was remote. Alexander Hamilton, who originally supported a motion to require Senate approval for treason pardons, later defended them in the context of restoring tranquility or harmony after an insurrection or rebellion. Randolph's motion was defeated, as were proposals to require legislative approval of pardons for treason.[102]

97 *Id.* at art. 42(12)(c).
98 *Id.* at art. 42(13).
99 William F. Duker, *The President's Power to Pardon: A Constitutional History*, 18 Wm. & Mary L. Rev. 475, 478 n. 22 (1977).
100 Ariz. Const. art. 5, § 5 (1912); Ark. Const. art. 6, § 18 (1874); Colo. Const. art. 4, § 7 (1876); Fla. Const., art. 4, § 8(a) (1968); Idaho Const. art. 4 § 7 (1890); Ind. Const. art. 5 § 17 (1851); Iowa Const. art. 4 § 16 (1857); Ky. Const. § 77 (1891); Miss. Const. art. 5 § 124 (1890); Mo. Const. art. 4 § 7 (1945); Neb. Const. art. 4 § 13 (1875); Nev. Const. art. 5 § 14(1) (1864); N.M. Const. art. 5 § 6 (1911); N.J. Const. art. 5 § 2(1) (1947); N.Y. Const. art. 4 § 4 (1777); Ohio Const. art. 3 § 11 (1851); Ore. Const. art. 5 § 14 (1859); Tex. Const. art. 4 § 11(b) (1876); Utah Const. art. 7 § 12(2)(a) (1895); Vt. Const. art. 20 (1793); Wisc. Const. art. 5 § 6 (1848); Wyo. Const. art. 4 § 5 (1889).
101 Nida and Spiro, *supra* note 88 at 216.
102 Brian C. Kalt, *Pardon Me: The Constitutional Case Against Presidential Self-Pardons*, 106 Yale L.J. 779, 786–787 (1996); Crouch, *supra* note 51 at 16–17.

Several state constitutions exclude the treason power entirely from the governor's mercy power, including Arizona, Colorado, Mississippi, Missouri, Nevada, and New Mexico. In addition, some constitutions provide an alternate process – usually involving a legislative pardon – for convictions of treason. In Kentucky, the pardoning power for treason is vested in the legislature, though the governor can reprieve the sentence until the end of the subsequent session of the state assembly.[103] The constitution of Arkansas provides that the governor may reprieve or pardon treason with the approval of the state senate, and he may delay execution of the sentence when the senate is in recess.[104] In Idaho, the governor has the power to suspend the execution of a sentence for treason until the next regular session of the legislature, which must pardon or commute the sentence, direct execution of the sentence, or grant a further reprieve.[105] The constitutions of Indiana, Iowa, New York, Ohio, Oregon, Utah, Wisconsin, and Wyoming are almost identical to the Idaho provision.[106] Similarly, the constitution of Nebraska does not permit the governor to pardon treason and impeachment, but the governor may suspend execution of a sentence in the case of treason until the state legislature votes to grant a pardon or sentence commutation, though this does not apply to impeachment.[107] Like impeachment, Vermont's constitution provides for a legislative pardon for treason. However, though the governor can reprieve treason until the next legislative session, he or she has no ability to reprieve impeachment.[108]

Conditional pardons

At common law, a pardon from the sovereign could be subject to certain lawful conditions, often used to raise funds and armed forces or to accept banishment or transportation to a penal colony.[109] Conditional pardons served the dual purpose of populating new colonies and removing unwanted criminals from the realm. Return from such banishment without license was a felony punished by death. Pardons conditional on transportation to the colonies or compulsory banishment became common in the 1660s and 1670s for persons convicted of theft, robbery, or malicious damage. In addition to these specified categories of criminals, felons under sentence of death could petition the King for a pardon on the condition that they agree to self-transport to the colonies for life or a specified term, often

103 Ky. Const. § 77 (1891).
104 Ark. Const. art. 6 § 18 (1874).
105 Idaho Const. art. 4 § 7 (1890).
106 Ind. Const. art. 5 § 17 (1851); Iowa Const. art. 4 § 16 (1857); N.Y. Const. art. 4 § 4 (1777); Ohio Const. art. 3 § 11 (1851); Ore. Const. art. 5 § 14 (1859); Utah Const. art. 7 § 12 (1895); Wisc. Const. art. 5 § 6 (1848); Wyo. Const. art. 4 § 5 (1889).
107 Neb. Const. art. 4 § 13 (1875).
108 Vt. Const., art. 20 (1793).
109 Krent, *supra* note 48 at 1671 (2001).

providing a bond or surety to pay for the transportation.[110] Unlike "absolute" or "free" pardons, conditional pardons trigger the thorny question of whether a recipient is entitled to refuse a pardon because he or she refuses to accept the conditions.[111] Most common law constitutions provide explicit textual authorization for conditional pardons. In those constitutions drafted on the Commonwealth model, the mercy provision specifically includes pardons "either free or subject to lawful conditions" or a variation of this phrase.[112] However, conditional pardons are less common in US states after the rise of institutional parole; only twenty-four of the fifty states allow conditional pardon, typically supervised by parole officers.[113]

Writing of the United Kingdom and Commonwealth realms, Brett notes that conditional pardons raise the problem of consent. While some jurisdictions allow a person to refuse a pardon, many do not, as the pardon is effective automatically even if it is refused. He argues that in the United Kingdom, the Crown has never had the power to substitute a penalty of a different character from that imposed by a court by means of a conditional pardon unless the prisoner consented to the substitution. He adds that in practice, however, the Home Office does not strictly follow this rule.[114] Conditional pardons are common in the United Kingdom; since the late nineteenth century, free or absolute pardons have typically been reserved for cases of actual innocence.[115] This is contrary to the view of the US Supreme Court in *Biddle v. Perovich*, where Justice Holmes wrote for the Court that a conditional pardon does not need to be accepted in order to be valid.[116] In *Schick v. Reed*, the US Supreme Court upheld a conditional pardon when President Dwight D. Eisenhower commuted a military death sentence to life imprisonment without the possibility of parole, even though such a sentence did not exist in the Uniform Code of Military Justice.[117] According to the Court, "the pardoning power was intended to include the power to commute sentences on conditions which do not in themselves offend the Constitution, but which are not specifically provided for by

110 Peter Brett, *Conditional Pardons and the Commutation of Death Sentences*, 20 MOD. L. REV. 131, 134–135 (1957).

111 Smith, *supra* note 1 at 422–423; Schick v. Reed, 419 US 256 (1974).

112 *See, e.g.*, BAH. CONST. art. 90(1)(a) (1973) ("either free or subject to lawful conditions"); PAPUA N.G. CONST. art. 151(1)(a) (1975) ("either free or conditional"); NAMIB. CONST. art. 32(3)(d) (1990) ("either unconditionally or subject to such conditions as the President may deem fit"); SING. CONST. art. 22P(b) (1965) ("either free or subject to lawful conditions").

113 Clifford Dorne and Kenneth Gewerthe, *Mercy in a Climate of Retributive Justice: Interpretations from a National Survey of Executive Clemency Procedures*, 25 NEW ENG. J. ON CRIM. & CIV. CONFINEMENT 413, 430–31 (1999).

114 Brett, *supra* note 110 at 140–144.

115 David Caruso and Nicholas Crawford, *The Executive Institution of Mercy in Australia: The Case and Model for Reform*, 37 U.N.S.W. L.J. 312, 320 (2014).

116 Biddle v. Perovich, 274 US 480, 487 (1927).

117 Schick v. Reed, 419 US 256 (1974).

statute."[118] In the case *Queen v. Secretary of State for the Home Department (Ex Parte Bentley)*, an English court confirmed that the posthumous conditional pardon for Derek Bentley was valid where the death sentence had already been carried out, even though the conditions could not be fulfilled. According to the court, the prerogative of mercy was flexible, and a conditional pardon could accord with the purpose of a posthumous pardon recognizing that a mistake was made and that a reprieve should have been granted.[119]

A conditional pardon raises novel constitutional issues, as it could be used to limit a recipient's freedoms of travel, association, or speech, for instance. The US Supreme Court upheld conditional pardons in *Ex Parte Wells* in 1855, where the Court emphasized that the pardon power was "frequently conditional, as [the president] may extend his mercy upon what terms he pleases, and annex to his bounty a condition precedent or subsequent, on the performance of which the validity of the pardon will depend."[120] Over time, the use of the conditional pardon has faded with the rise of modern parole and probation statutes or other statutory means to shorten punishment and monitor recidivism. These new institutions were more efficient and expert in their analyses of a criminal's rehabilitative potential, as the executive branch had few means to monitor compliance with conditions, especially as the number of pardon requests increased exponentially over the twentieth century.[121] Early unsuccessful challenges to federal parole and probation statutes were based on a separation of powers claim that Congress was infringing on the President's pardon power. To date, no federal court has ever held any condition on a conditional pardon to be invalid.[122]

US President Abraham Lincoln used conditional pardons for former Confederate secessionists to require a loyalty oath in exchange for citizenship. Other conditions have included making restitution to victims, dropping claims against the government, accepting deportation, and avoiding alcohol. President Clinton's last-minute pardons before he left office in 2001 included many that were conditional, attaching requirements that some of the offenders take periodic drug tests and some serve a period of supervised release. Failure to comply with these conditions could lead to the rearrest of the offender. Prior to this, he offered conditional early

118 *Id.* at 264.

119 Queen v. Secretary of State for the Home Department (ex parte Bentley), [1993] EWHC Admin 2 (July 7, 1993).

120 Krent, *supra* note 48 at 1666–1670.

121 *Id.* at 1678.

122 *See*, for instance, Duehay v. Thompson, 223 F. 305, 307 (9th Cir. 1915) (upholding parole and probation); Schick v. Reed, 419 US 256 (1974); Lupo v. Zerbst, 92 F.2d 362 (5th Cir. 1937). *Lupo* concerns a conditional pardon that was revoked by the president because the pardoned man violated the conditions on the pardon. The appellant argued that conditional pardons were unconstitutional; the court disagreed. *Lupo*, 92 F.2d at 364.

release to members of a radical Puerto Rican pro-independence organization, which engineered several non-fatal but nonetheless destructive bombings, restricting travel and preventing association with known felons. Critics alleged that these conditional pardons were intended to bolster his wife's New York Senate campaign among Puerto Rican voters, but they were constitutional.[123]

Courts-martial or military crimes

Another exception relates to military crimes or sentences passed by courts-martial. A handful of constitutions, for the avoidance of doubt, specifically state that the pardon power applies to military crimes or convictions by court-martial, often because of historical circumstances in which such a right was denied. The constitution of Ghana specifically extends the president's pardon power to any conviction, punishment, or forfeiture imposed by a court-martial or other military tribunal.[124] Nigeria's constitution as well specifically provides that the president's mercy power extends to courts-martial and military offenses. However, the provision is slightly different for military and non-military offenses: while the President is required to consult with the Council of State in ordinary cases, he is not bound to their recommendation. However, for military crimes, the President must act "in accordance with the advice of the Council of State."[125] Similarly, the constitution of the Seychelles includes in the mercy provision the imposition of any punishment, sentence, penalty, or forfeiture imposed by a court-martial or other military court.[126] In federal systems, such as Malaysia and India, the constitution grants the mercy power to the federal executive in the cases of courts-martial, rather than to state governors. The Malaysian constitution indicates that the federal elective monarch rather than state governors possesses the prerogative of mercy for convictions under court-martial.[127] In India, the provision is similar, though the constitution notes that the presidential prerogative does not affect the ability of an officer of the armed forces, apart from the presidential mercy power, to suspend, remit, or commute a sentence passed by court-martial.[128]

On the other hand, the constitution of the Falkland Islands entirely excludes the pardon power for convictions by courts-martial.[129] Other constitutions provide an alternate procedure in these cases. In Guyana, where the president appoints a minister to preside over the Advisory

123 Krent, *supra* note 48 at 1666–1670.
124 GHANA CONST. art. 72(3) (1992).
125 NIGERIA CONST. art. 175(3) (1999).
126 SEY. CONST. art. 60(4) (1993).
127 MALAY. CONST. art. 42(1)-(2) (1957).
128 INDIA CONST. art. (1)(a)-(2) (1950).
129 FALKLAND IS. CONST. art. 71(2) (2009).

Council on the Prerogative of Mercy, an alternative provision allows the president to designate a *second* minister to consult with him or her on mercy for convictions by courts-martial.[130] In Nigeria, the constitution states that president exercises the mercy power "after consultation with" the general advisory body known as the Council of State. However, for military offenses or convictions or sentences passed by courts martial, the president must "act[] in accordance with the advice of the Council of State." This indicates that the president is bound by the Council's advice when he exercises the mercy power with regard to military offenses, but not bound in other cases.[131] Zambia's constitution contains yet another variation, providing for two advisory committees. The provision states that the president "may appoint different persons to the advisory committee for the purposes of advising him in relation to persons convicted by courts-martial and for purposes of advising him in relation to persons convicted by other courts."[132] Some constitutions provide alternative processes for military or courts martial cases only where the conviction resulted in a death sentence. In some Commonwealth Caribbean constitutions, the special provision in death penalty cases requiring consideration of a report written by the trial judge excludes death sentences by court-martial.[133] A similar provision exists in the constitutions of the Solomon Islands, Fiji, Mauritius, and Swaziland.[134] On the other hand, the constitution of Malta specifically *requires* the person presiding over a court-martial to submit a written report of the capital case to the minister responsible for justice.[135]

Uganda's constitution provides for a presidential pardon power for courts-martial and military offenses, but excludes a pardon in the case of a "field court martial," an ad hoc creation for when an army unit is engaged in a military operation and an ordinary court-martial is impractical.[136] The military's ongoing operations in Somalia, Sudan, and the Democratic Republic of the Congo against both extremists and the Lord's Resistance Army rebels have used courts-martial in death penalty and other cases as

130 Guy. Const. art. 188(3) (1980). It appears that this second minister-designate for convictions by courts martial does not consult with the Advisory Council on the Prerogative of Mercy. In addition, there is no provision stating that this minister-designate must consider a report by a trial judge or the person presiding over the court martial. *See id.* at arts. 189–190.

131 Nigeria Const. art. 175(2)-(3) (1999).

132 Zam. Const. art. 60(2) (1991).

133 Belize Const. art. 53 (1981); Dominica Const. art. 75(1) (1978); Gren. Const. art. 74(1) (1973); Guy. Const. art. 190(1) (1980); St. Kitts & Nevis Const. art. 68(1) (1983); St. Lucia Const. art. 76 (1978); St. Vincent Const. art. 67(1) (1979). Note that some constitutions pointedly do not contain this exception, such as those of the Bahamas, Barbados, Jamaica, and Trinidad and Tobago.

134 Solom. Is. Const. art. 45(7) (1978); Fiji Const. art. 115(4) (1997); Mauritius Const. art. 75(6) (1968); Swaz. Const. art. 78(5) (2005).

135 Malta Const. art. 93(2)(a) (1964).

136 Uganda Const. art. 121(6) (1995).

governed by the Uganda Peoples' Defence Forces Act of 2005.[137] In 2006, the Supreme Court of Uganda found portions of this law unconstitutional to the extent that it permitted civilians to be tried before military courts-martial in violation of international law.[138] Some jurisdictions have additional statutory enactments. In Bangladesh, by statute, military offenses may be pardoned by the chief of staff of the branch of the military of which the offender is a member. The chief of staff's mercy power is coextensive with the presidential prerogative.[139]

Other exclusions

Besides the traditional exclusions for impeachment and treason and the special circumstances of self-pardon, constitutions in the English-speaking world contain a broad variety of additional subject matter exclusions from the pardon.

Limitation on the commutation of the death penalty and life imprisonment

In several common law jurisdictions, the pardon authority is restricted in capital cases or those involving sentences of life imprisonment without the possibility of parole and mandatory minimum sentences. Some US state constitutional provisions allow the pardon authority only to commute death sentences to life imprisonment without the possibility of parole; no further commutation is possible. The constitution of Wyoming is one such provision, stating that the legislature may create a sentence of "life imprisonment without parole," which may not be commuted by the governor. The governor may only commute death sentences to life without parole; no further commutations are permitted (though he may still pardon the offender).[140] This Wyoming provision was ratified by a popular referendum in 1994. South Carolina's constitution contains a similar restriction, stating that the governor has the authority only to grant reprieves and commute death sentences to life imprisonment; all other clemency authority is vested in the Probation, Parole, and Pardon Board, which is appointed by the governor.[141]

Some states prohibit pardons, reprieves, or commutations where the prisoner has not served a sufficiently long period of the sentence, such as

137 Human Rights Watch, *Righting Military Injustice: Addressing Uganda's Unlawful Prosecutions of Civilians in Military Courts* (July 26, 2011), www.hrw.org/reports/2011/07/27/righting-military-injustice.

138 Attorney General v. Uganda Law Society, Const. App. No. 1 of 2006 (Jan. 31, 2006).

139 *See, e.g.*, Air Force Act, Cap. XIV, art. 177 (1953); Army Act, Cap. 12, art. 143 (1952) (Bangl.).

140 Wyo. Const. art. 3(53) (1889).

141 S.C. Const. art. 4 § 14 (1895); S.C. Code Ann. § 24-21-920.

a mandatory minimum term, unless guilt is in doubt. In Georgia, the constitution provides that when a sentence of death is commuted to life imprisonment, the State Board of Pardons and Paroles does not have authority to grant a pardon or parole to a convicted person unless he or she has served at least 25 years in prison.[142] Georgia's constitution also permits the establishment of the sentence of life without parole, which cannot be paroled or pardoned.[143] The constitution of Nevada states that a sentence of death or life imprisonment without possibility of parole may not be commuted to a sentence that allows parole.[144] In Oklahoma, where the governor is able to pardon only upon a favorable recommendation by the Pardon and Parole Board, the board has no authority to make recommendations regarding parole for persons sentenced to death or to life without parole. The governor does not have the power to grant parole in these cases.[145]

Islamic law offenses

The Malaysian constitution restricts the pardon of Islamic offenses by the four secular governors of Penang, Malacca, Sarawak and Sabah. The hereditary monarchs of the traditional Malay states have pardon power over all crimes, but the ceremonial governors of the non-Islamic coastal states and the Borneo districts do not have the ability to pardon offenses passed by Islamic courts. Only the federal elective monarch, as the head of the Islamic faith in those districts, can pardon offenses under Islamic law.[146] In addition, only the Federal elective monarch can pardon offenses committed in the Federal territories of Kuala Lumpur, Labuan, and Putrajaya, similar to the requirement that only the president of the United States (and not the executive mayor) has the ability to pardon offenses under the federal district law of Washington, DC.[147] Under the Malaysian constitution, where the federal elective monarch acts in place of a Malay hereditary monarch or a ceremonial governor of one of the non-Malay states, the other requirements of the pardon process still apply, including the requirement to consult with the relevant pardons board and consider any written opinions by the attorney general.[148]

142 Ga. Const. art. 4 § 2 para. II(b)(1) (1983).
143 *Id.* at para. II(b)(3).
144 Nev. Const. art. 5 § 14(2) (1864).
145 Okla. Const. art. 6 § 10 (1907).
146 Malay. Const., art. 42(10) (1957).
147 *Id.* at art. 42(1)-(2). The mercy provision of the constitution of Malaysia has been amended to include the new administrative capital of Putrajaya in addition to the federal territories of Kuala Lumpur, the federal capital city, and Labuan, the international financial center, in 2001. *See* Act A1095 § 12 (2001).
148 Malay. Const. art. 42(11) (1957).

International and extraterritorial offenses

A sovereign typically may only pardon an offense under the law of the sovereignty over which he or she rules. This is true for federal systems, as explored above, where federal and state governors each have the ability, and only the ability, to pardon offenses within their respective domains. Some constitutional orders expressly extend or limit the ability of sovereigns to pardon international crimes or crimes committed and prosecuted in another jurisdiction. A legal system may allow a pardon for crimes committed in other jurisdictions provided the person is a citizen; Slovenia, a civil law country, permits such pardons but, in conformity with international treaty, does not allow pardon of convictions by the International Criminal Court.[149] Several common law constitutions contain variations on this theme. Zimbabwe's 1979 and 2013 constitutions contain nearly identical provisions stating that where a person resident in Zimbabwe has been convicted in another country of a criminal offense, the president of Zimbabwe may declare that the conviction is not valid under the law of Zimbabwe.[150] The constitution of Seychelles states that the mercy power does not apply to any conviction of a court established by the law of a country other than Seychelles that has jurisdiction in Seychelles, pursuant to an international agreement, presumably including the International Criminal Court or a regional criminal tribunal.[151] The constitutions of Mauritius and Swaziland have provisions nearly identical to that of Seychelles.[152] Like the Zimbabwean provision, these constitutions restrict the pardon power with regard to the extraterritorial application of foreign or international criminal law.

Conclusion

Although the King's prerogative of mercy was expansive at common law, in practice the power was subject to certain limitations by convention in order to aid in executive accountability, assist in law enforcement, or right historical injustices such as wrongful convictions. The exclusions from the pardon power, as identified in this chapter, are marginal relative to the power itself, including in some jurisdictions impeachment, treason, offenses prior to conviction, and self-pardons. The mercy power generally includes both posthumous pardons and conditional pardons, both of which existed at common law, though their frequency and scope are highly dependent on local political conditions. Finally, this chapter looked at a host of unique

149 Dušica Miladinović, *An Overview of the Concept of Pardon in the Serbian Criminal Legislation*, 5 Facta Universitatis: L. & Pol. 47, 53 (2007).
150 Zim. Const. art. 31(I)(2) (1979); Zim. Const. art. 112(2) (2013).
151 Sey. Const. art. 60(5) (1993).
152 Mauritius Const. art. 75(7) (1968); Swaz. Const. art. 78(6) (2005).

provisions, sensitive to their local cultural and political contexts, relating to, for instance, the pardon of Islamic law offenses in Malaysia, corruption in Nigeria, military offenses in Uganda, and sentences of life imprisonment without the possibility of parole in some US states.

Posthumous pardons existed at common law, though they have been extremely rare until modern times with recent examples involving wrongful convictions or racial injustice, among others. Most common law constitutions do not permit the exercise of clemency prior to conviction. Though these advance pardons were an aid to law enforcement in Great Britain to facilitate accomplice testimony, they fell into disuse and the convention was widely transmitted to the colonies, with the United States federal constitution being a notable exception. The impeachment exception, which became part of the Act of Settlement of 1701, exists today in the US federal constitution and many state constitutions. An exception for treason is retained in the constitutions of 22 US states. In some jurisdictions, self-pardons by sitting officeholders or their close family members are excluded from the pardon power or trigger an alternative process, as in Malaysia and Micronesia. This chapter also considered the special challenges posed by conditional pardons, especially the thorny question of whether a recipient is entitled to refuse a pardon if he or she does not consent to a condition. Many Commonwealth constitutions make specific provision for conditional pardons, and their use has been upheld by courts in the United States.

6 Comparative mercy committees

Most Commonwealth nations require the input of a committee or a board in the mercy decision-making process, either as created in the constitutional text itself or subsequently established by statute. These committees vary as to the strength of this input: their recommendations may be purely advisory; they may be binding on the executive; or they may be the sole decision-maker. The makeup of a mercy committee or a pardon board may affect the quality of its decision-making. A committee that operates as an extension of the executive as a body of political patronage, for instance, may produce very different results than a committee composed of technocrats, experts, medical practitioners, law enforcement or career prosecutors, crime victims, or persons wrongfully convicted, even apart from whether the committee's advice is binding or non-binding. The terms and conditions of membership vary across the English-speaking world and among states of the United States. Some committees serve solely at the pleasure of the executive, while others are composed of members confirmed by the legislature, vetted by a judicial appointments authority, or selected by the opposition party or local government.

Membership of the committee

The membership of mercy committees may be provided for in the constitutional text itself. In a handful of jurisdictions, the makeup of the mercy committee is solely left to the discretion of the executive. Mauritius is emblematic: the constitution intentionally grants the governor-general, an appointed figure, broad discretion as to the mercy committee and other contentious political functions, removing them from the political branch as a result of prevailing communal tensions in the country at the time the constitution was drafted.[1] Several other constitutions provide for the creation of a mercy committee without specifying its structure or membership.[2]

1 S.A. de Smith, *Mauritius: Constitutionalism in a Plural Society*, 31 Mod. L. Rev. 601, 616 (1968).

2 *See, e.g.*, N. Mariana Is. Const. art. 3 § 9 (1978); Vanuatu Const. art. 38 (1980); Malawi Const. art. 89(2)(a) (1994).

More common is for the constitution to specify the involvement of a legal actor, such as the attorney general or the minister of justice.[3] As Bojosi writes with respect to Botswana, where the attorney general serves as a member of the Advisory Committee on the Prerogative of Mercy, "the Attorney General is responsible for prosecutions and would therefore have been involved in the prosecution of the condemned prisoner." She identifies a potential conflict of interest, explaining that there was "merit in an argument that his objectivity in advising the President is likely to be compromised."[4] Another commentator has referred to the "odd arrangement" in which the federal attorney general of Malaysia, responsible for the prosecution of criminal cases, is also a member of the federal and all state boards of pardon.[5] While the constitution of Cyprus does not specifically create a clemency committee, all mercy decisions must be made with the unanimous approval of the attorney general and deputy attorney general.[6] Besides the attorney general or minister of justice, several constitutions authorize another legal actor to sit on the mercy committee; examples include the Director of Public Prosecutions in Trinidad and Tobago; the cabinet minister responsible for corrections in Kenya; and a corrections expert in Pennsylvania.[7] Additional committees may require that a certain number of members have legal training.

In addition to a legal actor, some constitutions require the involvement of a medical practitioner in the mercy decision. These roles could take different forms. In Antigua and Barbuda, Cayman Islands, Falkland Islands, Grenada, and St. Lucia, the mercy committee includes the government's Chief Medical Officer.[8] In Botswana, Guyana, Solomon Islands, St. Vincent and the Grenadines, and Swaziland (with the recommendation of the health minister), the requirement is simply that one member must be a licensed medical practitioner.[9] The constitution of Pennsylvania requires that one

3 *See, e.g.*, BOTS. CONST. art. 54(1)(b) (1966); GUY. CONST. art. 189(b) (1980); ST. LUCIA CONST. art. 75(1)(b) (1978); UGANDA CONST. art. 121(1)(a) (1995). Sri Lanka's constitution involves both the attorney general (a career lawyer) and the minister of justice (a member of parliament) in the mercy process. Sri Lanka Const. art. 34(1) (1978).

4 Kealeboga N. Bojosi, *A Commentary on Recent Challenges to the Death Penalty in Botswana*, British Institute on International and Comparative Law (c. 2004), www.biicl.org/files/2191_bojosi_recent_constitutional_challenges.pdf (last accessed May 13, 2015).

5 Burton G. Burton-Bradley, *The Power of Mercy*, 24 AUST. & N.Z. J. PSYCHIATRY 397 (1990).

6 CYPRUS CONST. art. 53(4) (1960).

7 TRIN. & TOBAGO CONST. art. 88(c) (1976); KENYA CONST. art. 133(2) (2010); PENN. CONST. art. 4 § 9(b) (1968).

8 ANT. & BARB. CONST. art. 85(c) (1981); CAYMAN IS. CONST. art. 40(1) (2009); FALKLAND IS. CONST. art. 70(d) (2009); GRENADA CONST. art. 73(c) (1973); ST. LUCIA CONST. art. 75(1) (1978).

9 BOTS. CONST. art. 54(1)(c) (1966); GUY. CONST. art. 189(1)(c) (1980); SOLOMON IS. CONST. art. 45(2)(a) (1978); ST. VINCENT CONST. art. 66(1)(c) (1979); SWAZI. CONST. art. 78(2) (2005).

member of the Board of Pardons be a "doctor of medicine, psychiatrist or psychologist."[10] In addition to the attorney general, Botswana's advisory mercy committee includes the vice president or another designated minister, and an appointed medical practitioner, who would presumably be able to advise on a prisoner's mental health and situations of grave illness.[11] In the British Virgin Islands, the Director of Health Services is a member of the mercy committee.[12]

A range of constitutions require the involvement of other actors in the mercy process, such as religious leaders or representatives of crime victims. In Brunei Darussalam, the pardons board includes the head Islamic legal authority, the *Mufti Karajaan*, presumably as Brunei possesses an Islamic penal code and may punish religious offenses.[13] In Papua New Guinea, the Advisory Council on the Power of Mercy requires a representative of the Council of Churches, an umbrella alliance of Christian religious leadership in the country.[14] The constitution of the Solomon Islands requires a social worker on the mercy committee, and a social worker has also served on Papua New Guinea's advisory committee.[15] Connecticut requires all of the above. Of five members, all state residents, three must be attorneys, one must be skilled in the social sciences, one must be a physician, and not more than three may be of the same political party.[16] The inclusion of crime victims in the mercy decision is perhaps more perplexing, but may be a concession to either populism or a restorative justice perspective. The constitution of Pennsylvania requires that the governor appoint a crime victim, a corrections expert, and a medical practitioner to the Board of Pardons, which would also include the lieutenant governor as chairman and the attorney general.[17] In Colorado pursuant to a 2007 executive order, the governor established an advisory body of 7 appointed members, to include the executive directors of the departments of corrections and public safety and at least one member who is a crime victim or represents crime victims.[18] The presence of a representative of crime victims may ultimately reinforce a "pro-punishment" agenda. A counterpoint: in 2014, the governor

10 Penn. Const. art. 4 § 9 (1968).

11 Bots. Const. art. 54(1) (1966).

12 Virgin Is. Const. art. 44(1) (2007).

13 Brunei Const. art. 8A (1959), *suspended by* Constitution of Brunei Darussalam (Suspension) Order, 2006 (S 15/06).

14 Philip Gibbs, *Religion and Politics in Papua New Guinea*, 24 Point (Melanesian Inst. for Pastoral Services) 155, 169 (2001).

15 Solomon Is. Const. art. 45(2)(a) (1978); Dave Weisbrot, *Papua New Guinea: Judges and Politicians*, 5 Legal Service Bull. 214, 214 (1980).

16 Joseph N. Rupcich, *Abusing a Limitless Power: Executive Clemency in Illinois*, 28 S. Ill. U. L.J. 131, 148 (2003), *citing* Conn. Gen. Stat. § 18–26 (2003).

17 Penn. Const. art. 4 § 9 (1968).

18 Colorado Executive Order B-008 of 2007.

of Connecticut appointed to that state's statutory board of pardons and paroles a man who had been wrongfully convicted of murder and rape and spent two decades in prison.[19]

In some constitutions, members of the mercy committee must be chosen from outside government or even outside of the legal profession. The constitution of Uganda requires that members of the Advisory Committee on the Prerogative of Mercy be "six prominent citizens of Uganda appointed by the President," excluding members of parliament; members of the Uganda Law Society, including licensed lawyers; or a district council, a unit of local government. The attorney general presides as chairman.[20] Kenya's constitution establishes an Advisory Committee on the Prerogative of Mercy comprising the attorney general, the cabinet secretary responsible for corrections, and "at least five other members…none of whom may be a State officer or in public service."[21] Members of the advisory committee are typically selected from within civil society. Similarly, Malaysia's constitution forbids state and federal legislatures from being members of the pardons boards in that country.[22] Guyana's provision excludes sitting members of the National Assembly from the mercy committee and requires that at least three appointed members be private citizens.[23] Lesotho's committee excludes sitting members of either house of parliament.[24]

By contrast to these broad-based constitutions, the constitution of the Falkland Islands requires two elected members of the Legislative Assembly to be appointed the advisory committee by the governor in consultation with the elected members of the assembly for four-year terms. The committee also includes the Falklands' head of government (known as the Chief Executive), the attorney general, and the government's chief medical officer. Like the Caribbean constitutions, the Falklands' constitution allows the advisory committee to regulate its own procedure, but the Legislative Assembly must approve its rules of procedure.[25] Though not specifically requiring members of the legislature, Swaziland's constitution similarly draws from a pool within the political class. Two members of the Committee on the Prerogative of Mercy must be drawn from the king's Advisory Council (*liqoqo)*, a large body composed of male members of the royal family (*ligunqa*), traditional chiefs (*tikhulu*), and other persons of distinction. In addition to these two members, the committee also includes

19 Jenny Wilson and Alaine Griffin, *Malloy Appoints Man Wrongfully Convicted of Murder to Parole Board*, Hartford Courant, Oct. 8, 2014, www.courant.com/politics/hc-malloy-appointments-judges-board-20141008-story.html.

20 Uganda Const. art. 121(1)-(3) (1995).

21 Kenya Const. art. 133(2) (2010).

22 Malay. Const., arts. 42(7) (1957).

23 Guy. Const. art. 189(2) (1980).

24 Lesotho Const. art. 102(1) (1993).

25 Falkland Is. Const. art. 70(1)-(3) (2009).

the attorney general, the minister of justice, and a qualified medical practitioner recommended by the minister of justice and appointed by the king.[26]

In addition to constitutions requiring representation of different constituencies such as religious leaders, civil society, crime victims, or a royal family, the Committee on the Prerogative of Mercy in the Solomon Islands includes a rotating seat to reflect the country's different geographic regions. The committee is composed of a chairman and two other persons appointed by the governor-general, one of whom must be a qualified medical practitioner and one a social worker. In addition, a fourth seat on the committee is reserved for a representative of either the capital city, Honiara, appointed by the city council, or a representative of one of the provinces, appointed by the legislative assembly of that province. In each case, depending on where the applicant for clemency ordinarily resides, the representative of that jurisdiction sits in the fourth seat. The constitution requires that Honiara and all of the provinces select a person for the committee in the event that a case arises from that jurisdiction.[27]

In a 1990 article from the *Australian and New Zealand Journal of Psychiatry*, Burton G. Burton-Bradley describes in detail his experience as the longtime psychiatrist on Papua New Guinea's Advisory Committee on the Power of Mercy.[28] According to Burton-Bradley, the committee was established in 1976 in order to advise the National Executive Council (cabinet), which is required to consider a recommendation of the committee before making its own recommendation to the head of state. When it was first established, the committee required one member to be a woman, and included a religious minister, a social worker, Burton-Bradley as the psychiatrist, the justice minister, and several members of parliament. The committee considered applications made by, or on behalf of individual prisoners, along with legal documents in the cases before it, the expertise of its own members, and, with the applicant's consent, special medical and psychiatric examinations where those have been thought necessary.[29] The committee is purely an advisory body, and the National Executive Council is not bound by its recommendations. Nonetheless, Burton-Bradley indicates that because such advice is rendered after the committee investigates and in line with members' own expertise, the body produces information that may not be available from other sources. He also defends the committee's independence from other government departments.[30]

26 Swazi. Const. art. 78(2).
27 Solomon Is. Const. arts. 45(2), (3), (5); 137(2); 141(1), (2)(c) (1978).
28 Burton-Bradley, *supra* note 5 at 397 *et seq.*
29 *Id.* at 399.
30 *Id.* at 400, 403.

The committee chair

Typically, constitutions that establish a mercy committee designate one member to be the chairperson. In some countries, the president or executive presides over the committee, as in Botswana, Jamaica, and several British overseas dependencies in the Caribbean.[31] In Fiji and Uganda, the attorney general presides as chair of the mercy committee.[32] In Sierra Leone, the vice president presides.[33] In still others, including Lesotho, Mauritius, Solomon Islands, and Swaziland, the executive selects one member to be chairperson.[34] According to the constitution of Pennsylvania, the lieutenant-governor is designated as chairperson, while in Georgia the chair is selected from among the sitting members of the State Board of Pardons and Parole.[35]

In a number of Commonwealth Caribbean countries, the president is to designate a minister as chair of the committee. This is the practice in Antigua and Barbuda, Bahamas, Dominica, Grenada, Guyana, St. Kitts and Nevis, St. Lucia, St. Vincent and the Grenadines, and Trinidad and Tobago. In Antigua and Barbuda and Guyana, the attorney general is an *ex officio* member of the mercy committee but he or she may *also* be the designated minister serving as chair; in the others, the attorney general may not be chair.[36] This is the case in St. Kitts and Nevis, where the minister-designate presides over a committee of the attorney general and three to four appointed members.[37] In Saint Lucia, the minister-designate is chairman of a committee including the attorney general, the chief medical officer, and three appointed members.[38] St. Vincent and the Grenadines is substantially similar: a minister-designate is chairman, and the other members include the attorney general and three to four appointed members, one of whom must be a licensed medical practitioner.[39] The constitution of Trinidad and Tobago provides for a variation on this structure, requiring a minister-designate as chair, with other members including the attorney general, the director of public prosecutions, and four members appointed by the president after consultation with both the prime minister and the leader of the opposition.[40] Guyana's constitution provides for an Advisory Council on the

31 Bots. Const. art. 54(3) (1966); Jam. Const. art. 87 (1962); Bermuda Const. art. 23(3) (1968); Cayman Is. Const. art. 40(2) (2009); Virgin Is. Const. art. 44(2) (2007).

32 Fiji Const. art. 115(2)(a) (1997); Uganda Const. art. 121(1)(a) (1995).

33 Sierra Leone Const. art. 63(1) (1991).

34 Lesotho Const. art. 102(1) (1993); Mauritius Const. art. 75(2) (1968); Solomon Is. Const. art. 45(2)(a) (1978); Swazi. Const. art. 78(3) (2005).

35 Penn. Const. art. 4 § 9(b) (1968); Ga. Const. art. 4 § 2 para I (1983).

36 Ant. & Barb. Const. art. 85(b) (1981); Guy. Const. art. 189(1)(b) (1980).

37 St. Kitts & Nevis Const. art. 67(1) (1983).

38 St. Lucia Const. art. 75(1) (1978).

39 St. Vincent Const. art. 66(1) (1979).

40 Trin. & Tobago Const. art. 88 (1976).

Prerogative of Mercy with a designated minister as chairman, as well as the attorney general and between three and five other members, one of whom must be a qualified medical practitioner.[41] In the past, the minister designated to be chairman of Guyana's Advisory Council was the minister of local government when the Council met in 2002 and the minister of home affairs when the Council again met in 2007. Besides the minister of home affairs, the council included the attorney general, two social workers, a lieutenant-colonel of the armed forces, a civil servant with the ministry of home affairs, and a local government official known as an overseer.[42]

The constitution of Guyana indicates that the Advisory Council on the Prerogative of Mercy is to include a designated minister as chairman, the attorney general *if* the attorney general is *not* the designated minister, and between three and five other members appointed by the president, including a medical practitioner.[43] This membership structure has triggered concerns about whether the attorney general creates a conflict of interest when he or she sits as chairman in a case on which he or she has worked. In one case, the Court of Appeal addressed a situation where the attorney general had previously been defense counsel to a convicted murderer. As attorney general, he advised the president on the prerogative of mercy in the case of his former client. The Court of Appeal found that he ought not to have presided over the Advisory Council for those deliberations, and declared that the advice given to the president was null and void. As a result, the president's decision not to grant mercy in that case was vacated.[44] In that case, the attorney general served as the minister-designate and chairman of the Advisory Council instead of simply as a member.[45]

The lawyers for the prisoner contended that the attorney general's improper involvement in the deliberations of Guyana's Advisory Council were grounds for judicial review of the clemency decision. In response, the attorney general argued that clemency was purely a discretionary act, and even if it were justiciable, the constitution requires the involvement of the attorney general in mercy deliberations as an *ex officio* member of the Advisory Council. The court found for the prisoner, holding that Articles 189 and 190 of the constitution were prerequisites to the discretionary

41 Guy. Const. art. 189(1)-(3) (1980).

42 *Mercy Council Sitting Again After Two Years*, Stabroek News, Dec. 6, 2007, www.stabroeknews.com/2007/archives/12/06/mercy-council-sitting-again-after-two-years.

43 Guy. Const. art. 189(1) (1980).

44 Yassin v. A.G., (1996) 2 C.H.R.L.D. 39, *quoted in* Bertrand Ramcharan, The Guyana Court of Appeal: The Challenges of the Rule of Law in a Developing Country 8–9 (2002).

45 Unlike most other Commonwealth Caribbean constitutions, the Constitution of Guyana specifically allows the Attorney General to serve as an *ex officio* member *and* be the authorized minister-designate to serve as chairman of the Council. *See* Guy. Const. art. 189(b) (1980).

exercise of the mercy power, and therefore their violation could amount to a violation of the right to life. As the court ruled, "until the requirements of those Articles are adhered to, no execution can take place. The condemned person cannot be therefore lawfully deprived of his life."[46] Ultimately, mercy consideration was an "integral part" of the criminal justice system, and bound by the constitutional standards. However, the court made clear that the actual exercise of the mercy power was "outside the pale of justiciability."[47] The court found that the attorney general's participation on the committee was a conflict of interest since he was also defense counsel in the case, and this harm was not reduced simply because the attorney general did not take an active role in deliberations. According to the court, the attorney general had both a duty of confidentiality to this client and a duty to provide honest and frank advice to the president. The court found that while the constitution required the attorney general to be a member of the Advisory Council, it did *not* require that the attorney general be the designated minister authorized by the constitution and did not require that he chair the council. As simply an ordinary member and not the chair, the court found, the attorney general could have excused himself from the deliberations.[48] The constitution has no limitations on the president's ability to appoint a different minister as chair, which he may do "from time to time," though it prescribed 3 year terms for all members unless removed for cause.[49] This unique decision is one of the few times in the Commonwealth that a court has placed a limitation on the membership of an advisory mercy committee.

Appointment and removal of committee members

Provisions relating to the appointment and removal of committee members vary widely among constitutional systems. In some countries, members may be appointed by and serve at the pleasure of the president or executive. Botswana's committee functions as a strong presidential model, and the president must summon the committee and shall, as far as practicable, attend and preside at all meetings. In Botswana, the president appoints the members and determines the length of the terms.[50] Mauritius's constitution, which dates from the same era as Botswana's and is among the oldest on the African continent, provides a weaker presidential structure. The Commission on the Prerogative of Mercy consists of a chairman and at least two other members appointed by the President. As in Botswana, the president is empowered to set the length of the terms or revoke the instruments

46 *Yassin*, 2 C.H.R.L.D. 39, *quoted in* Ramcharan, *supra* note 44 at 79.
47 *Id.* at 79–80.
48 *Id.* at 80–81.
49 Guy. Const. art. 188(2), 189(2) (1980).
50 Bots. Const. art. 54(1)-(3) (1966).

of appointment. The commission does not require a quorum. However, unlike in Botswana, the president of Mauritius must act in accordance with the commission's advice.[51] Mauritius's commission was said to "meet frequently" and has included a retired judge, a lawyer, a medical practitioner, and a university professor.[52] In Sierra Leone, the executive role is even more limited, as the advisory mercy committee is appointed not by the president, but by the cabinet.[53]

Kenya has likewise moved to a model in which the president is less central to the committee's makeup and membership. The independence constitution established an advisory committee on the prerogative of mercy, consisting of the attorney general and up to five other members appointed by the president. The committee was tasked with advising the president in exercising the prerogative of mercy, although he was not bound by its advice.[54] Mbote and Akech write that though successive presidents routinely granted amnesties to groups of prisoners as part of annual independence day celebrations, the mercy power "has typically been exercised in a subjective manner" and presidents have faced criticism for abusing this power.[55] In particular, President Daniel arap Moi granted a pardon to the former attorney general Charles Njonjo in 1984, shortly after Njonjo had been found guilty of abusing his office and plotting against Moi. Another example is the 2004 pardon of Margaret Gachara, former president of the National AIDS Control Council, after she had been in prison only 12 months for a corruption conviction.[56] According to Mbote and Akech, it was "encouraging that article 133 of the new constitution imposes the much-needed obligation of the president to consult the Advisory Committee" in exercising the mercy power.[57] The new constitution also requires the legislature to regulate the membership and proceedings of the advisory committee and the criteria on which the committee bases its decisions; the committee may take into account the views of the victims of the offense when recommending a grant of mercy.[58] In 2012, based on a recommendation of the advisory committee, President Mwai Kibaki issued a blanket pardon for 2,850 prisoners, including those who were terminally ill, those over age 65, and those guilty of petty offenses who had served their time or had six months or less remaining on their sentences. He also released

51 MAURITIUS CONST. art. 75(4) (1968).

52 A.H. Angelo, *Mauritius: The Basis of the Legal System*, 3 COMP. & INT'L L.J. SOUTH. AFR. 228, 237 (1970).

53 SIERRA LEONE CONST. art. 63(1) (1991).

54 KENYA CONST. art. 89 (1963).

55 Patricia Kameri Mbote and Migai Akech, KENYA: JUSTICE SECTOR AND THE RULE OF LAW 68 (2011).

56 *Id.*

57 *Id.* at 69.

58 KENYA CONST. art. 133(3)-(4) (2010).

another 1,227 prisoners who had nine months remaining on their sentences in order to help ease prison overcrowding.[59]

In parliamentary systems in which a non-elected executive, often a governor-general or ceremonial president, appoints members of the mercy committee, the constitution may require input from an elected prime minister or legislative chamber. In Barbados, the governor-general appoints all members of the Privy Council (as the mercy committee is titled) upon consultation with the premier. The governor-general must act in accordance with the advice of the Privy Council.[60] The constitution of the Cayman Islands also requires consultation with the opposition leader. The Advisory Committee on the Prerogative of Mercy in that jurisdiction is composed of the attorney general, the chief medical officer, and four other members, two of whom are appointed by the governor acting in consultation with the premier and two appointed in consultation with the leader of the opposition.[61] Jamaica's constitution also provides for the establishment of a Privy Council. In Jamaica, the governor-general appoints the six members of the Privy Council after consultation with the prime minister, at least two of whom must hold or have held public office. Members typically serve for three-year terms, but may be removed or found incapacitated again by the governor-general after consulting with the prime minister, in which case the governor-general may appoint a provisional member.[62] Similarly, the constitutions of Bermuda and the Virgin Islands require that the governor consult with the premier in making appointments.[63]

The constitution of the Bahamas is illustrative of committees in which the Advisory Committee on the Prerogative of Mercy is appointed by the governor-general in collaboration with other actors. The committee is composed of a minister designated by the governor-general upon the advice of the prime minister, the attorney-general, and "not less than three or more than five other members" appointed by the governor-general. The minister designated by the governor-general, currently the Minister of National Security, is chair of the advisory committee and may consult with it before tendering advice to the governor-general, but he is not required to consult with the committee and is not bound by its advice. The committee currently is composed of four private citizens, including a medical doctor and two religious leaders, as well as the attorney general.[64]

59 *Kenyan President Pardons Dying Prisoners, Reformed Inmates*, PANAPRESS, Dec. 23, 2012, www.panapress.com/Kenyan-President-pardons-dying-prisoners,-reformed-inmates – 13-855851-0-lang2-index.html.

60 BARB. CONST. arts. 76(1) (on the makeup of the Privy Council); 78(2) (on the Governor-General's deference to the Privy Council) (1966).

61 CAYMAN IS. CONST. art. 40(1) (2009).

62 JAM. CONST. arts. 82–85 (1962).

63 BERM. CONST. art. 23(1)(a) (1968); VIRGIN IS. CONST. art. 44(1) (2007).

64 BAH. CONST. arts. 90(2), 91, 92(1)-(3) (1973).

Most Commonwealth Caribbean nations have a variation of the structure set up by the constitution of the Bahamas. Antigua and Barbuda's constitutional provision on the Advisory Committee on the Prerogative of Mercy requires consultation with both the prime minister and the leader of the opposition, except that the committee also includes the government's Chief Medical Officer.[65] The constitution of Grenada also establishes an advisory committee composed of a designated minister, the attorney general, the Chief Medical Officer, and three other members appointed by the governor-general, subject to removal or expiration of a term of office as defined by the governor-general acting in consultation with the prime minister.[66] Dominica's constitution is more elaborate. While the president only must act on the advice of the prime minister in making appointments to the Advisory Committee on the Prerogative of Mercy, for other offices (including public and police service commissioners, chief and deputy chief of police, and ombudsman) he must also consult with the leader of the opposition and prime minister.[67] Similarly, the president of Dominica is required to consult with the prime minister in removing members of the mercy committee, which is composed of a designated minister, the attorney general, and up to four other members appointed by the president.[68]

Another way of improving the mercy decision-making process is to require vetting of appointees. In Lesotho, the Pardons Committee on the Prerogative of Mercy, which consists of a chairman and two other members, is appointed by the king acting in accordance with the advice of the Judicial Services Commission. The king is not able to appoint public officers or members of parliament to the committee, and members serve for three-year terms unless removed by the king, again acting on the advice of the Judicial Services Commission.[69] In Sierra Leone, members of the advisory mercy committee are appointed by the cabinet, not the president, with the vice president presiding.[70] This may not necessarily remove the potential that the mercy committee might become political patronage positions, but it spreads the appointment power among a broader group of people. The constitution of Seychelles provides for both term limits and vetting of candidates by an appointments authority. The advisory committee on the power of pardon consists of between three and five members appointed by the president for seven-year terms from candidates proposed by the Constitutional Appointments Authority.[71]

65 Ant. & Barb. Const. art. 85(a)-(d) (1981).
66 Gren. Const. art. 73(1)-(5) (1973).
67 Nicholas Liverpool, *Address to Parliament*, July 10, 2008, www.presidentoffice.gov.dm/former-presidents/25-his-excellency-dr-nicholas-j-o-liverpool-2003-2012/20-constitutional-change-and-advancement.
68 Dominica Const. art. 74(1)-(2) (1978).
69 Lesotho Const. art. 102 (1993).
70 Sierra Leone Const. art. 63(1) (1991).
71 Sey. Const. art. 61 (60).

Some constitutions require explicit legislative confirmation of members of the advisory mercy committee. In The Gambia, the committee on the exercise of the prerogative of mercy is composed of the attorney general and three other persons appointed by the president and confirmed by the National Assembly.[72] Despite this provision, members of the advisory committee on the prerogative of mercy (along with the advisory committee on the conferment of honors, another traditional prerogative power) are not considered offices in the public service and therefore subject to civil service regulations.[73]

The elaborate constitution of Belize combines several of these mechanisms, including consultation with the prime minister and opposition and both legislative and judicial input. In Belize, the Advisory Council includes two "senior" members appointed by the governor-general acting in accordance with the advice of the prime minister and two "senior" members on the advice of the leader of the opposition. In addition, the governor-general appoints three other members on the advice of the prime minister after consultation with the leader of the opposition. All seven members must be "persons of integrity and high national standing."[74] Removal requires a two-thirds vote of the House of Representatives, which serves as additional insulation from political pressure. Members must be citizens of Belize unless they are current or former judges, in which they must be citizens of a Commonwealth country, presumably to permit appointment of Belize's contract judges.[75] The four senior members rotate chairmanship of the council for one-year terms, and the chair may be removed by the council and replaced by a current or former judge, appointed by the governor-general on the advice of the prime minister after consultation with the leader of the opposition. The deliberate involvement of former and active judges on the Belize Advisory Council is an additional safeguard against politicization of the body.[76]

US states show more variation in committee structure than is generally evident in the rest of the common law world. In the United States, two models of mercy committees predominate: those that are composed solely of *ex officio* members acting as a pardons board, and those that are appointed by the governor. Delaware is an example of the first model, which tends to be more common in states in which a board either solely exercises the power of mercy or where the governor requires the board's recommendation to do so. In Delaware, where the governor may only pardon on a recommendation of the Board of Pardons, the board includes

72 Gambia Const. art. 82(2) (1996).
73 *Id.* at art. 166(4)(b).
74 Belize Const. art. 54(2) (1981, *as amended in* 1988).
75 *Id.* at art. 54(3)-(5).
76 *Id.* at art. 54(6), (13).

the chancellor, lieutenant-governor, secretary of state, state treasurer, and auditor of accounts.[77] In Minnesota, the Board of Pardons is composed of the governor, attorney general, and chief justice of the state supreme court.[78] Similarly, in Nebraska, the Board of Parole includes the governor, attorney general, and secretary of state.[79] In Nevada, the board includes the governor, justices of the state supreme court, and the attorney general.[80] States that fall in the second model include Georgia and Utah, which both require legislative confirmation of gubernatorial appointees.[81] Other states with boards solely appointed by the governor include Connecticut, Idaho, Maine, Missouri, Montana, and Texas.[82] This second model tends to predominate with advisory mercy committees or those bodies that only issue non-binding recommendations. Pennsylvania has a hybrid of the two models, including two *ex officio* members and three members appointed by the governor.[83] As noted in the previous chapter, Massachusetts and New Hampshire have a unique model in which the governor is advised on the mercy power by a publicly-elected council.[84]

Conditions of appointment

Constitutions may regulate the conditions of appointment for members of the mercy committee. In a strong presidential system, membership is entirely at the discretion of the executive. In Zambia, members of the Advisory Committee on the Prerogative of Mercy serve at the pleasure of the president. The committee's decisions are not binding, and as the president chairs the committee's meetings and has the power to hire and fire its members, the committee's decisions may not be a true reflection of the individual members' perceptions of the application.[85] In addition, Zambia's constitution does not require that the president consult with the advisory committee except in death penalty cases, when such consultation is required.[86] Nonetheless, the constitution places few limits on the president's

77 Del. Const. art. 7 § 1 (1897).
78 Minn. Const. art. 5 § 7 (1857).
79 Neb. Const. art. 4 § 13 (1875).
80 Nev. Const. art. 5 § 13 (1864).
81 Ga. Const. art. 4 § 2 para. I (1983); Utah Const. art. 7 § 12(1) (1895).
82 *See* Kathleen M. Ridolfi and Seth Gordon, *Gubernatorial Clemency Powers: Justice or Mercy?*, Crim. Just. 26, 34–40 (table), Fall 2009; Texas Board of Pardons and Paroles, *Board Member Responsibilities*, www.tdcj.state.tx.us/bpp/brd_members/brd_members.html (last accessed Mar. 14, 2015).
83 Penn. Const. art. 4 § 9 (1968).
84 Mass. Const. ch. 2 art. 8 (1780) (Governor's Council); N.H. Const. part II art. 52 (1783) (Executive Council).
85 Bako Chipola, *Capital Punishment in Zambia and the Presidential Prerogative of Mercy*, LL.B. Thesis, University of Zambia 48 (2004).
86 Zam. Const. art. 60(4)-(5) (1991).

power. Similarly, under the constitution of Brunei Darussalam, the Sultan possesses "absolute discretion" over the mercy power, and "may have regard to, but is not bound to act in accordance with, the advice of the Pardons Board."[87] Unlike Zambia, however, the constitution does limit the size of the Brunei Pardons Board to the attorney general, the *Mufti Karajaan*, and not more than three other appointed members.[88]

One manner by which the membership of the committee is regulated is through the use of term limits. In Malaysia, members of state Pardons Boards are appointed for three-year terms and eligible for reappointment.[89] In Fiji, the Commission on the Prerogative of Mercy includes the attorney general as chairperson and two other members appointed by the president, who in turn "acts on" the commission's advice.[90] The members serve for two-year terms and may be appointed once; their salaries are paid out of the Consolidated Fund along with members of the judiciary, the ombudsman, and members of other commissions to prevent manipulation of the office by cutting members' salaries.[91] Several newer African constitutions also provide that persons appointed to advisory mercy committees serve for set terms. In Uganda, members serve for four-year terms.[92] Kenya's constitution delegates to the legislature the advisory committee's tenure, procedure, and criteria for formulating advice; unlike most Commonwealth constitutions, these are not left to the executive or to the committee itself.[93] In Guyana, members of the Advisory Council serve for three-year terms but may be removed by the president for cause, or upon their election to the legislature, as legislators are excluded from membership on the council.[94]

The constitution of Belize includes a mandatory retirement age. The four "senior" members are to hold office until reaching the age of 75, unless they resign or are removed for cause, though they may be reappointed after reaching age 75. The other three members are to hold office for terms of three years unless they resign or are removed for cause. Belize's Advisory Council also has functions besides the mercy prerogative. One of these functions includes advising the Governor-General on the selection of one

87 Brunei Const. arts. 8A, 9(1)-(2) (1959).

88 *Id.* at art. 8A. The Sultan suspended the Constitution of Brunei in 2006, including the provisions pertaining to the establishment of the Pardons Board (but not his own power to grant clemency). The Constitution of Brunei (Suspension) Order of 2006 confers the advisory responsibility of the Pardons Board on the Privy Council, one of the country's executive councils, which is composed of members of the royal family and close personal advisors to the Sultan. Constitution of Brunei Darussalam (Suspension) Order, S 15/06 (21 Feb. 2006).

89 Malay. Const., arts. 42(4)-(11) (1957, *as amended to* 1994).

90 Fiji Const. art. 115(2)-(3) (1997).

91 *Id.* at arts. 169(k), 170(2), 183(1)(l), 183(2).

92 Uganda Const. art. 121(1)-(3) (1995).

93 Kenya Const. art. 133(3) (2010).

94 Guy. Const. art. 189(3) (1980).

member of the Senate of Belize (five others are appointed on the advice of the Prime Minister and two others on the advice of the Leader of the Opposition for a total of eight members).[95] Fiji's constitution includes mandatory retirement ages for a number of government officials, but members of the Commission on the Prerogative of Mercy are specifically excluded.[96]

In some jurisdictions, membership on the board is without compensation. Although the constitution of Washington specifies that the governor holds the pardon power, by statute a 5-member clemency and pardons board is established within the office of governor. The members of the board must be confirmed by the state senate and serve staggered terms of four years without compensation.[97] In Michigan, the governor issued an executive order in 2007 creating the Executive Clemency Advisory Council, which is tasked with advising the state parole board on pardon applications. The members of the advisory council serve without compensation.[98] Similarly, in Missouri, the governor may appoint a "a board of inquiry whose duty it shall be to gather information…bearing upon whether or not a person condemned to death should be executed or reprieved or pardoned, or whether the person's sentence should be commuted."[99] Membership on such a board of inquiry is non-remunerative, and the board is to report to the governor in strict confidence.[100]

Quorum, voting thresholds, and vacancies

Only four constitutions require a quorum of members of the mercy committee to be present in order to conduct business. One is the Belize Advisory Council, which requires five of seven members to be present. Decisions are made by majority and the chairman or senior member permitted to cast a second vote in the case of a tie.[101] In addition, the committee may still act even with a vacancy.[102] In addition, the advisory committees of Bermuda, the Cayman Islands, and the Virgin Islands require three members present in order to conduct business; in the Cayman Islands and the Virgin Islands, the attorney general must be one of the three members present.[103] The

95 Dag Anckar, *Bicameral Microstates: A Commonwealth Category*, 347 Round Table: Commw. J. Int'l Aff. 367, 371 (1998).

96 Fiji Const. art. 170(3) (1997).

97 Wash. Rev. Code. sec. 9.94A.880.

98 Office of the Governor, Executive Order 2007-2, February 16, 2007, www.michigan.gov/documents/gov/Executive_Order_2007-2_187378_7.pdf.

99 Mo. Rev. Stat. § 552.070.

100 *Id.*

101 Belize Const. art. 54(14) (1981, *as amended*).

102 *Id.* at art. 54(17).

103 Berm. Const. art. 23(4) (1968); Cayman Is. Const. art. 40(3) (2009); Virgin Is. Const. art. 44(3).

constitution of the Solomon Islands, while not requiring a quorum, indicates that the committee may act even with a vacancy or absence of a member, with decisions made by majority and the chairman able to break a tie.[104] A number of other constitutions also have provisions indicating that the mercy committee may still conduct business even with a vacancy or with the absence of a committee member. In the Caribbean, the constitution of Dominica provides that the advisory committee may act even without the presence of any member and notwithstanding a vacancy; in addition, the participation of any person not entitled to be present at the meeting does not invalidate the committee's decisions.[105] The Commonwealth Caribbean constitutions of Grenada, St. Lucia, St. Kitts and Nevis, and St. Vincent and the Grenadines have an identical provision, as does the constitution of Swaziland.[106] The constitutions of several British overseas dependencies and Mauritius state that the presence of a person not entitled to participate in deliberations does not invalidate the decision.[107] In the United States, the state constitutions of Delaware, Oklahoma, Pennsylvania, and Texas (where the governor may only act on the board's recommendation) and Idaho and Utah (where the board alone makes the decision) require that members of the board make decisions or recommendations by majority, with Pennsylvania requiring unanimity in death penalty cases.[108] In Nevada, the governor as a member of the pardons board must be in the majority in order to grant clemency.[109] In Delaware, the Board of Pardons may have vacancies, but at least three members must be serving in order to lawfully make decisions.[110]

What works best?

An impartial committee, insulated from politics, is probably more likely to grant routine pardons and clemency requests than an elected official acting alone. As Margaret Colgate Love has written, this is true among US states, where clemency is most frequently granted by independently-appointed boards of experts that operate in regulated proceedings, hold hearings, and produce binding decisions. States where either a board produces the final

104 Solomon Is. Const. art. 137(2) (1978).
105 Dominica Const. art. 74(3) (1978).
106 Grenada Const. art. 73(3) (1973); St. Kitts & Nevis Const. art. 67(3) (1983); St. Lucia Const. art. 75(3) (1978); St. Vincent Const. art. 66(3) (1979); Swazi. Const. art. 78(4) (2005).
107 Cayman Is. Const. art. 40(5) (2009); Berm. Const. art. 23(6) (1968); Virgin Is. Const. art. 44(5) (2007); Mauritius Const. art. 75(5) (1968).
108 Del. Const. art. 7 §1 (1897); Idaho Const. art. 4 § 7 (1890); Okla. Const. art. 6 § 10 (1907); Penn. Const. art. 4 § 9 (1968); Tex. Const. art. 4 § 11(b) (1876); Utah Const. art. 7 § 12(2)(a) (1895).
109 Nev. Const. art. 5 § 14(1) (1864).
110 Del. Const. sched. 1 § 17 (1897).

mercy decision or where the governor requires a recommendation from a board are especially well-structured to grant clemency.[111] The most frequent grants of clemency are in states where independent boards possess the final mercy authority: more than 400 pardons are granted annually in Alabama, Connecticut, and Georgia, and more than 200 in South Carolina, typically amounting to 30–60 per cent of all applications for clemency.[112] Idaho as well grants more than half the total number of applications filed.[113] States where a board serves as gatekeeper and the governor makes the final decision are more mixed: three (Delaware, Pennsylvania, and Oklahoma) grant pardons frequently, while pardons in six other states are infrequent (Texas, Montana, and Louisiana) or extremely rare (Arizona, Massachusetts, and New Hampshire).[114] In states where a governor and board share power, only Ohio and Arkansas have a lively tradition of pardoning.[115] Even where a governor possesses final mercy authority, he or she may conclude that consulting with a board, even where it is not required, is politically safer: Illinois Governor Pat Quinn granted 825 pardons between 2009 and 2012, all of which were referred to him by the Prisoner Review Board. Other governors have done likewise.[116]

Extrapolating from this US-based evidence, one would expect that this is also likely to be true in Commonwealth countries where the ultimate decision-maker is nonpartisan (like a governor-general) and where he or she is bound by the advice of a technocratic committee of experts. The non-partisanship of the decision-maker may immunize him or her from immediate and direct political consequences; similarly, binding that executive to the advice of a committee of experts, especially after an open public application process and a hearing, may allow the clemency system to escape serious political liability for making a single bad decision.

Given the myriad of committee arrangements in the English-speaking world, it may be useful to consider how the membership of mercy committees may affect their decision-making. Here, most current evidence comes from the United States. According to Barkow, clemency boards "should not be mere arms of law enforcement interests," as this could cause them to be skeptical of clemency petitions and less likely to second-guess the criminal justice system in the event of error.[117] As Cooper writes, some administrative

111 Margaret Colgate Love, *Reinvigorating the Federal Pardon Process: What the President Can Learn From the States*, 9 U. St. Thomas L. J. 730, 744–47 (2012).

112 *Id.* at 744.

113 *Id.*

114 *Id.* at 746.

115 *Id.*

116 *Id.* at 749.

117 Rachel E. Barkow, *The Politics of Forgiveness: Reconceptualizing Clemency*, 21 Fed. Sent'g Rep. 153, 155–56 (2009), *quoted in* Sarah Lucy Cooper, *The State Clemency Power and Innocence Claims: The Influence of Finality and Its Implications For Innocents*, 51 Cal. W. L. Rev. 55, 81 (2014).

boards reflect broad diversity among their members: Kentucky, for instance, has experts in law, investigations, education, mental health, corrections, probation and parole, and child and adult protective services. Ohio's board includes persons experienced in victim's rights, rehabilitation and corrections, drug and alcohol services, and law. Pennsylvania adds experience in offender mentoring and criminal defense, while South Carolina adds military service. She concludes that many boards are "devoid of representation by individuals (such as lawyers, academics, and scientists) with a working knowledge of post-conviction review, state evidence and innocence rules, and the causes of wrongful convictions…"[118] Other administrative boards are more overtly state-aligned, such as in Delaware, Nebraska, and Nevada where all members are sitting officeholders; Colorado, where the board is mandated to include the heads of the corrections department and the department of public safety, as well as at least one crime victim; and Utah, where seven of eight members have backgrounds in state organizations.[119] This has not escaped notice elsewhere: a Boston Bar Association task force reported that the Massachusetts Advisory Board of Pardons, which advises the governor and Governor's Council in clemency decisions, is primarily staffed by officials with backgrounds in law enforcement and other criminal justice work, despite formal membership criteria that emphasize diversity in the Board's makeup. According to the task force, the lack of diversity among members of the Board statistically correlated to the decline in grants of clemency and parole.[120]

The existence of a state-aligned committee does not necessarily hamper grants of clemency. Love identifies, for instance, Delaware, Nebraska, Nevada, and Pennsylvania as being frequent granters of clemency with open application processes, public hearings, and binding recommendations.[121] Indeed, Matthew Denn, the Lieutenant Governor of Delaware and a member of that state's Board of Pardons, has praised the electoral accountability inherent in a board entirely composed of elected officeholders, calling it "uniquely answerable to the public." He notes that even though the board's deliberations are closed, a candidate for office would almost certainly disclose his or her vote on a particular clemency application.[122]

118 Cooper, *supra* note 117 at 83–84, *citing* Ky. Rev. Stat. Ann. § 439.320(1); Ohio Rev. Code Ann. § 5149.10; Penn. Const. art. 4 § 9(b) (1968).

119 *Id.* at 82–83, *citing* Neb. Rev. Stat. § 83–1,126; Nev. Const. art. 5 § 13 (1864); State of Utah Board of Pardons and Paroles, *Board Members*, www.bop.utah.gov/board-top-public-menu/ members.html (last visited March 13, 2015). *See also* Del. Const. art. 7 § 1 (1897).

120 Gavriel B. Wolfe, *I Beg Your Pardon: A Call for Renewal of Executive Clemency and Accountability in Massachusetts*, 27 B.C. Third World L.J. 417, 435–36 (2007).

121 Love, *supra* note 111 at 746. Of boards where the governor sits as a member, two grant clemency frequently (Nevada and Nebraska). Two do not (Florida and Minnesota). *Id.*

122 Matthew Denn, *Clemency in the State of Delaware: History and Proposals for Change*, 13 Del. L. Rev. 55 (2012).

The broader problem, however, is that there currently is no due process protection against an overly state-aligned board in most jurisdictions. Courts throughout the common law world have been resistant to opening the membership of a board to judicial review, even where the board is overtly-aligned with the prosecution in a given case. As Strasser writes with respect to *Ohio Adult Parole Authority v. Woodard,* where the US Supreme Court identified possible due process minimum guarantees in clemency proceedings, "it is not at all clear why coin-tossing would offend Due Process guarantees but packing a board with individuals who had a personal interest in the case would not."[123] Membership of mercy committees is an important area of future research in coming years, not just in the United States, but across the Commonwealth.

Conclusion

Most English-speaking jurisdictions provide for a mercy committee to advise the governor in exercising the clemency power, a continuation of the British colonial practice. These constitutions vary widely in committee structure, membership, and conditions and terms of appointment. Many require, for instance, the presence of a legal actor or a medical practitioner, while others involve legislative approval or vetting by an appointments authority. The makeup of mercy committees matters. According to empirical evidence from the United States, committees that have more diverse membership, that are insulated from the political process, and that operate in public proceedings with a hearing are most likely to grant clemency. On the other hand, reluctance to grant clemency may be greater for boards that are more overtly state-aligned or where membership disproportionately includes career law enforcement or prosecution officials. Although comparative evidence is not as widely available elsewhere in the common law world, the underlying principle may be extended to countries across the Commonwealth. The quality of a board's decision or advice may depend on the degree to which the board is a political patronage body or an independent and technocratic committee of experts.

123 Mark Strasser, *The Limits of the Clemency Power on Pardons, Retributivists, and the United States Constitution*, 41 Brandeis L.J. 85, 132 (2002).

7 Comparative clemency procedures

After discussing the form and scope of action of clemency authorities, this chapter will compare constitutional clemency procedures. The most common constitutional feature in the common law world is the requirement for a mercy report in capital cases, written by the trial judge and provided to the clemency authority. This chapter will also compare the modern bureaucratic procedures of large jurisdictions. Throughout the common law world the types of materials and testimony relied on by mercy committees vary, including whether they make decisions by consensus or by majority. Finally, this chapter will also explore the variety of notification, reporting, and publication requirements and the special challenges posed by mass grants of clemency.

The pardon procedure used in early modern England was formalistic and highly technical, though these traditions loosened as mercy became a more routine and bureaucratic process. Instead of being granted under the Great Seal, by the early 1800s pardons were issued by what is known as the royal sign-manual, the monarch's handwritten signature. With the passage of the Criminal Law Amendment Act of 1967, the Queen's royal sign-manual was countersigned by a Secretary of State, injecting a democratically-accountable actor into the clemency process. By convention the countersigning minister is the Home Secretary for England or the Secretaries of State for Scotland and Northern Ireland for those jurisdictions, each tasked with advising the monarch and countersigning the pardon.[1]

As discussed in the last chapter, the degree to which the pardon authority is aligned to the other powers of state, including law enforcement and prosecution, may be determinative of the frequency of clemency grants. The clemency process raises fundamental tensions where the mercy authority and the justice authority overlap. This chapter will bring in another model of clemency authority besides a mercy committee: the bureaucratic model, including the Office of the US Pardon Attorney in the Department

1 A.T.H. Smith, *The Prerogative of Mercy, the Power of Pardon and Criminal Justice*, 1983 Pub. L. 398, 427.

of Justice and India's Ministry of Home Affairs. Just as the quality of decision-making by clemency committees may vary, so too does the quality of bureaucratic recommendations reflect different institutional cultures. The US Department of Justice advocates a war on drugs and a tough-on-crime stance for criminal prosecutions and simultaneously is in charge of screening pardon applications. Thus an organization with a vested interest in prosecuting and convicting people is in charge of recommending whether those convictions should be put aside. Inevitably, the Department of Justice's pardon program has gradually come to reflect the unforgiving culture of federal prosecutors. As Schultz writes, "the fox is guarding the henhouse."[2]

The makeup of a pardon authority may affect the quality and substance of its decisions; likewise, the routineness and transparency of clemency procedures matter to the ultimate decision. This chapter will explore the application process, including to whom the clemency application is made; reporting and notification requirements; provision, if any, for a hearing; consideration of the petitions; and the ultimate grant or denial. Executive clemency has declined in a world-historical perspective with the rise of institutional parole and the decline of the mandatory death penalty. In addition, mercy's decline is reflective of an increasingly retributivist political culture, which may also impact the nature and quality of the mercy decision.

Application process

Jurisdictions differ as to whether applicants for clemency apply in a formal process or an informal one; whether they apply to the executive or to another authority, such as a parole board; and whether they are subject to waiting periods and notification requirements. In the Bahamas, for instance, applicants petition the mercy committee directly. According to the website of Ministry of Finance of the Bahamas, the Advisory Committee on the Prerogative of Mercy typically meets two or three times per year. Petitioners do not need to submit fees or forms and are notified within 21 days of consideration of the petition. The committee considers the petition along with reports from the police, the prison, a chaplain, a psychiatrist, and the trial judge.[3] Elsewhere, a parole board is responsible for screening initial applications and providing recommendations to the deciding officials. In the Northern Mariana Islands, the pardon and parole powers are effectively combined, as the constitution authorizes the governor to consult with the parole board prior to exercising his clemency power.[4] In Canada, the

2 Evan P. Schultz, *Does the Fox Control Pardons in the Henhouse?*, 13 FED. SENT'G REP. 177, 177 (2001).

3 BAH. CONST. art. 92(1) (1973); Ministry of Finance, *Clemency Petitions*, www.bahamas.gov.bs/wps/wcm/connect/mof_content/internet/all+services/c/clemency+petitions (last accessed Nov. 25, 2014).

4 N. MARIANA IS. CONST. art. 9(c) (1978).

National Parole Board reviews federal clemency applications to the governor-general, conducts investigations, and makes recommendations to the solicitor general.[5]

As clemency procedures became standardized, barriers to seeking clemency – a need for political connections, legal representation, or fees, for instance – were reduced, thereby increasing the volume of cases still further. Florida is illustrative. After the establishment of a pardons board in 1868, petitioners seeking clemency had to go through a relatively formal application process, as formalism served to protect the members of the pardon board from charges of bias and favoritism. In the early twentieth century, applicants were required to publish and post notices of their intentions to apply for pardon for at least ten days, and a written application had to include a record of convictions, trial transcripts, and recommendations from the sentencing judge and prosecuting attorney. These applications could be lengthy and quite costly, and applicants often had legal representation. By 1918, the application process had become standardized. In addition, this increase in clemency applications was a means by which African Americans and others expressed dissatisfaction with the court system.[6] Applicants generally began with a description of the applicant and details of the conviction and sentence, with an emphasis on the innocence, unintentionality, or legitimacy of the actions. Unlike at trial, the narrative in a clemency petition was presented on the applicant's terms, though often in the language of a lawyer.[7] A routine application process can reduce complaints of favoritism or bias. In 1957, due to persistent rumors of partiality or improper conduct, the Kansas legislature passed a modern parole and probation statute that provided for the filing of clemency applications with the parole board.[8]

In the United States, thirty states require or permit the victim or victim's representative to be notified of a pardon application; twenty-four require the trial judge be notified; thirty-one notify the prosecutor; eight notify the police chief; and twelve require a public posting, according to Dorne and Gewerthe. "The more rigorous and expansive the notice requirement statutes, the more reluctant the state appears to be in granting pardons."[9] Virginia is an example of a jurisdiction with a partially bureaucratized clemency process. Historically, Virginia has not required an applicant or a

5 Jean Teillet, *Exoneration for Louis Riel: Mercy, Justice, or Political Expediency?*, 67 Sask. L.Rev. 359, 375 (2004).

6 Vivien M.L. Miller, Crime, Sexual Violence, and Clemency: Florida's Pardon Board and Penal System in the Progressive Era 135–37 (2000).

7 *Id.* at 138–139.

8 Dale A. Spiegel, *Pardon, Probation and Parole in Kansas*, 6 U. Kan. L. Rev. 421, 422 (1958).

9 Clifford Dorne and Kenneth Gewerthe, *Mercy in a Climate of Retributive Justice: Interpretations from a National Survey of Executive Clemency Procedures*, 25 New Eng. J. on Crim. & Civ. Confinement 413, 436–37 (1999).

clemency authority to notify the public through a newspaper or to file notice of the application or a hearing with the trial judge and prosecuting attorney. In Virginia, the governor is the sole clemency authority and may pardon on his or her own initiative, though as a policy matter a written application was required from the prisoner, his counsel, a member of his family, or by another interested person. The superintendent of a penal institution or even the Probation and Parole Board may initiate a pardon recommendation if a prisoner is ineligible for parole. Applications for pardon are referred to the Secretary of the Commonwealth for processing. The Probation and Parole Board then initiates an investigation, obtaining the prisoner's personal file from the Department of Corrections, which includes a field report on the prisoner's background and home life. Letters from the trial judge and prosecuting attorney may be forwarded to the governor.[10] Virginia has no provision for a hearing. In 2004, the legislature provided an additional form of clemency known as an "absolute pardon," based on actual innocence. In all cases, the pardon process is orchestrated by the pardons specialist within the Office of the Secretary of the Commonwealth.[11]

Illinois has both a notice requirement and a gatekeeping mechanism for pardon applications. Applicants for clemency must mail a petition to the Prisoner Review Board addressed to the governor, detailing the circumstances of the crime and the reasons for seeking clemency. Applicants must also publish notice in the newspaper of their intention for seeking clemency, and the prisoner, victims, counsel, or any other interested parties may appear at a hearing on the petition. The recommendation of the Prisoner Review Board is purely advisory in Illinois; the governor possesses final clemency authority.[12] Additional forms of notice and input vary depending on the jurisdiction. In New Hampshire, if a petitioner for clemency is incarcerated, the commissioner for corrections will have an opportunity to comment on the petition (presumably on the petitioner's behavior in prison) before it is referred to the Executive Council, a body that advises the governor on clemency decisions.[13] In Ohio, applications for clemency are made in writing to the Ohio Adult Parole Authority, which has informally adopted a rule requiring applicants to wait two years between applications for clemency. The parole authority is required to investigate the clemency petition and may schedule a hearing. Notice of the clemency application must be sent to the prosecuting attorney, the judge of the trial court, and, for some enumerated crimes, to the victim or the

10 William F. Stone, *Pardons in Virginia*, 26 WASH. & LEE L. REV. 307, 313–15 (1969).

11 Secretary of the Commonwealth of Virginia, *Pardons*, https://commonwealth.virginia.gov/judicial-system/pardons (last accessed March 12, 2015).

12 Joseph Rupcich, *Abusing a Limitless Power: Executive Clemency in Illinois*, 28 S. ILL. U. L.J. 131, 144 (2003).

13 N.H. REV. STAT. ANN. § 4:22.

victim's family. The parole authority then issues a report and a non-binding recommendation to the governor.[14]

Even in states where the clemency power is held by the governor alone and not by a committee or board, applications may be processed through a parole authority. In Michigan, applications for pardons, commutations, and reprieves must be filed with the parole board.[15] By executive order in 2007, Michigan Governor Jennifer Granholm established the Executive Clemency Advisory Council to advise the parole board with respect to applications for pardons, commutations, and reprieves.[16] Similarly, in New York, the Executive Clemency Bureau within the Division of Parole screens clemency applications and responds to letters from applicants.[17] A parole board may provide the governor institutional capacity to investigate the clemency application and hold hearings, and, additionally, may provide political cover. In New Mexico, the governor may, in his or her discretion, refer requests for executive clemency to the parole board for investigation and recommendation.[18] Likewise, in North Carolina, the Parole Commission is authorized to assist the governor in exercising the clemency power.[19]

South Africa is another country with a well-established bureaucratic mercy process. However, similar to Virginia, South Africa's process is only partially bureaucratized, as the process typically involves senior-level government officials in lieu of an independent board of experts. Under the constitution of South Africa, the president has the power to pardon or reprieve offenders and to remit any fines, penalties, or forfeitures that have been imposed.[20] The general policy that has developed is that a pardon application is made to the Department of Justice and Constitutional Development, which considers each application on its own merits and advises the president accordingly. However, as in the United States, the president may decide to pardon someone of his own accord outside of this process, as he possesses sole authority and is not required to consult with anyone else. As it is considered a "head of state" power, it cannot be delegated or performed under another's instruction, but the president may consult with and take the advice of ministers and advisors.[21] The South African constitution provides that a written decision of the president

14 Daniel T. Kobil, *Do the Paperwork or Die: Clemency, Ohio Style?*, 52 Ohio St. L.J. 655, 669–71 (1991) (hereinafter, "Kobil, *Paperwork*").

15 Mich. Comp. Laws § 791.243.

16 Governor of Michigan Executive Order No. 2 of 2007, www.michigan.gov/formergovernors/0,4584,7-212-57648_21975-162403—,00.html (Feb. 16, 2007).

17 Kathleen M. Ridolfi and Seth Gordon, *Gubernatorial Clemency Powers: Justice or Mercy?*, Crim. Just. 31, 38 (Fall 2009).

18 *Id.*

19 N.C. Gen. Stat. § 143B-720A.

20 S. Afr. Const, art. 84(2)(j) (1996).

21 B.C. Naudé, *The Pardoning Power As a Duty of Justice*, 15 S. Afr. J. Crim. Just. 159, 160–161 (2002).

requires a countersignature by another cabinet member in order to ensure that the cabinet member is aware of the power's exercise, as it may affect his or her portfolio. However, the cabinet member cannot veto the decision by refusing to countersign; the exercise will only be invalid if the president deliberately withholds information from the cabinet member or is grossly negligent in informing the cabinet member of the power's exercise.[22]

The pardon application process is lengthy and involves officials from the South African Police Service, the Department of Justice and Constitutional Development, the President's Office, and the relevant cabinet minister. In general, applications include a statement of the motivation for the application, including reference to the detrimental effect of the conviction; a brief description of the circumstances surrounding the offense; three recent testimonials of the offender's character; identifying documents; and a set of fingerprints. The Department of Justice and Constitutional Development forwards a recommendation for a pardon to the relevant cabinet minister with a memorandum, a report to the president, and a draft reply to the applicant. A rejected applicant may seek reconsideration from the department or direct consideration by the president. Senior officials consider each case on its own merits, including claims of actual innocence and excuse or justification.[23] Naudé is critical of this process, as it is "cumbersome" and "not cost-effective" given that it requires the involvement of senior state officials to review a rapidly increasing number of relatively low-level matters. Poor record-keeping and spoliation of evidence pose additional challenges.[24]

California has a unique application process in which an applicant may apply for a judicial certificate of rehabilitation, which constitutes an application for a full pardon by the governor. The first step is to file an application for such a certificate with the county clerk and notify the sheriff or chief of police; then, the applicant must live a law-abiding, productive, and sober life for a period of time (the "period of rehabilitation") amounting to three years and thirty days for each year of the maximum term prescribed by law for the offense. Upon completing the period of rehabilitation, the offender then petitions for the certificate with a court, which then reviews the records, testimony of the trial, and prison record. If the court finds that rehabilitation has been proven, it issues a certificate of rehabilitation recommending to the governor that a full pardon be granted and all rights restored.[25] The governor may grant the pardon without further investigation, subject to the proviso in the California

22 *Id.* at 161. *See also*, S. AFR. CONST. art. 101(2) (1996) (requiring a countersignature for all written decisions of the president).

23 Naudé, *supra* note 21 at 167–171.

24 *Id.* at 171.

25 Helen R. MacGregor, *Adult Probation, Parole, and Pardon in California*, 38 TEX. L. REV. 887, 907–11 (1960). This process is still current at CAL. PENAL CODE § 4852.01.

constitution that a person twice convicted of a felony must receive the recommendation of a majority of the justices of the state supreme court.[26] While the certificate of rehabilitation accounts for a significant number – perhaps even a majority – of clemency grants in California, it does not replace the traditional process. For that process, a petition is made directly to the governor's office and then is forwarded to the Board of Parole Hearings for processing.[27]

Bureaucratisation of the clemency process

The routinization of executive mercy is a continuing process as the charismatic "act of grace" becomes one increasingly confined by public review and objective criteria. Administrative law has weakened the traditional institution of mercy in two ways. First, the rise of the administrative state has made unchecked discretion an anomaly in the law to be viewed with skepticism. As the power of agencies has grown, concerns about inequitable distribution of benefits have also increased judicial review of agency discretion. Discretionary decision-making sits uncomfortably within a heavily-scrutinized administrative state. Second, the development of the administrative state has changed our legal culture to focus on the judicial branch to prevent unfair application of the law.[28] Where clemency committees advise or share the mercy power with an executive, they are, in effect, attempting to check the executive's unguided and capricious use of the mercy power. Most of these pardon advisory boards – in the United States and across the Commonwealth – were created contemporaneously with the rise of the administrative state in the late nineteenth and early twentieth centuries. Boards created after the Second World War in particular tend to be modeled after independent regulatory agencies and less like political patronage bodies.[29]

While the bureaucratization of the mercy power is evident in most large jurisdictions, the United States federal system has attracted, by far, the most extensive academic study. For nearly a century after independence, the administration of pardons was not assigned to a specific executive office or position. In 1865, the office of Pardon Clerk was established to manage the pardon process, evolving into the Office of the US Pardon Attorney in the Department of Justice.[30] As early as 1789, the secretary of state and the attorney general shared the responsibility for exercising the pardon power.

26 *Id.*; *see also*, CAL. CONST. art. 5 § 8(a) (1879).

27 Office of Governor Edmund G. Brown, *How to Apply for a Pardon*, http://gov.ca.gov/docs/How_To_Apply_for_a_Pardon.pdf (last accessed March 12, 2015).

28 Rachel E. Barkow, *The Ascent of the Administrative State and the Demise of Mercy*, 121 HARV. L. REV. 1332, 1334–1335 (2008).

29 *Id.* at 1350–1351.

30 Jody C. Baumgartner and Mark. H. Morris, *Presidential Power Unbound: A Comparative Look at Presidential Pardon Power*, 29 POLITICS & POL'Y 209, 215–16 (2001).

Beginning in 1865, Congress began appropriating funds to the attorney general to pay for a pardon clerk, which grew into the Office of the Attorney in Charge of Pardons in 1891 and the Office of the US Pardon Attorney in 1894. In 1898, the regulations were promulgated establishing the administrative framework for presenting clemency petitions to the president for consideration, which were, and continue to be, only advisory.[31] Other executive agencies such as the Department of State could issue pardons on the president's behalf, but this power was consolidated in the Department of Justice by executive order in 1893.[32]

Although the Office of the US Pardon Attorney was created by Congress, it is located in the Department of Justice and the regulations under which the office operates are promulgated by the executive branch.[33] The US Code of Federal Regulations includes the executive clemency regulations that guide the administration of the pardon power, specifying the process of submission, review, and determination. The code sets forth as eligibility requirements a five year waiting period, submissions describing the individual, the crime, and the reasons for the request, subject to possible investigation by the Federal Bureau of Investigation. The Office of the Pardon Attorney then reviews the completed package and makes a recommendation to the president, who has final authority to grant or deny the pardon request. It is important to note that this process is advisory only; the President has full constitutional authority to act outside of this process.[34] However, the president has traditionally relied on it, and the instances where he did not – such as Ford's pardon of Nixon, Clinton's controversial late-term pardons, George H. W. Bush's pardon of prominent Iran-Contra figures, and George W. Bush's commutation of sentence for Scooter Libby – have triggered public outrage against the clemency process.[35] Handling pardons outside of the ordinary process, however, avoids giving the media advance notice that these pardons were under consideration.[36]

According to federal pardon regulations, a petitioner must have violated a law of the United States to be eligible for executive clemency at the federal level. In addition, a petitioner must have waited at least five years after the date of his or her release from confinement or five years after the date of conviction if the petitioner was not imprisoned. Commutations of lengthy prison terms or death sentences include different eligibility requirements. The Pardon Attorney conducts an investigation, often requesting an opinion from the US Attorney in the district where the conviction occurred

31 Lauren Schorr, *Breaking Into the Pardon Power: Congress and the Office of the Pardon Attorney*, 46 Am. Crim. L. Rev. 1535, 1542–43 (2009).
32 Jeffrey Crouch, The Presidential Pardon Power 21 (2009).
33 Schorr, *supra* note 31 at 1535.
34 Baumgartner and Morris, *supra* note 30 at 215–16.
35 Schorr, *supra* note 31 at 1535.
36 Crouch, *supra* note 32 at 22.

and from the victim. The Department of Justice relies on such factors as post-conviction character, seriousness of the offense, acceptance of responsibility and remorse, need for relief, and official recommendations and reports from the prosecutor and sentencing judge.[37] The petition process requires strict application requirements and waiting periods to keep the applicant pool relatively small, typically requiring "exceptional circumstances" before filing a petition if other forms of judicial or administrative relief are available.[38]

Much of what we know about the inner workings of the Office of the US Pardon Attorney come from Margaret Colgate Love, who has written extensively on her time as Pardon Attorney under President Bill Clinton.[39] She explains that the pardon power has declined since 1980 in part because of the hostility of federal prosecutors and a reconfiguration of the Office of the Pardon Attorney to leave prosecutors in charge of advising on clemency decisions. Officials simply rubber stamped the recommendations of prosecutors without subjecting them to thorough review.[40] "By the time President Clinton entered office in 1993, the pardon program at Justice had lost whatever independence and integrity it once enjoyed within the Department, and was functioning primarily to ratify the results achieved by prosecutors, not to provide any real possibility of revising them." She continues, "[t]o be sure, the pardon process was disciplined and regular. But it had no sense of mission and produced very little."[41] She describes how this pardon paradox eventually ensnared Bill Clinton, who began to express interest in exercising clemency more frequently only late in his term. The Department of Justice made no effort to warn President Clinton about the perils of pardoning outside of the bureaucratic system; to the contrary, the department seems to have shut down its production of pardon recommendations entirely by the end of Clinton's term. As a result, President Clinton set up an ad hoc procedure in the White House Counsel's office, and, in the last months of Clinton's tenure in office, White House staff at all levels worked around the clock compiling and revising lists of pardon applicants, fielding calls from influential supporters, and attending meetings at which the merits of applications were debated. Clinton, regarding the pardon power as personal to the presidency, used many public opportunities to talk about the forthcoming pardons, but even he was surprised when, on the morning of January 20, 2001, the 177 pardons and sentence commutations he issued ballooned into the second-most damaging scandal of his

37 Schorr, *supra* note 31 at 1543–1544.

38 Crouch, *supra* note 32 at 23.

39 *See* Jeffrey Crouch, *The President's Power to Commute: Is It Still Relevant?*, 9 U. St. Thomas L.J. 681, 696 (2011).

40 Margaret Colgate Love, *The Pardon Paradox: Lessons of Clinton's Last Pardons*, 32 Cap. U. L. Rev. 185, 192 (2002) (hereinafter, "Love, *Pardon Paradox*").

41 *Id.* at 193.

presidency.[42] Love explains that the clemency power "was abandoned to the chaos that reigned at the White House during Clinton's final weeks in office."[43] Erler writes that Clinton found it difficult to steer the Department of Justice to his policy preferences on pardons, in part because he lacked a close relationship with his attorney general.[44]

The bureaucratization of the pardon power is not without its critics. Harrison writes that pardon was intended to be like a lightning bolt, relatively rare and in principle hard to predict because it served as an exception to generally-accepted rules of criminal law. He explains that the current Department of Justice pardon process instead creates a form of legislation by anticipating the grounds on which pardons should be granted that will apply to crimes yet to be committed. "Granting significant legislative power to a single individual, even the President of the United States, is contrary to the genius of our constitution," he asserts, indicating that even if federal sentencing is too draconian, the pardon power should not be used to cure Congressional inaction.[45] Freed and Chanenson object on similar grounds, arguing that rules that guide the sentencing discretion of judges at trial and institutional parole mechanisms are preferable to a system "that relies exclusively upon the unstructured, unexplained discretion of a president to grant or deny individual pardons or commutations." They concede that presidents may wish to use this power to motivate a recalcitrant Congress, but they should resist the motivation to convert the presidency into a legislature of one in lieu of systemic sentencing reform.[46]

Indeed, experience shows that this bureaucratic process is not appropriate for all types of clemency petitions. For instance, the office of the US Pardon Attorney may be peculiarly ill-suited to claims based on actual innocence, as a presidential pardon is only a sign of forgiveness and not of vindication. In addition, the applicant ordinarily must wait five years before applying and has no right to submit new evidence beyond that included on the application form and no right to appear before the Pardon Attorney in person. If denied, the applicant has no right to receive an explanation for a denial of clemency.[47] This is true even though the US Supreme Court has ruled that actual innocence, absent a procedural violation in a convict's

42 *Id.* at 198–200.

43 *Id.* at 205.

44 H. Abbie Erler, *Executive Clemency or Bureaucratic Discretion? Two Models of the Pardons Process*, 37 Pres. Stud. Q. 427, 445 (2007). A significant part of the problem was that responsibility for reviewing pardon recommendations had shifted from the deputy attorney general to the associate attorney general, whose staff was composed of career prosecutors. *Id.* at 443.

45 John Harrison, *Pardon as Prerogative*, 13 Fed. Sent'g Rep. 147, 148–49 (2001).

46 Daniel J. Freed and Steven J. Chanenson, *Pardon Power and Sentencing Policy*, 13 Fed. Sent'g Rep. 119, 124 (2001).

47 Brian M. Hoffstadt, *Normalizing the Federal Clemency Power*, 79 Tex. L. Rev. 561, 580–81 (2001).

underlying case, is not a constitutional ground for relief; rather, executive clemency is the proper mechanism for assessing claims of innocence.[48] Similarly, the office is not well-suited to evaluate merits of wholly political claims, which are best handled by close advisors to the president, outside of the Pardon Attorney mechanism.[49] The Pardon Attorney is designed to emphasize clemency as a tool of rehabilitation and not a means of correcting egregious legal error, as evident in the waiting periods and other barriers to the application process.[50]

Consideration of mercy petitions

One of the most common constitutional mercy procedures in the Commonwealth is to require that the trial judge provide a written report and other information about a case to the clemency authority specifically in death penalty cases. Where the trial judge is unavailable, many constitutions require the chief justice to produce such a report. In Uganda, a trial judge or the chief justice must provide a written report in all capital cases to the Advisory Committee on the Prerogative of Mercy.[51] Botswana's constitution contains a similar provision, requiring the Advisory Committee on the Prerogative of Mercy to consider a mercy report in death penalty cases. However, no mercy report is necessary in non-capital cases, as the president is not required to consult with the committee.[52] The mercy report may contain other information as well. In Sierra Leone, the package must include a written report of the trial judge as well as a medical report on the prisoner.[53] Singapore requires not only a report by the trial judge, but also a report by appellate judges that affirmed the death sentence.[54] Whether this report is prepared for an advisory mercy committee, for the cabinet, or for the attorney general or another minister depends on that constitution's mercy framework. Sri Lanka's constitution does not create an advisory mercy committee; in that country, the report is made available to the attorney general and the minister of justice for recommendations.[55] In death penalty cases in Brunei prior to the suspension of some constitutional provisions in 2006, the attorney general was required to supply the Pardons Board with any material information in the possession of the prosecutor concerning the case. In all cases, the Pardons Board was required to consider a written opinion from the attorney general and by the *Mufti*

48 Herrera v. Collins, 506 US 390, 400 (1993).
49 Hoffstadt, *supra* note 47 at 591.
50 *Id.* at 583.
51 Uganda Const. art. 121(5) (1995).
52 Bots. Const. art. 55 (1966).
53 Sierra Leone Const. art. 63(2) (1991).
54 Sing. Const. art. 22P(2) (1965).
55 Sri Lanka Const. art. 34 (1978).

Karajaan if the offense arose under Islamic law.[56] In total, twenty-three Commonwealth jurisdictions include some requirement that a trial judge or chief justice write a report for consideration of clemency in capital cases.[57]

Some constitutions contain exclusions from this requirement. In Swaziland, capital convictions by court-martial are excluded from the requirement of a mercy report.[58] The exclusion of courts-martial is especially common in the Caribbean. The constitutions of Belize, Dominica, Grenada, Guyana, St. Kitts and Nevis, St. Lucia, and St. Vincent and the Grenadines contain a similar exception, as do those of Fiji, Mauritius, and the Solomon Islands.[59] The Constitution of Malta contains the reverse provision, specifically *including* courts-martial. In capital cases, the officer presiding must prepare a written mercy report to the executive.[60]

The Canadian procedure illustrates the role that the mercy report played in the consideration process – and the risks. Prior to 1961, the Canadian Criminal Code provided for the exercise of executive clemency by the Governor General in Council (the equivalent of the federal cabinet), but the code did not guide the use of the power, nor did it require the cabinet to explain a clemency decision. In practice, all capital cases have been referred to the cabinet since shortly after Confederation, and the cabinet decided whether to allow a mandatory death sentence to stand or to commute it to life imprisonment.[61] Upon receiving notice of a conviction for murder, the Remissions Service of the Justice Department gathered all relevant information on the case, including court records, a report of the trial judge, representations on behalf of the accused, psychiatric reports, and police reports. Then, consultation occurred between the Director of the Remissions Service and either the minister of justice or the solicitor general. Shortly before the appointed execution date, the minister or solicitor general took

56 Brunei Const. arts. 8A, 9(4)-(5) (1959).

57 Ant. & Barb. Const. art. 86(1) (1981); Bah. Const. art. 92(1) (1973); Barb. Const. art. 78(3) (1966); Belize Const. art. 53 (1981); Bots. Const. art. 55(1) (1966); Dominica Const. art. 75 (1978); Fiji Const. art. 115(4) (1997); Ghana Const. art. 72(2) (1992); Gren. Const. art. 74(1) (1973); Guy. Const. art. 190(1) (1980); Jam. Const. art. 91(1) (1962); Malta Const. art. 93(2)(a) (1964); Mauritius Const. art. 75(6) (1968); Sierra Leone Const. art. 63(2) (1991); Sing. Const. art. 22P(2) (1965); Solomon Is. Const. art. 45(7) (1978); Sri Lanka Const. art. 34 (1978); St. Kitts & Nevis Const. art. 68(1) (1983); St. Lucia Const. art. 76 (1978); St. Vincent Const. art. 67(1) (1979); Swaz. Const. art. 78(5) (2005); Trin. & Tobago Const. art. 89(1) (1976); Uganda Const. art. 121(5) (1995).

58 Swaz. Const. art. 78(5) (2005).

59 Swaz. Const. art. 78(5) (2005); Belize Const. art. 53 (1981); Dominica Const. art. 75 (1978); Gren. Const. art. 74(1) (1973); Mauritius Const. art. 75(6) (1968); St. Kitts & Nevis Const. art. 68(1) (1983); St. Lucia Const. art. 76 (1978); St. Vincent Const. art. 67(1) (1979); Fiji Const. art. 115(4) (1997); Solomon Is. Const. art. 45(7) (1978); Guy. Const. art. 190(1) (1980).

60 Malta Const. art. 93(2)(a) (1964).

61 Kenneth L. Avio, *The Quality of Mercy: Exercise of the Royal Prerogative in Canada*, 13 Can. Pub. Pol'y 366, 367–8 (1987).

the case to the cabinet for a final decision.[62] The cabinet did not produce a written record explaining its decision, though the Remissions Service prepared a summary in each case for the cabinet's review. Empirical analysis of the cabinet's clemency decisions generally shows that grants of executive clemency were not arbitrary or random, and conformed to constitutional expectations of mitigating and aggravating circumstances. However, a statistical analysis for the years 1926 to 1957 does reveal that gender, ethnicity of the offender, the offender-victim racial configuration, and the offender's occupational status were correlated to clemency decisions.[63]

Since constitutions typically do not provide significant detail as to the mechanics of the mercy process, the procedures may be informal. In Sudan after independence, a criminal court circular described the process whereby judges would make mercy reports to the executive. According to the circular, a judge was to give reasons for a recommendation for mercy, including notes on the accused person's ethnic or cultural background and the state of security in the area. If a judge's mercy recommendation in a death penalty case was based on insanity or mental illness, the judge was first required to find the accused legally responsible for the act and explain why the insanity or mental illness was not exculpatory. In death penalty cases confirmed by the Supreme Court, the president was required to review judicial mercy recommendations. Prior to 1960, the practice was to allow the governor of the province where the crime was committed to comment on a court's mercy recommendation. Generally, judges are requested not to inform the accused that a recommendation to mercy has been made, since the president could refuse to commute the sentence. However, because of early government policy commuting death sentences for women or for persons who played a minor role in a joint crime, the circular allowed judges to tell the condemned prisoners of its recommendation in these cases.[64] An informal procedure authorizing more intensive review in capital cases is common. In Tennessee, where the governor alone holds the clemency power, a practice has developed in which governors seek "non-binding recommendations from the Board of Probation and Parole on whether clemency should be granted in a capital case." The board considers a set of specific criteria, but the governor may not limit him or herself to those criteria, and indeed the governor is not required to consider any of the board's findings. The board's hearings and the prisoner's presentation to the governor are generally open to the public, with greater emphasis placed on the trial evidence rather than the defendant's post-trial conduct.[65]

62 *Id.* at 368.

63 *Id.* at 372.

64 Krishna Vasdev, LAW OF HOMICIDE IN THE SUDAN 363–64 (1978).

65 Dwight Aarons, *Adjudicating Claims of Innocence for the Capitally Condemned in Tennessee: Embracing a Truth Forum*, 76 TENN. L. REV. 511, 545 (2009).

The clemency consideration process in US states varies widely in complexity and in the involvement of additional actors. Massachusetts has a two-stage review process: the Advisory Board of Pardons conducts initial reviews of all clemency applications before they reach the governor and the Governor's Council, a specially-elected body that advises the governor on mercy grants and other executive powers. The Advisory Board is composed of seven full-time, salaried employees appointed by the governor to five-year terms. Upon receiving an application for a pardon, the Advisory Board conducts a preliminary investigation and compiles a case summary with the petitioner's criminal, social, and institutional histories and statements from officials within the justice system. For a pardon petition, a hearing before the Advisory Board is required; for a commutation, it is optional. The Board passes recommendations on to the governor and the Governor's Council along with a statement of reasons; the governor requires a favorable recommendation from the Governor's Council to grant clemency but is not required to follow the recommendation. The Governor's Council must hold a public hearing of its own if the crime to be pardoned was a felony, and ultimately disposes of a case by a recorded majority vote.[66] The clemency scheme used in Massachusetts is complex and peculiarly susceptible to political pressure, as the governor and the Governor's Council are both elected, and the two-tiered review process requires two layers of proceedings (often including two separate hearings), increasing the structural costs of granting clemency.[67] The overly-bureaucratic process makes pardons in Massachusetts "vanishingly rare."[68]

Besides mercy reports in death penalty cases, jurisdictions may emphasize different parts of the clemency application package. In Missouri, the affidavits accompanying the application are an important tool of evaluation not only based on what the affiant says but also for who the affiant is – the applicant's local police chief is likely more influential than his former cellmate. Affidavits made by persons of political substance not only show reliable information about the applicant, but in theory might also protect the governor politically. If the upholder of the law in closest contact with the applicant felt he was worthy, the governor could hardly be faulted for following the recommendation.[69] Alaska's relatively new provisions, passed in 2007, often require the involvement of victims. Upon a clemency application the governor must provide 120 day notice to the Board of Parole, which will investigate the application and send a notice of the proposed act

66 Gavriel B. Wolfe, *I Beg Your Pardon: A Call for Renewal of Executive Clemency and Accountability in Massachusetts*, 27 B.C. Third World L.J. 417 (2007).

67 *Id.* at 433.

68 Margaret Colgate Love, *Reinvigorating the Federal Pardon Process: What the President Can Learn From the States*, 9 U. St. Thomas L. J. 730, 746 (2012) (hereinafter, "Love, *Reinvigorating*").

69 James G. Lindsay, *Pardons in Missouri: Procedure and Policy*, 48 U.M.K.C. L. Rev. 33, 46 (1979).

of clemency to all relevant government actors and to any victims in the case who suffered domestic violence, a crime against the person, or first-degree arson. The victims may comment on the proposed clemency, and their comments must be forwarded to the governor, though he or she has no statutory obligation to consider the comments or follow any of the board's recommendations. The new statute eliminates the direct request to the governor, and requires the application go through the Board of Parole and, within the Board of Parole, the Executive Clemency Advisory Board.[70]

Some jurisdictions resist pressure to reveal the considerations that go into a grant or denial of clemency. In India, the Ministry of Home Affairs has resisted identifying clemency guidelines, indicating as recently as February 2014 that "[n]o specific guidelines can be framed for examining the mercy petitions due to the vast majority of different types of cases and varied circumstances."[71] Human rights organizations have called grants of clemency arbitrary in a country where more than one convict is sentenced to death every day. Between 2001 and 2012, nearly 6,000 convicts were awarded the death penalty, of which nearly 1,600 were confirmed while 4,400 were commuted to life imprisonment – and only one was executed.[72] However, informal guidance in the form of circulars and instructions requires the Ministry of Home Affairs to examine the personality of the accused person and the circumstances of the case; cases in which the appellate court doubted the reliability of evidence but nonetheless decided on conviction; cases in which fresh evidence may be available; cases in which appellate courts enhanced the sentence or reversed an acquittal; disagreement among judges; and long delays in investigation and trial.[73] In 2005, President A.P.J. Abdul Kalam requested that the Ministry of Home Affairs additionally consider the sociological aspects of a case; humanist and compassionate grounds, such as the age of the convict and his physical and mental condition; the scope for recidivism in capital cases; and the financial liabilities of the convict's family.[74]

Other jurisdictions have been more forthcoming about the considerations involved in the mercy decision. In Papua New Guinea, the Advisory Committee on the Power of Mercy looks into submissions in great detail. Circumstances that might be grounds for mercy include a referral by a judge; a change in the law that has altered a penalty subsequent to the prisoner's sentencing; a harsh or oppressive punishment out of proportion with

70 Ronald S. Everett and Deborah Periman, *"The Governor's Court of Last Resort:" An Introduction to Executive Clemency in Alaska*, 28 ALASKA L.REV. 57, 91–92 (2011).

71 Asian Centre for Human Rights, ARBITRARY ON ALL COUNTS: CONSIDERATION OF MERCY PLEAS BY PRESIDENT OF INDIA 10 (2014).

72 *Id.*

73 *Id.* at 12.

74 Bikram Jeet Batra, *"Court" of Last Resort: A Study of Constitutional Clemency for Capital Crimes in India*, Jawaharlal Nehru University Centre for the Study of Law and Governance Working Paper Series, CSLG/WP/11, April 2009.

that originally intended; new evidence unavailable to a judge at trial; long-term detainees; mental or physical medical issues; or exceptionally meritorious conduct by a prisoner in saving the life of another or assisting in apprehension of escaped detainees.[75] As a member of the mercy committee indicated, these grounds for clemency were not dissimilar to the prevailing practice in the United Kingdom.[76] Opinions as to what factors are most important may even differ among the members themselves. In Delaware, some members of the current Board of Pardons believe the applicant should make a practical need for clemency, for example, to pursue specific types of employment, while others place less emphasis on this practical need. In addition, members disagree about the weight to give an applicant's immigration status, remorse for the crime, and the duration of time since the conviction.[77]

Whether an applicant is entitled to a public hearing before a pardon or parole board in clemency cases varies widely across jurisdictions. In Connecticut, for instance, the Board of Pardons, a creature of statute, holds clemency hearings as a matter of course.[78] However, in New York hearings are ordinarily not held; instead, the governor bases a decision on a report from the corrections facility, recommendations from the sentencing judge and prosecuting attorney, and medical and psychiatric evaluations.[79] According to Dorne and Gewerth, a total of twenty-four US states expressly indicated that they permitted hearings for pardon applicants, eleven of which allowed *ex parte* proceedings. Ten required the applicant's presence at the hearings. The degree of procedural formality varies, but they tend not to be directly adversarial, with the applicant and other interested parties testifying in the narrative. In Louisiana, the pardon board even travels to prisons so that an inmate-applicant can appear.[80] Four state constitutions (Delaware, Idaho, Pennsylvania, and Utah) provide for the right to a hearing in clemency proceedings.[81]

Investigations that cross jurisdictional lines add additional complexity. Missouri is illustrative of pardon applications from out-of-state residents. For applicants living out of state, local authorities contact the agency

75 Burton G. Burton-Bradley, *The Power of Mercy*, 24 Aust. & N.Z. J. Psychiatry 397, 401 (1990).

76 *Id.*

77 Matthew Denn, *Clemency in the State of Delaware: History and Proposals for Change*, 13 Del. L. Rev. 55, 61 (2012).

78 Meah Dell Rothman, *The Pardoning Power: Historical Perspective and Case Study of New York and Connecticut*, 12 Colum. J.L. & Soc. Probs. 149, 163 (1976).

79 State of New York Department of Corrections and Community Supervision, *Information Concerning Executive Clemency*, Dec. 31, 2014, www.ny.gov/sites/ny.gov/files/atoms/files/6901_signed_12312014.pdf.

80 Dorne and Gewerthe, *supra* note 9 at 446.

81 Del. Const. art. 7 § 1(1) (1897); Idaho Const. art. 4 § 7 (1890); Penn. Const. art. 4 § 9(a) (1968); Utah Const. art. 7 § 12 (1895).

equivalent to the Missouri parole board in the applicant's home state and request an investigation, though these may produce sketchy background information. Certainly, Missouri officials closest to where the offense was committed will investigate, but if the information gathered is too sparse, the pardon could be denied simply for that reason. Missouri's interests are lessened with regard to out-of-state pardons, but cooperation by the state of residence reflects favorably on the applicant.[82] In the United States, the Supreme Court has held that states need not accord the same consequences to a federal pardon that the federal government does.[83] Nor must federal authorities treat a state pardon just as the state does.[84] Indeed, despite the Full Faith and Credit Clause of the US constitution, which would seem to mandate mutual reciprocal recognition of pardons among states, federal courts have not required that states give effect to one another's pardons.[85] However, some states, like California, have chosen to do so as a matter of policy, and for the sake of uniformity courts seem likely to accord an out-of-state pardon the same status as a local pardon.[86]

The most common complaint against the clemency process is that it may be secretive, opaque, and closed to participation and review. In the United Kingdom, the clemency process may require a police investigation, even though the Home Office, which reviews clemency decisions, is politically responsible for the police force. If the police find that no injustice has been done, the Home Office is in no position to reach a different conclusion. "Doubts have been expressed about whether the Home Office is really the most appropriate body to conduct the ultimate review of criminal convictions, and about whether a politician is the most appropriate ultimate judge in such a matter."[87] Additional complaints include the lack of public openness and the unwillingness of the Home Office to explain or give reasons for its decisions, with proceedings effectively limited to a review of the papers. There is no provision for a hearing.[88] As the only state in the United States without guidelines regulating the mercy power, Texas is a particularly egregious target of this complaint. In 1998, a state judge ruled that the Texas Board of Pardons and Paroles was required to make public its meetings, deliberate clemency petitions, hold a public vote, and record its reasoning, though the Texas Supreme Court suspended the ruling.[89] In a

82 Lindsay, *supra* note 69 at 46–47.
83 *Id.* at 33, *citing* Carlesi v. New York, 233 US 51 (1914).
84 Lindsay, *supra* note 69 at 49 n. 114, *citing* US v. Matassini, 565 F.2d 1297, 1300 n. 5 (5th Cir. 1978); Thrall v. Wolfe, 503 F.2d 313 (7th Cir. 1974), *cert. denied*, 420 US 972 (1975).
85 *See, e.g.*, Groseclose v. Plummer, 106 F.2d 311 (9th Cir.), *cert. denied*, 308 US 614 (1939).
86 Lindsay, *supra* note 69 at 50.
87 Smith, *supra* note 1 at 430.
88 *Id.* at 430–31.
89 In Re Texas Bd. of Pardons and Paroles, 989 S.W.2d 360 (Tex. 1998), *quoted in* Allen L. Williamson, *Clemency in Texas: A Question of Mercy?*, 6 TEX. WESLEYAN L.REV. 131, 147 n. 128 (1999).

subsequent challenge, a federal judge called Texas's clemency process "extremely poor and certainly minimal," but noted that the US Supreme Court only requires minimal due process in clemency decisions. Indeed, the Texas Board of Pardons and Paroles virtually never meets to discuss *any* petitions for clemency, and its members are allowed to meet in private or by telephone. No record is kept, and typically members call or fax in their votes. Yet, the board must favorably recommend clemency – a breathtakingly rare event – before the governor can even consider the merits of a case.[90] This does not mean that the governor is completely without influence. In one clemency case, Texas Governor George W. Bush was forced to pressure the Board of Pardons and Paroles to grant clemency in a case where a defendant had not even been in the state at the time the crime was committed. By the end of his governorship, Bush, who approved 152 executions as governor, had appointed all eighteen members of the Board and could request reconsideration of mercy decisions.[91]

The clemency decision

The ultimate clemency decision is often a deeply personal and individual one, connected to the facts of a specific case and sensitive to the surrounding political and social context. The bureaucratization of the mercy process has not completely erased the personal role of the executive him or herself in the process. In Missouri in January 1999, the scheduled execution of Darrell Mease, an unrepentant triple-murderer, on the same day that Pope John Paul II visited St. Louis resulted in an accidental face-to-face plea for Mease's life by the Pope to then-Missouri Governor Mel Carnahan. In deference to the Pope's wishes, though acknowledging that Mease was hardly the most deserving candidate for clemency then on Missouri's death row, Carnahan commuted his sentence to life imprisonment without parole.[92] The Pope did not protest Mease's case for any intrinsic reason, and had never met Mease, but the coincidence of the chance encounter with the Pope and the weight of a personal appeal moved Carnahan to acknowledge a higher authority than the state. It was not to last: executions proceeded almost monthly in Missouri afterward.[93] The pardon power is not merely an executive privilege, but an official duty of the head of state,

90 Williamson, *supra* note 89 at 148–49.

91 Alan Berlow, *The Texas Clemency Memos*, ATLANTIC MONTHLY, July/August 2003.

92 Linda Ross Meyer, *The Merciful State*, *in* FORGIVENESS, MERCY, AND CLEMENCY 64, 75–6 (Austin Sarat and Nasser Hussain eds., 2007). Kobil notes that even after the Mease commutation, Carnahan avoided characterizing the commutation in merciful terms, indicating that he refused to know the facts of the case and that he granted the commutation solely out of respect for the Pope. Daniel T. Kobil, *Should Mercy Have a Place in Clemency Decisions?*, *in* FORGIVENESS, MERCY, AND CLEMENCY 36, 40–41 (Austin Sarat and Nasser Hussain eds., 2007) (hereinafter, "Kobil, *Mercy*").

93 Meyer, *supra* note 92 at 102.

requiring great forethought, patience, and accountability. In making a pardon decision, an executive inquires into the circumstances of a case, sifting through factual data, judicial proceedings, the law itself, public opinion, and character of the accused. Following this, he or she must reach his or her own decision on the matter by seeking an unbiased answer to the question of whether the public welfare would be better served by exercising the clemency power.[94]

Narratives of executive decision-making in clemency cases help provide a semblance of order by connecting the unlimited sovereign prerogative power and the lived experiences of most citizens in a democratic society, who view clemency as a form of "lawful lawlessness," outside the world of laws and rules. Former Ohio Governor Michael DiSalle (1959–1963), a longtime opponent of capital punishment, commuted six death sentences but allowed six more to proceed – more executions in his one term than in the terms of the subsequent four governors combined.[95] Once he left office, DiSalle wrote an unusual book entitled *The Power of Life and Death*, detailing his decision-making process in each of the twelve clemency petitions placed on his desk as governor.[96] He used great care in making each decision, reviewing extensive case files, reading pleadings, asking questions, visiting crime scenes, even interviewing prisoners on death row. In an article in the *Ohio State Law Journal*, DiSalle reflected on his clemency power as governor in greater detail. He explained that although he personally opposed the death penalty, he felt that he had to enforce it unless there were mitigating circumstances present since it was a part of the law of Ohio.[97] He did not do that lightly:

> The governor's role…is one in which there can be no transfer of responsibility. When he reviews an application for clemency he knows that this is the individual's last resort. This cannot be done in the secrecy of a jury room. He cannot salve his conscience by saying, "Maybe my switch did not cause the man to die."
>
> If we take a man's freedom in error we might compensate for that mistake. If we take a man's life the damage is irreparable. Clemency is an essential part of our system of justice. It is for this reason alone, if for no other, that there will be a more general recognition of its need, its purpose, and the difficulties incumbent with its administration.

94 Christopher C. Joyner, *Rethinking the President's Power of Executive Pardon*, 43 FED. PROBATION 16, 19 (1979).

95 Austin Sarat, *Mercy, Clemency, and Capital Punishment: Two Accounts*, 3 OHIO ST. J. CRIM. L. 273, 281 (2005).

96 Michael DiSalle, THE POWER OF LIFE OR DEATH (1965), *quoted in* Sarat, *supra* note 95 at 281.

97 Michael V. DiSalle, *Comments on Capital Punishment and Clemency*, 25 OHIO ST. L.J. 71, 72 (1964).

> It is because of the solitude in which he must make his decision that the governor's method of arriving at the result is not hampered by rules of evidence. He is free to secure information in whatever manner he feels will best serve the cause of ultimate justice.[98]

The "solitude" of the clemency decision is a reminder of the unique and unclassifiable nature of mercy within a legal system. As Sarat describes, the book casts DiSalle as "an agonizing and agonized decision-maker, as if by recounting the pain associated with his clemency decision he could enlist some measure of sympathy and convince his readers that his use of the sovereign prerogative was reluctant and responsible."[99] DiSalle described being haunted long after one execution, even when he was convinced of the man's guilt. As Sarat writes, "DiSalle deploys language, detail, and order to tell a story of conflict between his conscience and his duty, his moral principles and the oath of office that binds chief executives to faithfully execute the law of the land even when they find it morally abhorrent."[100] As governor of Texas, George W. Bush faced criticism that his review of clemency petitions was cursory and based only a brief memorandum from the state attorney general that was designed to minimize his legal and moral responsibility for executions, though Bush argues in his autobiography that his review was thoughtful and thorough.[101]

Maryland Governor Bob Ehrlich has also reflected on his frequent grants of clemency in deeply personal detail. He recalled how lawyers, judges, and clemency petitioners made inappropriate contact with him to influence the clemency process until his personal attorney took his cellular phone away. In making the clemency decision, Ehrlich noted that he had a series of personal markers or red flags; among the most important of these was where a petitioner for clemency had arrears in child support payments. He explained that he would meet monthly with his lieutenant governor, his policy director, and several other lawyers to review thirty or forty cases over four or five hours. Some of these cases were easy and some were difficult, he recalled; some he would hold over to the next month pending additional investigation.[102] Barkow writes that Governor Ehrlich sought input from victims before granting a clemency application, which helped to neutralize political opposition. Ehrlich granted an unusually high number of pardons and commutations during his single term as governor, and though he was defeated for reelection, his grants of clemency did not play a role in that defeat.[103]

98 *Id.* at 80.
99 Sarat, *supra* note 95 at 284.
100 *Id.* at 281.
101 Berlow, *supra* note 91.
102 Robert L. Ehrlich, *Pardons and Commutations: Observations from the Front Lines*, 9 U. St. Thomas L.J. 669, 672–75 (2012).
103 Rachel E. Barkow, *The Politics of Forgiveness: Reconceptualizing Clemency*, 21 Fed. Sent'g Rep. 153, 153–56 (2009).

It may be difficult to predict public reaction to grants of clemency. The pardons issued by US President Bill Clinton shortly before he left office dominated headlines and talk shows for weeks, inflicting lasting damage to Clinton's popularity.[104] "By moving the process into the White House, Clinton was able to exercise greater control over the pardons process, but in return opened himself up to charges of corruption, bribery, and favoritism," Erler writes.[105] Crouch describes the public outrage at Clinton's pardon for Marc Rich, a large donor to Clinton's presidential library, and then at the efforts of Hillary Clinton's brother and Bill Clinton's half-brother to lobby for pardons.[106] However, one federal judge, reflecting on President Clinton's pardon of a low-level drug offender on his last day in office in 2001, believed that the president's pardon was merited as the offender had no previous convictions, proved his commitment to rehabilitation by completing college courses, expressed remorse for the crime, and worked to teach others to avoid drugs.[107] Indeed, most grants of clemency are not controversial. Since the start of the Carter administration in 1977, 95 percent of all those granted clemency received post-*sentence* pardons, which typically go to people who have been tried and convicted, served their full sentence, and went on to live productive, law-abiding lives for at least five years. These types of pardons are routine and generally unnoticed; they provide offenders some measure of self-respect and help them reclaim their civil rights to vote, obtain certain types of jobs and licenses, adopt a child, carry a weapon, sell alcohol, or race cars or horses, among other rights.[108]

The consequences of an executive pardon vary among jurisdictions. As is generally accepted throughout the common law world, a full pardon removes the legal consequences of an offense but does not create a legal status identical with an innocent person, though some jurisdictions have established separate processes for claims based on actual innocence.[109] A pardon merely forgives the offense; it does not acquit. Finally, pardons generally do not restore rights previously forfeited by the conviction; they

104 Love, *Pardon Paradox*, *supra* note 40 at 203.

105 Erler, *supra* note 44 at 446.

106 Crouch, *supra* note 32 at 116–117.

107 David S. Doty, *A View from the Bench of Two Commutations – Vignali and Willis*, 13 FED. SENT'G REP. 161, 161 (2001).

108 Kathleen Dean Moore, *Mr. President, Misusing This Pardon Power Is Unpardonable*, 13 FED. SENT'G REP. 159, 159 (2001).

109 *See, e.g.*, Henry Weihofen, *The Effect of a Pardon*, 88 U. Penn. L. Rev. 177, 179 (1939). As Weihofen writes, "no rational rule as to the effect of a pardon can be stated without distinguishing clearly between pardons granted for innocence and pardons granted for other reasons. A pardon for innocence is an acquittal, and must be given all the effects of an acquittal. A pardon for other reasons is not an acquittal; it leaves the determination of the convict's guilt stand, and only relieves him from the legal consequences of that guilt." *Id. See also*, Ashley M. Steiner, *Remission of Guilt or Removal of Punishment? The Effects of a Presidential Pardon*, 46 EMORY L.J. 959 (1997).

only apply prospectively.[110] The disabilities of criminal convictions also vary. In South Africa, criminal convictions can prevent a person from obtaining travel documentation, becoming a police officer, obtaining a firearm license or professional driving permit, or successfully applying for employment, among other disabilities.[111]

Reporting and publication procedures

Jurisdictions in the common law world differ as to the requirements for making grants of clemency public and as to whether executives or mercy committees must provide reasons for their actions. The constitution of Belize is typical, authorizing a transparency requirement in the form of an annual report to the prime minister and subject to consideration by the National Assembly.[112] Several modern constitutions require legislative notification or official publication for all reprieves, commutations, and pardons. The new constitution of Zimbabwe states that the "grant of a pardon or respite from execution of sentence or the substitution or suspension of a sentence must be published in the Gazette."[113] The previous constitution contained no such requirement.[114] Some jurisdictions require that the executive provide reasons for a pardon. In Tuvalu, if the governor-general exercises the mercy power in accordance with the advice of the cabinet, the prime minister must present at the next session of parliament a statement giving details of the exercise of that power and of the reasons for it.[115]

Twenty-seven US states require that the governor report his or her clemency actions to the state legislature, a provision codified either in the state constitution or in subsequent legislation.[116] In addition, seven states require that a pardon board or parole board serving as a pardon board give a periodic report to the governor; one state, Georgia, requires that the board report to the legislature.[117] In Massachusetts, the governor is not required to issue any reasons for granting, ignoring, or denying a pardon petition; he or she is only required to provide an annual list to the state legislature of pardons granted the previous year. No explanations are required.[118] This creates a form of selection bias, as the governor is not required to report denials of clemency, or petitions that were ignored. It is politically safer for the governor to ignore recommendations of clemency.[119]

110 Joyner, *supra* note 94 at 16.
111 Naudé, *supra* note 21 at 167–71.
112 Belize Const. art 54(14), (18), (19) (1981).
113 Zim. Const. art. 47(4) (2013).
114 *See* Zim. Const. art. 31 (1979).
115 Tuvalu Const. art. 80(2) (1986).
116 Ridolfi and Gordon, *supra* note 17 at 31.
117 Dorne and Gewerth, *supra* note 9 at 438.
118 Wolfe, *supra* note 66 at 432.
119 *Id.* at 434.

By contrast, Connecticut's independent Board of Pardons has no duty to report its decisions to the legislature.[120]

Some US states have a more robust requirement. By the early twentieth century, the nature of pardons and the abuse of the pardoning power were deeply controversial among legal scholars, criminologists, and the general public. In Florida, for instance, governors were required to report all pardons, commutations, reprieves, and remissions to the legislature, including details of the crimes, offenders, and sentences.[121] As in England a hundred years earlier, the recommendations of court and judicial personnel, victims, community and family members, and employers were highly relevant to any pardon board decision on whether to release an offender back into the community as an independent probation or parole service did not yet exist.[122] Under the constitution of Colorado, the governor must report to the legislature the reasons for granting a pardon, the purpose of which is to furnish a moral restraint upon the granting of pardons in cases without just reason, though in practice no case has arisen where valid reasons were not assigned to an act of executive clemency.[123] The constitution of Arkansas requires that the governor communicate to the legislature each case of reprieve, commutation, or pardon, with reasons provided.[124] The constitution of Pennsylvania, which creates a Board of Pardons, states that the board shall keep records available for public inspection.[125]

At the US federal level, the mercy power does not require that justifications or reasons be given for a pardon. Even states that lack transparency requirements have no such requirements either. In *Connecticut Board of Pardons v. Dumschat*, the US Supreme Court found that the state clemency authority can deny clemency for any constitutionally-permissible reason or no reason at all.[126] However, some observers have argued that even though justification is not required, it would serve some benefits. Prior to 1931, the Department of Justice's official pardon records disclosed a wide range of reasons for exercise of the pardons, from doubt about guilt or suspected lack of capacity to pragmatic or humanitarian concerns such as illness, and even idiosyncratic ones. In the modern era, detailed explanations for clemency usually accompany only the most controversial pardons.[127] In 2001, President Clinton took the unprecedented step of publishing an opinion piece in the *New York Times* justifying his pardon a month earlier of

120 Rothman, *supra* note 78 at 169.

121 Miller, *supra* note 6 at 4.

122 *Id.* at 267.

123 Ernest Morris, *Some Phases of the Pardoning Power*, 12 A.B.A. Journal 183, 187–88 (1926).

124 Ark. Const. art. 6 § 18 (1874).

125 Penn. Const. art. 4, § 9(b) (1968).

126 Connecticut Board of Pardons v. Dumschat, 452 US 458, 467 (1981).

127 Daniel T. Kobil, *Should Clemency Decisions Be Subject to a Reasons Requirement?*, 13 Fed. Sent'g Rep. 151, 151–52 (2001) (hereinafter, "Kobil, *Reasons Requirement*").

Marc Rich, a wealthy fugitive who was suspected of several tax offenses.[128] President Ford included a statement of reasons with his pardon of Richard Nixon; George H.W. Bush also did so with his pardon of the defendants in the Iran-Contra scandal.[129]

Yet these exercises are the exception rather than the rule; most are never explained by the president or the Pardon Attorney. Justifications for clemency could help improve public confidence in the quality of clemency decisions and could serve valuable civic functions. They would also force a clemency authority to assess and evaluate the strength and persuasiveness of the justifications. Even more importantly, such reasons would allow those denied clemency to understand the reasons for their denial. On the other hand, a transparency requirement would discourage use of the clemency power in some cases, perhaps for fear of political fallout, and could invite judicial scrutiny if the reasons provided appear inadequate.[130] Too much transparency, of course, can work to an applicant's detriment. Louisiana's process is unusually public: upon an application for clemency, the Board of Pardons must give notice to the district attorney and the sheriff in the parish where the applicant was convicted, to the injured victim or the spouse or next-of-kin if the victim is deceased, and to any other interested person. All have the opportunity to testify at a clemency hearing. The offender is required to advertie his petition for clemency three times in a local newspaper. The sessions of the pardon board are public, and all recommendations for clemency may be opened to public inspection, which may discourage public officials from supporting bids for clemency. A life-term prisoner is ineligible to apply for clemency for fifteen years after being sentenced, and, if denied, may not apply again for six years and every three years subsequent to that. Legislative changes continue to make negative information about the applicant widely available, presumably to fuel opposition to grants of clemency.[131]

One possibility for middle ground would be to require an executive to specify the charges being pardoned at the time the pardon is issued without necessarily providing reasons for the pardon, which would focus the attention of the news media and allow inquiry of the underlying crimes. In addition, unspecified charges would remain fair targets for prosecution. This has historical support in England, where Richard II was required by

128 William Jefferson Clinton, *My Reasons for the Pardons*, N.Y. TIMES, Feb. 18, 2001.

129 *President Gerald Ford's Pardon of Richard Nixon, Sept. 8, 1974*, 13 FED. SENT'G REP. 207, 207–08 (2001); *President George Bush's Pardon of the Iran-Contra Defendants, Dec. 24, 1992*, 13 FED. SENT'G REP. 209, 209–10 (2001).

130 *See* Kobil, *Reasons Requirement, supra* note 127 at 151–52.

131 Helen Ginger Berrigan, *Executive Clemency, First-Offender Pardons; Automatic Restoration of Rights*, 62 LA. L. REV. 49, 55–56 (2001), *citing* LA. REV. STAT. 15:572.4. Berrigan also notes that after 1997, the five-member Board of Pardons must vote at least 4 to 1 to support a recommendation for clemency, instead of 3 to 2. *Id., citing* 1997 La. Acts No. 828.

statute to specify the circumstances of the crime upon issuance of pardons for murder, treason, and rape.[132] Another possibility exists in South Dakota, where two parallel pardon processes exist: a direct application process to the governor, and an indirect one to the Board of Pardons and Paroles. If a petitioner first seeks a recommendation from the board and undergoes a public application process and an open hearing, a pardon by the governor on the board's recommendation seals the record of conviction and the pardon itself. Since 2004, all grants of clemency in South Dakota have been on the board's recommendation and the pardons have been sealed.[133]

Mass clemency decisions

Where an executive (or, more rarely, a board) grants a blanket clemency to a category of prisoners, a different set of considerations is at issue. First, the fact-finding role inherent in a bureaucratic process is less important as clemency is granted not based on individual factors but on factors common to the group. Second, such grants may be policy-driven and may generate public opposition on the grounds that the executive has usurped the role of the legislature, particularly in jurisdictions that otherwise have modern parole mechanisms. This having been said, mass clemency decisions are not uncommon in the Commonwealth. In fact, in some jurisdictions, clemency is so common at holidays or the anniversary of independence that prosecutors have considerable frustration with the executive branch.[134] Mass commutations may be given to commemorate important holidays or anniversaries or may be performed for policy reasons. In 2012, former Kenyan President Mwai Kibaki pardoned 6,700 prisoners to ease prison congestion.[135] Three years earlier, he commuted more than 4,000 death sentences in one of the largest commutations of death sentences in the modern era.[136]

In the United States, mass clemencies are uncommon because most states have either heavily bureaucratic processes or strictly political ones – both of which discourage grants of mass clemency in different ways. Governor Lee Cruce of Oklahoma commuted twenty-two death sentences between 1911 and 1915. He did so under a system in which the governor was the ultimate decision-maker, but the mass clemency proved controversial. By

132 Christopher E. Smith and Scott P. Johnson, *Presidential Pardons and Accountability in the Executive Branch*, 35 WAYNE L.REV. 1113, 1125, 1130 (1989).

133 Love, *Reinvigorating*, *supra* note 68 at 750.

134 This is the case in Vanuatu. *Vanuatu Pardon Raises Response from Government*, THE WORLD TODAY, Nov. 25, 2002, www.abc.net.au/worldtoday/stories/s734239.htm.

135 Lordrick Mayabi, *Kibaki Pardons 6,700 Prisoners*, CAPITAL NEWS, Dec. 21, 2012, www.capitalfm.co.ke/news/2012/12/kibaki-pardons-6700-prisoners.

136 *Kenya Commutes All Death Sentences*, ASSOCIATED PRESS, Aug. 3, 2009, www.deathpenaltyinfo.org/international-clemency-kenya-commutes-4000-death-sentences.

constitutional amendment in 1944, Oklahoma created a pardon and parole board that investigates applications for pardons and commutations and makes a recommendation to the governor; the governor today is only able to pardon with a favorable recommendation from the board.[137] More recently, Governors Winthrop Rockefeller of Arkansas (1967–1971), Terry Sanford of North Carolina (1961–1965), and Toney Anaya of New Mexico (1983–1987) each cleared their states' death rows before leaving office.[138] All were opponents of capital punishment. Shortly before leaving office in 2001, Ohio Governor Richard Celeste commuted the death sentences of four men and four women to life imprisonment, as well as the prison sentences of 25 battered women who had killed or assaulted their purported abusers.[139] For seven of the eight death row prisoners, Celeste intentionally deviated from normal procedures and did not file applications for clemency with the Ohio Adult Parole Authority prior to remitting punishment, which became the basis for future legal challenges.[140] Mass clemencies frequently set up a constitutional battle over the separation of powers. Shortly before leaving office in 2012, Mississippi Governor Haley Barbour pardoned more than 200 convicted criminals, with most receiving full, unconditional, and complete pardons, clearing their records. The Mississippi attorney general subsequently challenged 21 of the pardons for failing to comply with the publication requirements as contained in the state constitution.[141] The Mississippi Supreme Court refused to void the pardons finding that the governor possessed not only plenary pardon authority but also authority to determine whether the constitution's publication requirement was met.[142]

No grant of mass clemency in the modern era is as famous or as controversial as that of Illinois Governor George Ryan in 2003. On January 10, 2003, Ryan announced a decision to pardon four African-American inmates on death row after concluding that none of them had committed the crimes for which they had been sentenced. The next day, Ryan spoke at Northwestern University Law School, where the Center on Wrongful Convictions had documented egregious errors and mistakes in Illinois's capital sentencing process. Despite inaugurating a commission that recommended extensive changes to Illinois's capital sentencing system, Ryan was unable to convince the state legislature to adopt any of the suggested reforms. He decided to take unilateral action, announcing at Northwestern University that he was commuting the death sentences of all 167 inmates on death row in Illinois, the largest grant of executive clemency by an

137 Rupcich, *supra* note 12 at 145.

138 Austin Sarat, Mercy on Trial: What It Means to Stop an Execution 36–7 (2005).

139 Rupcich, *supra* note 12 at 146.

140 Kobil, *Paperwork*, *supra* note 14 at 656–57.

141 Michael Heise, *The Death of Death Row Clemency and the Evolving Politics of Unequal Grace*, 66 Ala. L. Rev. (forthcoming 2014).

142 *Id., citing* In re Hooker, 87 So. 3d 401, 401, 414 (Miss. 2012).

American governor in history.[143] Ryan was elected as a pro-death penalty candidate, and he would likely not have won election had his position been different. His decision to wait two days before leaving office raised questions about his political courage, and he "unintentionally" misled victims' families only a short time earlier by announcing that he was leaning against granting clemency. In the media firestorm that followed, the names of some of Illinois's most notorious murderers once again became household names.[144] Yet, perhaps because of his honesty as a troubled death penalty supporter, his act of clemency was transformational – the most consequential act of mercy since Ford's pardon of Nixon – and it proved to be a precursor to death penalty abolition in Illinois.

Ryan's wholesale clemency was less an act of grace or forgiveness than it was a concession to the inadequacies of a death penalty system gone awry and to a political system unable to redress those inadequacies. Ryan's hour-long "I Must Act" speech was "both deeply personal and yet flatly bureaucratic, presenting … his decision as if it were 'compelled,' an act of duty not a personal choice."[145] Ryan did not use the language of mercy in his speech; rather, he emphasized the role of victims and the failures of legal institutions. In his speech, Ryan tried to allay public doubts about the nature of executive clemency and meticulously justify his use of the clemency power.[146] He assured listeners that he was no stranger to the violent loss that accompanied homicide, recounting how a brutal murder had taken the life of a close family friend and neighbor. He recounted his meetings with the families of victims and "poured out his mounting distress with the error and capriciousness" that he found in the Illinois criminal justice system.[147] As Markel argues, the mercy power can be understood in two ways: as an act of compassion for offenders who have some redeeming characteristics unrelated to their offense, and as an equitable consideration that addresses an offender's reduced culpability for an offense. In retributive philosophy, a blanket commutation such as that issued by Ryan is not justifiable on the first ground, since no individual determination is made that an offender is "mercy-eligible," but may be justified on the second ground as accuracy in adjudication is central to the retributive project. Although Ryan faced criticism from many quarters – including that he was insensitive to the interests of victims and their families and that he usurped power from the legislature and jury members – his

143 John Charles Boger, *Acts of Capital Clemency: The Words and Deeds of Governor George Ryan*, 82 N.C. L. Rev. 1279, 1279–80 (2004).

144 David A. Wallace, *Dead Man Walking: An Abuse of Executive Clemency Power in Illinois*, 29 U. Dayton L. Rev. 379, 389 (2004).

145 Sarat, *supra* note 95 at 277.

146 *Id.* at 280.

147 Boger, *supra* note 143 at 1280.

reliance, in part, on mercy considerations is not fundamentally incompatible with an increasingly retributive strain in American criminal justice.[148]

Decline of clemency?

Undoubtedly, clemency has declined across the English-speaking world over the course of the twentieth century, in large part because of the decline of mandatory death sentences and the rise of the institution of parole. In addition, popular skepticism and judicial and administrative review have also contributed to clemency's vulnerability. Presidential clemency has declined considerably in the course of American history. Between 1860 and 1900, nearly half of all applications for presidential pardons were granted, though this was in a time before widespread probation and parole procedures, and the development of special considerations for women, juveniles, and persons with mental illness.[149] Since the Office of the US Pardon Attorney started keeping records on the number of pardons and commutations granted by the president since 1945, there has been a steady decline in the use of executive clemency.[150] The decline of clemency has accelerated with each successive president. From Franklin D. Roosevelt's presidency through Jimmy Carter's, more than 200 people each year were granted some form of presidential clemency on average. Under Ronald Reagan, however, this number fell to only about 200 each term, and President George H.W. Bush even fewer: only 77 in four years. Clinton followed the trend, pardoning or commuting the sentences an average of only 35 people per year, increasing the odds that the few pardons issued would be more closely scrutinized.[151] The infrequency of pardons may increase their arbitrariness, perpetuating racial, political, and class disparities in the criminal justice system generally. During George W. Bush's two terms in office, 176 pardons went to Caucasians and only 13 went to non-whites. In addition, petitioners enjoying the support of a member of Congress were three times as likely to win a pardon as those without such backing.[152]

Individualized executive clemency for death row inmates has functionally disappeared in the United States. While clemency was regularly dispensed in order to help offset the harshness of automatic death sentences, the abolition of the mandatory death penalty has resulted in a drastic decline in the use of the clemency power to the point of insignificance.[153] Clemency has generally not been a successful path for relief for

148 Dan Markel, *State, Be Not Proud: A Retributivist Defense of the Commutation of Death Row and the Abolition of the Death Penalty*, 40 HARV. C.R.-C.L. L.REV. 407, 418–21, 447–49 (2005).

149 Kathleen Dean Moore, PARDONS: JUSTICE, MERCY, AND THE PUBLIC INTEREST 53 (1989).

150 Hoffstadt, *supra* note 47 at 582–83.

151 Moore, *supra* note 108 at 159.

152 Crouch, *supra* note 39 at 696.

153 Heise, *supra* note 141.

capital defendants. From 1977 through May 2009, 1,165 death row inmates were executed, and 245 received executive clemency, which includes the 167 commutations and 4 pardons granted by Illinois Governor George Ryan in 2003.[154] During the 1990s, between one and eight death row inmates had their sentences commuted each year, as compared to between twenty and ninety executions. This was a radical shift from several decades previously, in which governors granted clemency in about one-quarter of the death penalty cases that they reviewed. The increasing scarcity of executive clemency is not solely a phenomenon of the South, and even in Washington, Pennsylvania, and Illinois (before 2003) commutations of death sentences had grown extremely rare.[155]

The retributivist impulse, ascendant in American criminal sentencing since the 1980s, was reflected in another subtle shift beyond simply declining numbers of pardons and commutations. The manner in which clemency was framed changed: no longer did executives use the language of compassion and forgiveness, but rather of legalism, emphasizing abuses of process, unsafe verdicts, racial discrimination in sentencing, or other perceived shortcomings of the criminal justice process. "The removal of mercy from clemency and the prevailing focus on justice-based rationales have also coincided with an overall decline in clemency in most jurisdictions."[156] As Sarat writes, clemency in the United States is in decline as political leaders respond to forces such as victims' rights and retributivism that are increasingly powerful in American political culture. Even executives who grant clemency do so in as unmerciful a way as possible.[157]

Prior to the creation of modern parole systems, conditional pardons served a similar purpose and were used as regular releasing devices in lieu of parole, though unlike parole authorities governors had no staff to ensure that conditions were complied with. One of the most frequently-used forms of executive clemency was to make eligible for parole prisoners who were ineligible either because they were excluded from parole or because they had not yet served the minimum amount of time in prison.[158] Only twenty-four US states have conditional pardons, and in these states typically parole officers must supervise recipients of conditional pardons and enforce the conditions.[159]

Some constitutions, especially in the United States, effectively combine pardons and parole. On the one hand are states such as Missouri and North Carolina, which specifically separate the pardon and parole powers and

154 Aarons, *supra* note 65 at 546.
155 Sarat, *supra* note 138 at 35.
156 Kobil, *Mercy*, supra note 92 at 37.
157 Sarat, *supra* note 138 at 28.
158 Henry Weihofen, *Consolidation of Pardon and Parole: A Wrong Approach*, 30 Am. Inst. Crim. L. & Criminology 534, 534–538 (1939).
159 Dorne and Gewerthe, *supra* note 9 at 430–31.

indicate that parole is not a form of executive clemency.[160] On the other are states that merge the powers of pardon and parole by either creating a single board of pardons and parole to perform both functions, such as Georgia, Texas, Nebraska, and Utah, or by specifically including the power to parole as a form of executive clemency, as in Oklahoma and Alabama.[161] These provisions are strikingly varied. In Georgia, the State Board of Pardons and Paroles is solely vested with the power of executive clemency, including reprieves, pardons, and paroles.[162] Utah's constitution is functionally similar.[163] By contrast, under the Texas constitution, the Board of Pardons and Paroles treats pardons and paroles differently; parole is performed by the board alone, while the governor pardons on the recommendation of the board.[164] Nebraska's constitution similarly separates the pardon and parole functions, though it creates a single Board of Parole. The board performs two functions: it grants paroles as permitted by law and advises the governor, attorney general, and secretary of state on executive clemency.[165] Oklahoma's constitution creates a Pardon and Parole Board that has the power to grant parole by majority vote; in addition, the governor has the power to grant pardons *or* paroles by favorable recommendation of the board. Neither the board nor the governor can parole death sentences or life sentences without the possibility of parole.[166] In Alabama, the governor may "grant reprieves, paroles, commutations of sentence, and pardons," but unlike Oklahoma, the board is only advisory and does not need to recommend parole or clemency. In California, the governor reviews and may overturn a grant of parole in a murder case, a kind of reverse clemency provision.[167]

Clemency may have some life left. In April 2014, the US Department of Justice announced a "New Clemency Initiative," described as "the most sweeping reinvigoration of the clemency power in nearly four decades." The initiative seeks to prioritize certain clemency applications from federal inmates, with a special emphasis on the application of mandatory minimum sentences to low-level drug offenders where it has generated unduly harsh sentences.[168] Nonetheless, US President Barack Obama has issued about 65 pardons by 2015, or about a dozen per year, lower than any of his

160 Mo. Const. art. 4 § 7 (1945); N.C. Const. art. 3 § 5 (1971).

161 Ga. Const. art. 4, sec. 2 (1983); Tex. Const. art. 4 § 11 (1876); Neb. Const. art. 4 § 13 (1875); Okla. Const. art. 6 § 10 (1907); Utah Const. art. 7 § 12 (1895); Ala. Const. art. 5 § 124 (1901).

162 Ga. Const. art. 4 § 2 ¶ 2(a) (1983).

163 Utah Const. art. 7 § 12 (1895).

164 Tex. Const. art. 4 § 11(a)-(b) (1876).

165 Neb. Const. art. 4 § 13 (1875).

166 Okla. Const. art. 6 § 10 (1907).

167 Cal. Const. art. 5 § 8 (1879).

168 Heise, *supra* note 141.

predecessors.[169] Currently, California Governor Jerry Brown has famously used several mass grants of clemency during his term to effect broader criminal justice reform, including 79 grants of clemency on Christmas Eve 2012; 127 on Christmas Eve 2013; 63 on Good Friday 2014; and 104 on Christmas Eve 2014, mostly for low-level drug offenses. By contrast, the three previous governors issued only 29 grants of clemency combined over 20 years.[170]

Conclusion

The procedures for applying for mercy and the process of decision-making vary widely across the common law world, and yet the process itself has an impact on the outcome. Jurisdictions differ as to how routine and institutionalized the mercy process is, and how public and transparent proceedings are. This chapter explores another model of mercy mechanism besides the committees analyzed in Chapter 6: here the focus is on bureaucratized mercy structures such as the Office of the US Pardon Attorney, the Ministry of Home Affairs in India, and the Department of Justice and Constitutional Development in South Africa. These bureaucracies differ as to whether formal criteria are used in the decision-making process and whether the clemency authority must provide reasons or justifications for its decisions. In the United States, the president can grant clemency outside of the bureaucratic process, though this has political risks, while in India the president is bound to the bureaucratic mechanism. The ultimate clemency decision is deeply personal, often made by an executive in isolation, no matter the strength and forcefulness of recommendations. Mass grants of clemency, by contrast, often reflect greater policy rationales rather than factors individual to the applicant. The role of clemency in the modern world is changing, and institutional structures are changing as well. Parole mechanisms, for instance, play a role in pardon investigations and often provide recommendations to the clemency authority.

169 US Department of Justice, *Pardons Granted by President Barack Obama*, www.justice.gov/pardon/obama-pardons (last accessed March 14, 2015).

170 *See, e.g.*, *Jerry Brown Grants Clemency to 79 Criminals*, L.A. TIMES, Dec. 24, 2012, http://latimesblogs.latimes.com/california-politics/2012/12/jerry-brown-clemency-list.html; *California Governor Jerry Brown Pardons 127, Mostly for Drugs*, SACRAMENTO BEE, Dec. 24, 2013, http://blogs.sacbee.com/capitolalertlatest/2013/12/california-governor-jerry-brown-pardons-127.html; *Gov. Jerry Brown Pardons 104 for Christmas*, SACRAMENTO BEE, Dec. 24, 2014, www.sacbee.com/news/politics-government/capitol-alert/article4928388.html; *Gov. Jerry Brown Grants 63 More Pardons*, L.A. TIMES, Apr. 18, 2014, www.latimes.com/local/political/la-me-ff-brown-grants-63-more-pardons-20140418-story.html.

8 Legislative and judicial review of executive clemency

At common law, the executive prerogative of mercy was generally not subject to judicial review. In recent years, principles of constitutional and administrative review have opened at least some aspects of the clemency process to judicial inquiry. In the Commonwealth Caribbean, for instance, a prisoner has the right to a hearing and the right to see the information put before the mercy committee, while in India, a grant of clemency that is arbitrary or discriminatory is unconstitutional. By contrast, courts in Singapore have resisted opening clemency to judicial oversight, and a number of constitutions specifically limit judicial reviewability in the clemency process. This chapter also explores legislative involvement in clemency cases, including the possibility of impeachment for an executive who misuses the clemency power and the constitutionality of legislatively-enacted guidelines or limitations.

The prerogative of mercy is one of a host of common law royal prerogatives that were uncodified by statute and outside the reach of judicial inquiry, though the courts were often required to determine the existence of the prerogative in specific cases. This traditionally insular conception of the prerogative powers has, since the 1980s, given way to principles of administrative law, which have imposed some outer boundaries on the exercise of the prerogative. British courts generally show deference to those who exercise the prerogative powers, in the expectation that they will do so fairly, reasonably, and in accordance with law.[1] However, in many common law nations, judges are no longer reluctant to determine whether the constitutional mercy procedure was followed, a defendant was provided minimal due process protections, and the grant of clemency was not arbitrary or discriminatory – though judges typically stop short of reviewing the ultimate decision. This chapter will explore both conventional and constitutional limitations on judicial review of the pardon power before turning to the role legislatures play in the exercise of the clemency power.

1 Noel Cox, *The Gradual Curtailment of the Royal Prerogative*, 25 Denning L.J. 1, 12–3 (2012).

Constitutional limits on judicial reviewability

A number of common law constitutions specifically shield the prerogative of mercy from judicial or administrative review. The constitution of Belize states that "[t]he question whether or not the [Advisory] Council has validly performed any functions conferred or imposed on it by this Constitution or any other law shall not be enquired into in any court of law."[2] The constitutions of Ghana and Uganda limit the reviewability of clemency decisions by their constitutional human rights commissions. In Ghana, the constitution prohibits review of the prerogative of mercy by the Commission on Human Rights and Administrative Justice, which serves as Ghana's institutional ombudsman and anti-corruption mechanism. This provision shields pardon and clemency decisions from administrative investigation and review.[3] A similar provision in the Ugandan constitution restricts the Uganda Human Rights Commission from inquiring into any matter relating to the exercise of the prerogative of mercy, such as a claim that the power's exercise was discriminatory, arbitrary, or corrupt.[4] The constitution of Dominica prevents investigation by the parliamentary commissioner, the country's corruption ombudsman, into any exercise of the prerogative of mercy.[5] On the other hand, in Papua New Guinea, the question of whether and, if so, what report was made to the cabinet (the National Executive Council) by the Advisory Committee on the Power of Mercy, is not reviewable in court, though this provision specifically does *not* limit the jurisdiction or power of the ombudsman.[6]

Opening the royal prerogative of mercy to judicial review

In traditional theory, courts will determine the existence and extent of a royal prerogative power, but will not review the manner of its exercise. This includes, among other powers, the royal prerogative of mercy, though judges frequently had considerable influence on whether mercy should be extended in specific cases.[7] In *De Freitas v. Benny*, the Judicial Committee of the Privy Council in London, then the highest court of appeal for the Commonwealth Caribbean, stated the traditional case in a death penalty challenge arising from Trinidad and Tobago:

2 Belize Const. art. 52(18) (1981).
3 Ghana Const. art. 219(2)(c) (1992).
4 Uganda Const. art. 53(4)(c) (1995). The Commission is also restricted from any matter pending before a court or judicial tribunal and any matter involving the relations or dealings between the government and a foreign nation or international organization. *Id.* at art. 53(4)(a)-(b).
5 Dominica Const. sched. 3(6) (1978).
6 Papua N.G. Const. art. 153 (1975).
7 A.T.H. Smith, *The Prerogative of Mercy, the Power of Pardon and Criminal Justice*, [1983] Pub.L. 398, 432–33.

> At common law [the prerogative of mercy] has always been a matter which lies solely in the discretion of the sovereign, who by constitutional convention exercises it in respect of England on the advice of the Home Secretary to whom Her Majesty delegates her discretion. Mercy is not the subject of legal rights. It begins where legal rights end. A convicted person has no legal right even to have his case considered by the Home Secretary in connection with the exercise of the prerogative of mercy. In tendering his advice to the sovereign, the Home Secretary is doing something that is often cited as the exemplar of a purely discretionary act as contrasted with the exercise of a quasi judicial function.[8]

The historically sacrosanct nature of the royal prerogative powers has, in recent years, come under increasing scrutiny by courts. In *Council of Civil Service Unions (CCSU) v. Minister for the Civil Service*, a majority of the Law Lords in the House of Lords found that it would be archaic to maintain that traditional monarchical prerogative powers were immune from judicial review on administrative law grounds. That case involved a challenge to the royal Order-in-Council prerogative, whereby the Queen could issue primary legislation with the assent of the government but without a vote of Parliament.[9] According to the House of Lords, the absolute non-interference of the judicial branch in royal exercise of the prerogative powers (except where the prerogative's use was wholly illegal) was anachronistic in a representative democracy, though the House ultimately upheld the specific Order-in-Council in the case preventing unionization of a government agency based on the grounds of national security.[10] *CCSU* had a broad impact not only in the United Kingdom, but in all Commonwealth realms that inherited the royal prerogative powers. For instance, *CCSU* was extended into the law of South Africa and Zimbabwe, where courts also opened up the traditional royal prerogative powers to judicial review on the basis of illegality, irrationality, or procedural impropriety, though, like *CCSU*, these did not concern the prerogative of mercy per se.[11]

Although *CCSU* declared that the prerogative powers are, in principle, open to judicial review, the Lords acknowledged that some prerogatives, owing to their nature, cannot be made the subject of judicial review. Several courts have determined that mercy is one of these exceptions. In

8 De Freitas v. Benny, (1976) A.C. 234 (P.C.).

9 Council of Civil Service Unions v. Minister for the Civil Service, [1983] UKHL 6.

10 *Id.*

11 George N. Barrie, *Judicial Review of the Royal Prerogative*, 111 S. Afr. L.J. 788, 790 (1994), *citing* Boesak v. Minister of Home Affairs, 1987 (3) S.A. 665 (Cape Prov. Div.); Patriotic Front-ZAPU v. Minister of Justice, Legal and Parliamentary Affairs, 1986 (1) S.A. 532 (Zim.). Barrie explains that beginning with South Africa's 1993 constitution, all executive power emanated from the constitution and therefore the president no longer possessed traditional prerogative powers. *Id.* at 790–91.

New Zealand, a High Court judge found that the prerogative of mercy was not subject to judicial review in *Burt v. Governor-General*, distinguishing *CCSU*.[12] In that case, a life-term prisoner convicted of murder exhausted his remedies on appeal and petitioned the governor-general for a full pardon on the basis that exculpatory evidence was misstated or withheld in his case. The governor-general, acting on ministerial advice, declined to exercise the prerogative of mercy. The judge in that case distinguished *CCSU*, which found that executive action was not immune from judicial review merely because it was carried out in pursuance of the prerogative power.[13] According to the court, mercy decisions involved policy determinations properly left to the other branches of government, though arguably the case only involved low-level policy considerations as it was based on a mistake by the criminal justice system.[14] He expressed concern that judicial review of the mercy prerogative would be contrary to the public interest in the finality of litigation and would "second guess" decisions of criminal courts. As Wheeler writes, however, *Burt* was not the final word, as "[t]here is no *a priori* reason for excluding judicial review of the prerogative of mercy in all cases," as the interests of administrative justice would be better served by conceding the possibility of review and perhaps refusing relief where strong policy elements rendered judicial intervention inappropriate.[15] Barrie explains that on appeal in *Burt* the New Zealand Court of Appeal held that the prerogative of mercy was a unique and extralegal power, but did not rule out the possibility that there might be exceptional circumstances in which the court could exercise a power of review.[16]

The United Kingdom followed suit in distinguishing the prerogative of mercy from other prerogative powers in a subsequent case, *Queen v. Secretary of State for the Home Department, Ex Parte Bentley*. In that case, the Queen's Bench ruled that the prerogative of mercy was one prerogative power that was not subject to judicial review.[17] However, the court also ruled that mercy was a constitutional safeguard against mistakes and not a monarchical act of grace; as a result, the court determined that the Home Secretary had not given adequate consideration to his power of mercy as concerned Derek Bentley, who was hanged in 1953 for a crime committed at age 19. As a result of the Court's request, the Home Secretary

12 Burt v. Governor-General, [1989] 3 NZLR 64 (High Ct.).

13 *CCSU*, [1983] UKHL 6. *See also*, Fiona Wheeler, *Judicial Review of Prerogative Power in Australia: Issues and Prospects*, 14 SYD. L. REV. 432, 432, 453–455 (1992) (explaining the impact of this decision in Australia and New Zealand).

14 *Burt*, 3 NZLR at 73; *see also* Wheeler, *supra* note 13 at 454.

15 Wheeler, *supra* note 13 at 455.

16 Barrie, *supra* note 11 at 791, *citing* Burt v. Governor-General, [1992] 3 NZLR 672 (Ct. App.).

17 Queen v. Secretary of State for the Home Department (Ex parte Bentley), [1993] EWHC Admin 2 (July 7, 1993).

recommended a posthumous grant of a pardon to Bentley in 1993.[18] Citing *Burt*, the New Zealand case, the Queen's Bench determined that "some aspects of the exercise of the Royal prerogative are amenable to judicial process," though the criteria used in determining whether a pardon should be granted was not justiciable.[19] Interestingly, the court nonetheless believed that the Home Secretary failed to recognize the flexibility and broad scope of the prerogative of mercy in denying Bentley a free pardon, ordinarily reserved for cases of actual innocence, as the Home Secretary could have considered a conditional pardon that would posthumously recognize that the sentence was imposed in error. It found that the Home Secretary's failure to consider all aspects of the prerogative of mercy was reviewable.[20]

The opacity of the royal prerogative of mercy renders it an imperfect tool to redress the problem of wrongful convictions in the event of actual innocence. Some jurisdictions, such as Australia, have reconciled this through alternative processes for reviewing a conviction. In Australia, a petition for pardon must go to the governor of a state, who may issue a pardon as an executive decision or refer the case to the Court of Appeal for reconsideration.[21] For claims that are unsuccessful, a letter stating that the application for pardon has been unsuccessful and the case has not been referred to the Court of Appeal may be the only clue to the entire process. The executive's decision-making process is "non-transparent and purely discretionary," and "[v]irtually no guidelines exist as to when, why or how the decision on whether to refer the case to the Court of Appeal is made."[22] In addition, the reliance on the executive for referral to the Court of Appeal to reopen a case leaves the process open to political considerations and public pressure. The referral may be insufficiently independent from an original

18 *Id.* The request of the court to the Home Minister to reconsider a posthumous pardon for Bentley has come in for some criticism. It appears that the court established some level of judicial scrutiny over the prerogative of mercy but did so in a way that was not necessary to decide the case and did not respect the established and proper boundaries of remedial intervention. Ivan Hare, *The Prerogative of Mercy: Judicial Review of Whether to "Let Him Have It,"* [1994] CAMBRIDGE L.J. 4, 6.

19 *Bentley*, [1993] EWHC Admin 2.

20 *Id.*

21 *See* Australia Act, 1986, § 7(1)-(2): "Powers and functions of Her Majesty and Governors in respect of States (1) Her Majesty's representative in each state shall be the Governor; (2)...all powers and functions of Her Majesty in respect of a State are exercisable only by the Governor of the State." For the complete list of pardon procedures in Australian states, *see* Criminal Code Act, 1899, §§ 18, 672A (Queensland); Crimes Act, 1958, § 584 (Victoria); Criminal Law Consolidation Act, 1935, § 369 (South Australia); Sentencing Act, 1995, § 140 (Western Australia); Criminal Code Act, 1924, § 419 (Tasmania); Crimes Act, 1900, § 433 (Australian Capital Terr.); Crimes Act, 1900, §§ 474B, 474C-G (New South Wales); Criminal Code of the Northern Territory of Australia, § 431.

22 Lynne Weathered, *Pardon Me: Current Avenues for Correction of Wrongful Conviction in Australia*, 17 CURRENT ISSUES IN CRIM. JUST. 203, 212 (2005).

wrongful conviction, as the Court of Appeal is limited in considering evidence already adjudicated upon and in admitting evidence that fails to satisfy the fresh evidence criteria.[23] The result is a system that is imperfect at resolving wrongful convictions.

New South Wales differs from other Australian states by providing an expanded appeal avenue, first passed in 1993 after a spate of wrongful convictions across the country. Under the new provisions, a pardon need not necessarily go to the governor of New South Wales. While that option remains, an applicant may alternatively apply directly to the state supreme court, and either the governor or the supreme court may direct an inquiry into the case. Of 69 reported applications to the supreme court between 1994 and 2003 under this policy, seven inquiries were directed and five cases resulted in the quashing of a conviction.[24] Australian state governors may also direct a royal commission to investigate a wrongful conviction. The recommendations from such commissions are highly influential, but this mechanism is, in practice, limited to cases that generate extensive media coverage or implicate major systemic failings.[25]

Australia has also considered the application of *CCSU* in challenges to open the traditional prerogative powers to judicial review in the interests of administrative justice. In *Van Einem v. Griffin*, the Supreme Court of South Australia held that the prerogative of mercy was not subject to judicial review. Like *Burt*, the case was brought by a life-term prisoner convicted of murder after exhausting his appeals and he sought clemency based on non-disclosure of evidence at trial. The clemency petition was considered by the provincial attorney-general and the solicitor-general, who advised the premier and the governor that the verdict was safe despite the failure to disclose certain evidence. The court was guided by earlier Australian precedent that the prerogative of mercy was unreviewable, citing to the 1908 case *Horwitz v. Connor*, which was later confirmed by the Australian High Court and courts in New Zealand.[26] According to the South Australian Supreme Court, to "allow judicial review in this case would involve intrusion by the court into an executive sphere," and though Australian courts had followed the British decision in *CCSU* in opening executive discretion to judicial review, this did not apply to the prerogative of mercy.[27] Despite the rise of the modern administrative state in Australia, *Horwitz* remains good law after a century.

Other Commonwealth jurisdictions are in accord with this line of cases. In *Harewood v. Attorney General*, the Supreme Court of Barbados

23 *Id.*
24 *Id.* at 212.
25 *Id.* at 213.
26 Horwitz v. Connor [1908] HCA 33; (1908) 6 CLR 38.
27 Van Einem v. Griffin, [1998] SASC 6858 (23 December 1998), *citing* R v. Toohey ex parte Northern Land Council [1981] HCA 74; (1980) 151 CLR 170.

commuted two death sentences to life imprisonment as a result of unreasonable delay in carrying out the executions, accepting the prisoners' claim that the death sentences constituted inhumane punishment under section 15 of the constitution of Barbados. However, the court dismissed their challenges that the Barbados Privy Council (as the advisory mercy committee is known) unlawfully considered their claims while they had appeals pending before the Inter-American Commission on Human Rights. Finding that the prerogative of mercy was not the subject of legal rights and not subject to judicial review, the Court dismissed their claim that executions with appeals pending violated the constitutional right to a fair trial.[28]

The Judicial Committee of the Privy Council in London likewise determined that mercy was not the subject of legal rights, confirming the traditional rule of *de Freitas v. Benny*. In *Reckley v. Minister of Public Safety and Immigration*, a case arising from the Bahamas, the Privy Council rejected a claim by a death row inmate that the failure of the governor-general to grant clemency in his case was unconstitutional.[29] The decision came in for criticism as a result of its failure to reconcile more recent precedent that altered the common law rule, including *CCSU* and *Bentley*. The Privy Council's decision in *Reckley* was ultimately "at odds with the principle underlying a broad approach to the availability of judicial review of the prerogative of mercy."[30] The petitioner Reckley was executed shortly after.

By the turn of the twenty-first century, the traditional non-justiciability of the prerogative of mercy yielded to judicial review. In 2000, the Privy Council reversed the Trinidadian case *de Freitas v. Benny* and the Bahamian case *Reckley* in *Lewis v. Attorney General of Jamaica*, a groundbreaking case consolidated with appeals from Belize and in which the attorneys-general of the Bahamas and Trinidad and Tobago intervened. According to the Judicial Committee of the Privy Council, the exercise of mercy is for the governor-general acting on the recommendations of the Jamaican Privy Council, as the advisory mercy committee is known in that country; the merits are not for review in court.[31] However, this did not mean that the whole process is completely beyond review at all. According to Lords of the Privy Council in London, since a petitioner had the right to seek mercy from the governor-general the court could inquire into, for instance, whether the governor-general consulted with the Jamaican Privy Council, whether the Jamaican Privy Council refused to look at required information, or whether the recommendation was made by people not qualified to sit as members of the Jamaican Privy Council.[32] Ultimately, the Court emphasized

28 Harewood v. Attorney General, (1996) 2 C.H.R.L.D. 15.
29 Reckley v. Minister of Public Safety and Immigration, [1996] 1 A.C. 527 (P.C.).
30 Christopher Gelber, Reckley (No2) *and the Prerogative of Mercy: Act of Grace or Constitutional Safeguard?*, 60 MOD. L. REV. 572, 574, 581–82 (1997).
31 Lewis v. A.G. of Jam., [2000] UKPC 35 at ¶ 47.
32 *Id.*

the unique and irreversible nature of the death penalty, particular where, as in Jamaica, it was mandatory for the crime of murder. The Privy Council in London determined that it was necessary to provide a condemned man notice of the date when the Jamaican Privy Council would consider his case and an opportunity to make representations to the Council.[33] The Caribbean Court of Justice has confirmed *Lewis* in *Attorney General of Barbados v. Joseph and Boyce*. The court ruled that only once all national and international proceedings were concluded should the mercy committee in Barbados consider the petition for clemency; provide to the petitioner all the material upon which the committee proposes to make its decision; give him or her reasonable notice of the date of the meeting; and invite him or her to submit written representations.[34]

Citing *Lewis*, the Hong Kong Court of First Instance rejected a challenge to a clemency decision by the Chief Executive of Hong Kong Special Administrative Region based on the failure of the Chief Executive to provide reasons for the rejection of the petition, the failure to provide a hearing, and the failure to obtain independent advice outside of the Department of Justice.[35] According to the court, the petitioner could not point to a conflict of interest or risk of injustice as a result of the summary and advice tendered to the Chief Executive by a Department of Justice solicitor. In rejecting a hearing, the court ruled that the Chief Executive "is exercising a purely discretionary function and not a judicial one," unconstrained by the laws of evidence.[36] Although the advice provided to the Chief Executive may have been aligned with the prosecution and was written by an employee of the Department of Justice, this did not rise to the level of the arbitrariness or bias that the Lords feared in *Lewis*. As in *Lewis*, the petitioner was entitled to see the documents placed before the Chief Executive, though he was not entitled to reasons for the decision, a hearing, or an external review.[37]

In 2007, the Supreme Court of the Australian Capital Territory favorably cited *Lewis* in holding that where an executive power affects the rights or interests of an individual, the statutory process – though not the exercise of discretion itself – is amenable to judicial review even if it is made by the Crown's representative or the cabinet.[38] In a subsequent case, the Australian Federal Court reiterated that where an executive has a duty to consider a case, a court may inquire into whether the executive has considered it, but a court cannot second-guess the executive where no duty exists to consider

33 *Id.* at ¶ 63.

34 A.G. of Barb. v. Joseph and Boyce, [2006] CariCJ 3 at ¶ 153 (de la Bastide, J., Saunders, J., *joint judgment*).

35 Ch'ng Poh v. Chief Executive of H.K.S.A.R., [2003] HKCFI 496 at ¶¶ 11–12.

36 *Id.* at 111.

37 *Id.* at ¶¶ 112–13.

38 Eastman v. A.G. of the Aust. Capital Terr., [2007] ACTSC 28 (Jan. 29, 2007) at ¶¶ 49–50, 68–70.

the case.[39] However, the Australian High Court has refused to use laws pertaining to the freedom of information and disclosure of government records to allow a petitioner for clemency to see documents relied on by a clemency authority in the decision-making process. According to the High Court, this information was privileged as it constituted legal advice to the governor.[40] British courts have also continued to open up the prerogative of mercy to limited review where the process, and not the ultimate decision, is at issue. In the case of *In re: Dunn*, the Queen's Bench in Northern Ireland came to this conclusion in a case where a prisoner had been provided an erroneous release date, some ten months before the end of his sentence, and applied for mercy based on this disappointed expectation. The Secretary of State for Northern Ireland responded that the case did not fall within the criteria used for early release. The Court found in that case that the mercy power was justiciable, as the case did not review government policy or the competing factors in the decision-making process. Rather, the Court found that the Secretary of State was guided by overly restrictive criteria and had a duty to hear the applicant.[41]

The Queen's Bench has refused to intervene in denials of clemency that derived from the peace process that ended Northern Ireland's sectarian violence. In *In re: McGeough*, the court refused to find that a refusal to grant clemency for a political offense was discriminatory or arbitrary, even though similar cases had been granted in the past as a part of the Good Friday Agreement and other peace initiatives. According to the court, those cases were not analogous as they had occurred a decade earlier and in a different political context.[42] Similarly, in *In re: Rodger*, the court considered a case where an applicant convicted of murder had been pardoned as part of the peace process, after which he became rehabilitated. However, the applicant was, some years later, found to have committed a second murder, which rendered him ineligible for the mercy initiatives that accompanied the peace process. The court refused to intervene, finding that the comparator cases noted by the applicant were not analogous to show arbitrariness or discrimination.[43] However, in another case, the court came to a different

39 Yasmin v. A.G., [2015] FCA 91 at ¶¶ 44–48.

40 Osland v. Sec. to Dept. of Just., [2008] HCA 37. Osland reversed a decision of the Civil and Administrative Tribunal of the state of Victoria releasing such records. In that case, the judge found that the public interest favored such release, as the exercise of the prerogative of mercy in circumstances that are not transparent had the potential to undermine public confidence in the judicial system. The court also noted that the media interest in the case was high, and members of the public wished to know whether justice was done. According to the court, the attorney-general released a press release denying clemency, and explicitly named those who provided advice in the matter. The court found that "public interest requires that access be granted" to the documents. Osland v. Dept. of Justice, [2005] VCAT 1648 (Aug. 16, 2005) at ¶¶ 48–55.

41 Dunn, Re: Judicial Review, [2010] NIQB 54 at ¶¶ 8–9, 18–19.

42 McGeough's Application, [2012] NIQB 11 at ¶ 46.

43 Rodger's Application, [2014] NIQB 79.

conclusion, strongly recommending clemency on behalf of the petitioner. In that case, a British citizen in Bulgaria was convicted in that country of attempted murder as a result of hooliganism during a football match, but another person later confessed to the crime in the United Kingdom. The British citizen was unable to achieve redress in Bulgarian courts, and sought a pardon when he was repatriated to the United Kingdom to serve the balance of his sentence. The court disagreed with the Secretary of State that the European Convention on Human Rights limited exercise of the mercy power. The court noted that it was not for it "to say whether or how" the mercy power was used, but it advocated a free pardon in the petitioner's case, as the evidence "justifies a conclusion that Michael Shields is morally and technically innocent."[44]

A similar state of affairs prevails in Canada as well. In Canada, courts have shown a willingness to exercise judicial review over exercises of the prerogative power that breaches written law, including possible violations of the Canadian Charter on Rights and Freedoms. In *Black v. Chretien (Prime Minister)*, the Court observed that the scope and application of the Crown prerogatives are defined by the judiciary and not by the executive.[45] Nonetheless, the prerogative powers retain a certain resiliency due to the reluctance of judges to impose robust remedies on the executive when these powers are used, and because Acts of Parliament have left room for continued executive discretion. Prerogative powers, in effect, fill the gaps in the statutory frameworks, and executives can continue to do what Parliament has not expressly forbidden.[46] The legislative and judicial branches have the ability to sharply curtail these powers, but in practice have not done so. In Canada, as elsewhere, many of the prerogative powers are administrative in nature: besides mercy and pardons, these include the power of civil service appointments; honors and military decorations; disposal of public lands; declaration of federal holidays; prosecutorial discretion; collection of tolls; and establishment of royal commissions of inquiry. Some, however, are more robust, such as the foreign affairs prerogative (making treaties, sharing intelligence, revoking passports), the war prerogative (declaring war), and the national defense prerogative (maintaining foreign troops on Canadian soil, testing weapons). The policing authority of the Royal Canadian Mounted Police flows from the executive's public order prerogative.[47]

Like the other prerogative powers, Canada has slowly opened the prerogative of mercy to judicial review. In *Thatcher v. Attorney General*, the Canadian Federal Court ruled that the minister of justice's decision to deny

44 Shields v. Secretary of State for Justice, [2008] EWHC 3102 (Dec. 17, 2008) at ¶¶ 2–5, 34–35.

45 Black v. Chretien, (2001) 199 D.L.R. (4th) 228 (Can. C.A.).

46 Philippe Lagassé, *Parliamentary and Judicial Ambivalence Toward Executive Prerogative Powers in Canada*, 55 CAN. PUB. ADMIN. 157, 158–9, 168 (2012).

47 *Id.* at 162–3.

clemency may result in a breach of a defendant's liberty, and therefore it triggered Section 7 of the Canadian Charter on Rights and Freedoms.[48] According to the Court, "[t]he Minister must act in good faith and conduct a meaningful review. The convicted person should have a reasonable opportunity to state his case and adequate disclosure of new relevant information revealed by the Minister's investigation. Where the Minister deems it necessary to consider material in police or prosecution files, the material or at least the gist of it, if not already known, must be disclosed."[49] Citing *Lewis*, the Court found that the minister conducted a meaningful review and met the standards of fairness. In addition, the applicant had a reasonable opportunity to present his case. The minister of justice was bound by the Charter's duty of fairness in making the clemency decision, but he had no legal obligations to the applicant.[50]

In 2014, the Court of Appeal of Trinidad and Tobago considered a challenge by former death row prisoners whose death sentences were commuted to life imprisonment as a result of undue delay in carrying out the sentence. Consequently, the prisoners challenged their commutations on the basis that their due process rights were breached when they were not permitted to make representations on their own behalf before the Advisory Committee on the Power of Pardon.[51] The court ultimately did not quash the commutation orders, but ordered that the Advisory Committee convene meetings at which the appellants could make representations in individual hearings and in accordance with the requirements of fairness and natural justice. The Committee was to review the circumstances that might affect the proper calculation of the commuted term by the president, on the advice of the minister of national security.[52] According to the court, the constitutional principle in *Lewis* applied retroactively; in this respect, the court overruled the attorney general's "floodgates" argument by noting that any significant increase in the work of the Advisory Committee was the consequence of adherence to the correct procedure. The court confirmed that the appellants were entitled to adequate notice of the date when the Advisory Committee would hear their cases; a copy of all documents available to the Advisory Committee; and an opportunity to make representations on their behalf, though these representations need not be oral. The Advisory Committee was required to review the representations. Because the appellants did not receive adequate notice of the review of their cases and were not afforded a hearing, the procedure adopted for the commutation of their death sentences was unconstitutional. The sole

48 Thatcher v. Attorney General, [1997] 1 F.C. 289 (Can.).

49 *Id.*

50 *Id.*

51 Lendore v. A.G. of Trin. & Tobago, Civ. App. Nos. 01, 10, 13, 14 and 19 of 2010 (Dec. 5, 2014) (C.A. Trin. & Tobago).

52 *Id.* at ¶ 119.

remedy, according to the court, was for the Advisory Committee to reconsider the cases.[53]

Judicial review of the constitutional pardon power

According to the constitution of India, "No person shall be deprived of his life or personal liberty except according to a procedure established by law."[54] According to the Indian Supreme Court in *Maneka Gandhi v. Union of India*, the procedure prescribed had to be "fair, just, and reasonable, not fanciful, oppressive or arbitrary," which imported nascent principles of due process into the Indian constitution.[55] Following *Maneka Gandhi*, the Supreme Court ruled that the constitutional clemency power is subject to such minimum due process guarantees. In the *Maru Ram v. Union of India* in 1980, the Court laid down the rule that "no consideration nor occasion [for clemency] can be wholly irrelevant, irrational, discriminatory, or *mala fide*. Only in these rare cases will the court examine the exercise."[56] Given the sharply polarized views on the death penalty among the justices of the Indian Supreme Court during the 1970s and early 1980s, Batra describes how several decisions from this period encouraged clemency on compassionate grounds and noted the general trend away from capital punishment.[57] In *Goud v. State of Andhra Pradesh*, the Court stated that it would not turn a blind eye where public power is exercised in an arbitrary way or in bad faith, including where the president exercises the pardon power discriminatorily.[58] In *Kehar Singh v. Union of India*, the Supreme Court recognized the existence of its power to review executive grants of clemency in a limited class of instances, including procedural impropriety and violations of individual rights though not on the substantive merits of the decision.[59] In *Kehar Singh*, the petitioner sought an oral hearing, which the Court refused, noting that the clemency power was within the president's discretion. The Court also refused to lay down guidelines regulating the exercise of the clemency power.[60]

53 *Id.* at ¶¶ 98–101.

54 India Const. art. 21 (1950).

55 Maneka Gandhi v. Union of India, (1978) 2 S.C.R. 621, 658.

56 Maru Ram v. Union of India, (1981) 1 S.C.C. 107.

57 Bikram Jeet Batra, *"Court" of Last Resort: A Study of Constitutional Clemency for Capital Crimes in India*, Centre for the Study of Law and Governance, Jawaharlal Nehru University, Working Paper Series, CSLG/WP/11 (April 2009) at 42–45, *citing* Bishan Dass v. State of Punjab, A.I.R. 1975 S.C. 573; Joseph Peter v. State of Goa, Daman and Diu, (1977) 3 S.C.C. 280; Harbans Singh v. State of Uttar Pradesh, (1982) 2 S.C.C. 101.

58 G. Krishta Goud v. State of Andhra Pradesh, (1976) 1 S.C.C. 157.

59 Kehar Singh v. Union of India, A.I.R. 1989 S.C. 653.

60 *Id.*; Rohan Sahai, *Limits of the Pardoning Power under the Indian Constitution*, 2 N.U.J.S. L. Rev. 283, 293 (2009). As Sahai notes, the Supreme Court confirmed *Kehar Singh*'s holding resisting clemency guidelines in Ashok Kumar v. Union of India, A.I.R. 1991 S.C. 1792. *See* Sahai, *supra* note 60 at 294.

The constitutional clemency power in India is plenary; when issued, it takes priority over any court orders or enforcement.[61] According to the Indian Supreme Court, delay in the disposition of a clemency petition may render a death sentence unconstitutional. The Supreme Court has held that a fair and just procedure in line with *Maneka Gandhi* includes the carrying out of a sentence. In *Vatheeswaran v. State of Tamil Nadu* in 1983, the Court held that delay exceeding two years in the execution of a death sentence was sufficient to entitle the person under a sentence of death to invoke Article 21 and demand the quashing of the sentence.[62] The consequence of this decision was to require the executive to dispose of a mercy petition within the two year time period or a death sentence could not be carried out.[63] However, in *Sher Singh v. State of Punjab* later that year, the Court walked back from a strict time limit of two years, which it believed did not accord with the common experience of the time normally consumed by litigation and clemency proceedings.[64] The Court expressed concern that an accused person might misuse the process of clemency in order to delay execution. Although the Court confirmed the *Sher Singh* decision in *Triveniben v. State of Gujarat*, a different panel of the Court returned to the holding of *Vatheeswaran* in 1985 in *Javed Ahmed Pawala v. State of Maharashtra.*[65] The delays in India's clemency process are notorious. Even Supreme Court orders to the Home Ministry to act expeditiously were in vain, despite the social strains caused by endemic delays in India's judicial system.[66]

Other than delay, the Supreme Court has been careful in confronting the executive over its exercise of the constitutional clemency powers. The Supreme Court has rarely found procedural defects to merit judicial intervention, refusing to require an oral hearing, lay down guidelines, or adjudicate the rejection of a clemency petition. The Court has also been inconsistent in whether it will review the material that the Ministry of Home Affairs places before the president; its failure to do so in the case of Dhanajoy Chatterjee, despite a 10-year delay in the disposition of the clemency petition, led to India's only execution between 1998 and 2012.[67] In *Swaran Singh v. State of Uttar Pradesh*, the Court quashed a clemency order with a direction to reconsider the petition of the prisoner where the

61 Nanavati v. State of Bombay, 1961 (1) S.C.R. 497, 563–64 (India 1960).

62 Vatheeswaran v. State of Tamil Nadu, (1983) 2 S.C.C. 68.

63 Poornima Sampath and Priyadarshini Narayanan, *Mercy Petitions: Inadequacies in Practice*, 12 Student Advoc. 72, 72–73 (2000).

64 Sher Singh v. State of Punjab, 1983 S.C.R. (2) 582 (India) ("the fixation of the time limit of two years does not seem to us to accord with the common experience of the time normally consumed by the litigative process and the proceedings before the executive").

65 Javed Ahmed Pawala v. State of Maharashtra, (1985) 1 S.C.C. 275; Triveniben v. State of Gujarat, (1989) 1 S.C.C. 678.

66 Sampath and Narayanan, *supra* note 63 at 74, *quoting* K.P. Mohammed v. State of Kerala, (1984) Supp. S.C.C. 684.

67 Batra, *supra* note 57 at 52–53.

Governor was not told of certain facts concerning the prisoner's case.[68] In that case, however, the Court pointedly refused to go into the merits of the governor's decision. More recently, in *Satpal v. State of Haryana*, the Supreme Court found that the clemency decisions of state governors were open to judicial review on limited grounds, such as where the governor based a grant of clemency on extraneous considerations.[69] In *Satpal*, the Court noted the "uncanny haste with which the file has been processed and the unusual interest and zeal shown by authorities" in the clemency process. The Court determined that the decision was made mechanically and the governor had not applied his mind to the material on record. In a third decision, *Epuru Sudhakar v. State of Andhra Pradesh*, the Court quashed the release of a murder convict on the grounds that irrelevant and extraneous materials entered into the decision making process. The report to the state governor made several false statements about the circumstances of the crime and the prisoner's background.[70] The pardon for Sudhakar was granted as part of a blanket pardon order for 1500 people in commemoration of the ruling party's sixtieth anniversary. The Court found that the order was motivated by political expediency and resembled an act of grace, which did not fit within India's constitutional scheme.[71]

Singapore's president may grant pardons, reprieves, respites, and remissions under Article 22P of Singapore's constitution.[72] The Singapore Court of Appeal reviewed the justiciability of the pardon power in *Yong Vui Kong v. Attorney General*, ruling that the exercise of the pardon power was governed by the fundamental rules of natural justice and was therefore reviewable on the classic grounds of illegality, irrationality, and procedural impropriety.[73] However, the Court limited the practical value of this holding by finding that the condemned person did not have the right to be heard. The Court even ruled that the constitution did not provide for any right on the part of the offender in a death sentence to file a clemency petition.[74] The Court also ruled that a condemned person was not entitled to see the material presented to the cabinet, including reports from the trial judge, the presiding judge on appeal, and the views of the Public Prosecutor. In this, the Court rejected *Lewis v. Attorney General of Jamaica*, which held that a condemned person does have the right to see materials presented to the clemency authority.[75] As Dam explains, the Court emphasized the "local

68 Swaran Singh v. State of Uttar Pradesh, (1998) 4 S.C.C. 72.

69 Satpal v. State of Haryana, (2000) 5 S.C.C. 170. *See also* Parul Kumar, *The Executive Power to Pardon: Dilemmas of the Constitutional Discourse*, 2 N.U.J.S. L. Rev. 9, 28–29 (2009).

70 Epuru Sudhakar v. State of Andhra Pradesh, A.I.R. 2006 SC 3385. *See also* Batra, *supra* note 57 at 55–56.

71 *Sudhakar*, A.I.R. 2006 S.C. 3385.

72 Sing. Const. art. 22P (1965).

73 Yong Vui Kong v. Attorney General, [2011] SGCA 9.

74 *Id.*

75 *Id.* at 134–35.

context" in refusing to follow precedent from other common law jurisdictions in recognizing the right of disclosure, as Singapore's constitution confers no right to petition for clemency. This is "internally inconsistent," as the Court recognized that the mercy procedure may be open to judicial review, but refused to provide a mechanism by which a petitioner is able to access the information on which the cabinet and president relied in order to determine whether the clemency decision was validly made.[76]

Hor finds puzzling the juxtaposition of a progressive holding on the issue of justiciability and a conservative holding on the right of a prisoner to be heard. "Surely a far more sensible foundation for the power of pardon in modern Singapore is the realization that the process of the criminal law – investigation, prosecution, trial, and sentence – are not perfect and that at the end of the day, although due process might have been accorded, the result may still not be quite right."[77] This is especially true for a mandatory death sentence, in which courts lack the power to tailor an appropriate sentence. Hor notes that the Chief Justice, who wrote the decision in *Yong Vui Kong*, served on the bench that decided the seminal administrative law decision in *Chng Suan Tze v. Minister for Home Affairs* in 1988, which shockingly held that the government's power to detain indefinitely without trial for national security reasons under the Internal Security Act was subject to judicial review.[78] Although the Internal Security Act was later amended to prevent such review, the Court in *Yong Vui Kong* noted that judicial review in other contexts was preserved. In 2008, a joint panel of the High Court and the Court of Appeal ruled that prosecutorial discretion – another jealously guarded discretionary power – was subject to judicial review where the prosecutorial power is exercised in bad faith and where its application violates the Constitution, such as where it is applied in a discriminatory manner.[79] As Hor writes, disclosing the materials before the clemency authority to the condemned person would certainly benefit due process and place the prisoner in a much better position to make representations to the tribunal about any perceived deficiencies. In addition, the adverse consequences of doing so, including possible disclosure of secret information, do not seem to outweigh the costs of disclosure as a blanket rule.[80] In essence, the holding of *Yong Vui Kong* limits judicial review to the realm of the theoretical: "The door is open, but the crack is too small for anyone to pass through."[81]

76 Shubhankar Dan, *Presidential Pardon in Singapore: A Comment on* Yong Vui Kong v. Attorney-General, 42 COMM. L. WORLD REV. 48, 57–59 (2013).

77 Michael Hor, *Singapore's Death Penalty: The Beginning of the End?*, *in* CONFRONTING CAPITAL PUNISHMENT IN ASIA: HUMAN RIGHTS, POLITICS, AND PUBLIC OPINION 141, 152 (Roger Hood and Surya Deva eds., 2013).

78 *Id.* at 150–51.

79 Law Society v. Tan Guat Neo Phyllis, [2008] 2 S.L.R. 239, ¶ 148.

80 Hor, *supra* note 77 at 153.

81 *Id.* at 154.

Following Yong Vui Kong's challenge to the judicial reviewability of clemency decisions, the Court of Appeal returned to the issue of reviewability of prosecutorial discretion in *Ramalingam Ravinthran v. Attorney General.* In that case, the petitioner argued that bringing different charges to co-conspirators who engaged in the same criminal act such that one faced the mandatory death penalty and the other did not, resulted in the arbitrary infliction of capital punishment and violated equality before the law.[82] The prosecutor charged the co-conspirators as transporting different quantities of the drug in question, such that one met the death-eligible threshold while the other did not. The Court acknowledged outer limits on prosecutorial discretion, just as it did in *Yong Vui Kong*: "He must compare and treat like with like, and must not unlawfully discriminate against one offender as compared to another," but he also had to consider other factors, including the sufficiency of evidence and the likelihood of a co-accused to testify against the other. "Where relevant, these factors may justify offenders in the same criminal enterprise being prosecuted differently."[83] Building on these cases, the Singapore High Court found that it had the ability to interpret a commutation order by the president in *Mathavakannan v. Attorney General* in 2012. According to the commutation order, the defendant had a death sentence reduced to "life imprisonment," but the order did not say whether this meant life imprisonment for a term of 20 years, as provided by Singapore law, or natural life imprisonment. Because the order was ambiguous, the Court interpreted the commutation order to give the defendant the benefit of the lesser punishment.[84]

In South Africa, Article 84(2)(j) of the 1996 constitution provides that the president is responsible for "pardoning or reprieving offenders and remitting any fines, penalties or forfeitures."[85] In *President v. Hugo*, the Constitutional Court upheld the president's remission of sentences for all mothers of children younger than twelve years old from a constitutional challenge based on sex discrimination by a father of a young child.[86] The Constitutional Court relied heavily on British precedent to interpret the pardon power analogously with the royal prerogative of mercy. Although the president was required to exercise this power in consultation with the cabinet, he was not obligated to follow the cabinet's advice and his discretion was unfettered.[87] In *Hugo*, the Court relied on the conception of a

82 Ramalingam Ravinthran v. A.G., [2012] SGCA 2 (Jan. 10, 2012).

83 *Id.* at ¶ 52.

84 Mathavakannan v. Attorney General, [2012] SGHC 39 (Feb. 27, 2012) at ¶¶ 23–27.

85 S. Afr. Const. art. 84(2)(j) (1996). Although the 1961 constitution conferred the pardon power on a figurehead non-political head of state, the 1983 and 1996 constitutions conferred it on a powerful political executive. L. Wolf, *Pre- and Post-Trial Equality in Criminal Justice in the Context of the Separation of Powers*, 14(5) Potchefstroom Electronic L.J. (2011) at 118–119.

86 President v. Hugo, 1997 (4) SA 1 (CC). This case arose under the pardon power of South Africa's interim constitution of 1993. S. Afr. Interim Const. art. 82(1)(k) (1993).

87 *Id.* at ¶¶ 11–14.

pardon variously as both an act of grace and an act of public welfare. The Bill of Rights applied to pardon decisions and may be considered by courts in the same way as the exercise of other constitutional powers; consequently, the Court found that pardons were open to judicial review.[88] South African courts have wrestled with the degree to which the pardon power is an administrative action and therefore bound by the administrative justice provisions of the constitution or of the Promotion of Administrative Justice Act to challenge a pardon decision.[89] In September 2009, the Constitutional Court ruled in *Minister of Justice v. Chonco* that although there was "no right to be pardoned," the presidential power to make clemency decisions "entails a corresponding right to have a pardon application considered and decided upon rationally, in good faith, in accordance with the principle of legality, diligently and without delay."[90]

Some common law jurisdictions have explicitly confirmed the traditional rule that the clemency power is not subject to judicial review. The High Court of Swaziland has ruled that the King's prerogative of mercy is non-justiciable. In that case, the King commuted the death sentence of the appellant to life imprisonment with release at the age of 75. The defendant appealed, arguing that a sentence of life imprisonment in Swaziland could not exceed 20 years under the Prisons Act of 1964. The Court dismissed the complaint, indicating that "the prerogative of mercy is not susceptible to judicial review" and the King had "wide discretion" to impose conditions on sentences. The Court also indicated that the provision of the Prisons Act did not apply to capital defendants who had their sentences commuted.[91] The High Court of Malaysia has also determined that the prerogative of mercy is not reviewable in court. In *Juraimi bin Husin v Lembaga Pengampuanan Negeri Pahang*, the High Court adopted the traditional definition of clemency, holding that it was not the subject of legal rights and began only where legal rights ended.[92] The Botswana Court of Appeal, in rejecting a stay in a death penalty case, found it irrelevant that the current president had never granted clemency and rejected concerns from a human rights organization that it was "highly unlikely that the current death-row inmates and subsequent inmates will be granted clemency by the President." The court called the concern "presumptuous."[93]

Other common law jurisdictions, however, appear to be following the majority trend toward opening clemency to judicial review. In *Maniau v. Governor General*, the High Court of the Solomon Islands ruled that the

88 Wolf, *supra* note 85 at 130–132.

89 B.C. Naudé, *The Pardoning Power As a Duty of Justice*, 15 S. Afr. J. Crim. Just. 159, 162 (2002).

90 Minister of Justice v. Chonco, (2010) 1 S.A.C.R. 325 (CC) at ¶ 30.

91 Nkosi v. Attorney General, [2004] SZHC 79 (June 17, 2004).

92 Juraimi bin Husin v Lembaga Pengampuanan Negeri Pahang, [2001] 3 M.L.J. 458.

93 Kgafela v. A.G. (In re: Gabaokelwe), Crim. App. No. CLCGB-027-12 (April 27, 2012) (Bots. C.A.).

petitioner, a convicted murderer, never received any evidence that his petition was acknowledged, received, read, referred to a committee, or just ignored, which raised "the question of fairness."[94] The court had a "positive obligation" to ensure that an aggrieved person had a continued right to petition for clemency, but noted that the governor-general's ultimate decision was entirely a matter for his discretion. The court also distinguished the *Burt* case as the governor-general of New Zealand operated solely on the common law prerogative of mercy, while the governor-general of the Solomon Islands exercised the clemency power based on the constitution.[95] In Vanuatu, the Supreme Court rejected a challenge by the attorney general to certain presidential pardons; there, the attorney general argued that the petitioners had not put forth evidence of actual innocence and that there were less serious offenders more deserving of clemency. After comparing the traditional conception of the pardon prerogatives in both Britain and France, Vanuatu's colonial powers, the court rejected the claims, finding that "there may be cases in which the court will review the grant of a pardon, e.g. where corruption is established," but the current case was "within his discretion."[96] According to the court, the grant of a pardon may be properly made on a national anniversary, as a gesture of reconciliation, or because of ill-health; a comparison of the severity of offenses or the fact of innocence are not decisive factors in a grant of clemency.[97]

A few jurisdictions have even gone so far as to strike down exercises of executive clemency. In *Commissioner of Prisons v. Raikali*, the High Court of Fiji struck down a conditional pardon. In that case, a defendant who had served 11 years of a term of life imprisonment had been released with a 12-month compulsory supervision order by the President. According to the Court, the Prisons Act of Fiji specifically gives the power to impose a compulsory supervision order to the Minister for Home Affairs as the minister responsible for prisons. The president had the power to grant pardons either free or subject to lawful conditions, but the president had no power to attach a compulsory supervision order to a pardon – only the Minister of Home Affairs could issue such an order. The Court ordered the defendant's release without the condition attached.[98] The Supreme Court of Palau has invalidated presidential pardons where the president did not follow "procedures prescribed by law," as required by the constitution, including the legislatively-enacted Executive Clemency Act. Under the Act, a clemency petition goes to the minister of justice, who then distributes it to the attorney-general, the director of the Bureau of Public Safety, and the parole board, which will in turn review it and submit written recommendations to

94 Maniau v. Governor General, [2004] SBHC 118 (Oct. 6, 2004).
95 *Id.*
96 A.G. v. President of Vanuatu, [1994] VUSC 2 (Jan. 1, 1994).
97 *Id.*
98 Commissioner of Prisons v. Raikali, [1998] 44 F.L.R. 205.

the minister. The president was required to consult these recommendations.[99] In *Llecholch v. Republic*, the president of Palau granted executive clemency to two convicted persons without receiving the required recommendations. The Supreme Court upheld the Act and invalidated the pardons.[100] As discussed in an earlier chapter, the Guyana Court of Appeal vacated a denial of clemency where the attorney general previously served as defense lawyer in the petitioners' case and subsequently chaired the Advisory Council on the Prerogative of Mercy. The president of Guyana ultimately denied clemency. According to the court, the procedural impropriety based on the attorney general's role as both defense lawyer and chairman of the mercy committee nullified the constitutional procedure relating to the exercise of mercy.[101]

In the United States, federal restrictions on the state exercise of the clemency power are founded on the Due Process Clause of the Fourteenth Amendment. The Supreme Court held in *Connecticut Board of Pardons v. Dumschat* that the Due Process Clause did not apply in non-capital clemency proceedings, because there is no constitutionally-protected interest in such proceedings as an inmate's liberty interest was obviated once a valid conviction was obtained.[102] Not until 1998 did the Supreme Court finally address the constitutional standards for clemency proceedings in death penalty cases in *Ohio Adult Parole Authority v. Woodard*.[103] *Woodard* did not produce a majority opinion on the issue of whether due process protection applied to capital clemency proceedings. The plurality writing for the Court found that *Dumschat* also applied in death penalty cases, but five other justices concluded that "some minimal procedural safeguards apply to clemency proceedings," though it found Ohio's proceedings to meet the due process standard.[104] As Justice Sandra Day O'Connor wrote, "[a] prisoner under a death sentence remains a living person and consequently has an interest in his life," noting that judicial intervention might be warranted where a state official merely flipped a coin or where a state arbitrarily denied a prisoner any access to its clemency procedures.[105] Justice John Paul Stevens took a harsher tone, citing instances of bribery, personal or political animosity, and fabrication of false evidence.[106] As Clarke writes, this holding "fundamentally alter[s] clemency proceedings in many states,"

99 *See* Palau Const. art. 8 § 7(5) (1979), 17 P.N.C. § 3201–3205.
100 Llecholch v. Republic, Civ. App. No. 14-003 (July 24, 2014) (Palau).
101 Yassin v. A.G., (1996) 2 C.H.R.L.D. 39 (Guy.).
102 Connecticut Board of Pardons v. Dumschat, 452 US 458, 464–65 (1981).
103 Ohio Adult Parole Authority v. Woodard, 118 S.Ct. 1244 (1998).
104 *Id.* at 1253–54 (O'Connor, J., concurring in part and concurring in the judgment).
105 *Id.* at 288 (O'Connor, J., concurring in part and concurring in the judgment).
106 *Id.* at 290 (Stevens, J., concurring in part and dissenting in part).

and represents "the first time … that the Court has recognized the existence of a 'life' interest in any capital proceeding."[107]

Egregious cases have been found to violate *Woodard*. In a case arising from Missouri, the United States Court of Appeals for the Eighth Circuit ruled in favor of a death row inmate when the city attorney threatened to fire a lawyer under her supervision if the lawyer provided information to the governor or to the state board of probation and parole concerning the inmate's clemency petition.[108] In that case, the lawyer had concerns about the adequacy of the inmate's counsel, but was under pressure not to embarrass the city attorney's office. According to the Eighth Circuit, "[t]he Constitution of the United States does not require that a state have a clemency procedure, but, in our view, it does require that, if such a procedure is created, the state's own officials refrain from frustrating it by threatening the job of a witness."[109] In a subsequent decision, a split Eighth Circuit distinguished this case when senior employees of a corrections facility pressured a staff member who worked in the laundry of the prison not to testify in support of a claim of clemency by a death row inmate. Because the laundry employee eventually provided a signed affidavit to the governor, the Eighth Circuit ruled that the inmate had sufficient access to the clemency process to satisfy due process.[110] The court has also rejected a claim for relief when a prisoner alleged that he did not have sufficient time for his mercy petition and where a death row prisoner argued that a clemency proceeding was unfair because the governor was running for reelection and would be predisposed to deny clemency for political reasons.[111] Williamson has described the impact of *Woodard* on Texas courts, as the Board of Pardons and Paroles has come under scrutiny for its lack of procedure: no record is kept, no reasons are provided, no public proceedings are held, and frequently no deliberations take place. Although a state judge found this system violated *Woodard*, the Texas Supreme Court and a federal judge upheld the board's proceedings.[112]

Legislative involvement in clemency decisions

Constitutional regimes in the common law world vary as to the role of the legislature in grants of clemency. Although clemency by legislative action

107 Brian S. Clarke, *In Search of Clemency Procedures We Can Live With: What Process Is Due in Capital Clemency Proceedings After* Ohio Adult Parole Authority v. Woodard, 11 Cap. Def. J. 5, 11.

108 Young v. Hayes, 218 F.3d 850 (8th Cir. 2000).

109 *Id.* at 853.

110 Winfield v. Steele, No. 14–2392, 2014 WL 2766782 (8th Cir. June 17, 2014).

111 Noel v. Norris, 336 F.3d 648, 649 (8th Cir. 2003); Roll v. Carnahan, 225 F.3d 1016 (8th Cir. 2000).

112 Allen L. Williamson, *Clemency in Texas: A Question of Mercy?*, 6 Tex. Wesleyan L. Rev. 131, 147–48 (1999).

is unusual, there is some precedent for it. In New Zealand, defendant John James Miekle was convicted of sheep stealing in 1877 and sentenced to seven years in prison. Because New Zealand had no appellate procedure at that time, his only redress was to petition parliament claiming wrongful conviction. As a result of the petition, two judges were appointed to inquire into the matter and concluded that he should have been acquitted. In response the New Zealand legislature enacted the Meikle Acquittal Act. The private act – that is, it only applied to him and could not be used for the benefit of others – reversed the conviction and expunged his record.[113] On the other hand, some constitutions specifically make provision for a legislative grant of clemency in specific cases. In Nepal, the interim constitution grants to the legislature the ability to pardon or alter a sentence for contempt of parliament if a person submits a satisfactory apology.[114] In the United Kingdom, while the Crown and Parliament both have the ability to grant pardons, at times the Crown has brought a bill before Parliament with royal assent already given in a sort of combination procedure in which both the Crown and Parliament agree to the pardon.[115] Canada also allows legislative pardon, either by a government-sponsored or private member bill. There was no standard form in which a pardon must be issued. In 1998, the Federal Department of Justice drafted a bill to posthumously exonerate Métis rebel leader Louis Riel, which considered using the word "pardon" over the objection of the Riel family and the Métis community.[116]

The Parliament of India can check the Union president's pardon power in two ways: impeachment of the president and legislation that may impact the carrying out of the pardon power. As Kumar explains, the constitution of India vests the pardon power in the president and state governors rather than in the prime minister or legislatures in order to prevent legislative debate. Unlike the United States, however, the president and state governors are not directly elected, which reduces the possibility of public accountability for misuse of the pardon power. Although the Indian constitution provides for impeachment of the president, it does not permit impeachment of state governors. The amendments requiring the president to follow the advice of the council of ministers also makes impeachment of the president unlikely for misuse of the pardon power. The Indian constitution places strict limits on impeachment of the president, requiring two-thirds of legislators to vote in favor.[117] Courts in India, including differently-composed panels of the Supreme Court, have made inconsistent

113 Jean Teillet, *Exoneration for Louis Riel: Mercy, Justice, or Political Expediency?*, 67 Sask. L.Rev. 359, 387–388 (2004), *citing* Meikle Acquittal Act, (N.Z.) 1908, No. 1 (Private).

114 Interim Constitution of Nepal, art. 56 (2007).

115 Henry Weihofen, *Legislative Pardons*, 28 Cal. L. Rev. 371, 373 (1939).

116 Teillet, *supra* note 113 at 389.

117 Kumar, *supra* note 69 at 25–26.

rulings about whether the legislature could enact guidelines for the executive to follow in making clemency decisions. In *Maru Ram v. Union of India*, the Supreme Court emphasized the need for non-binding guidelines, encouraging the government to make rules for its own guidance in the exercise of the pardon power in order to exclude the possibility of discrimination. Absent such guidelines, however, the Court observed that until such guidelines were framed, the remission rules under the Prisons Act and similar legislation by state governments would fill the void.[118] The Supreme Court has also held in *Ashok Kumar v. Union of India* that the Prisons Act rules and similar state legislation should be treated as guidelines by the president and state governors while exercising their power to remit sentences.[119] However, this appears to be in tension with an earlier decision of the Supreme Court, which found that since the power to pardon is of the broadest scope, that the Court itself was not able to suggest guidelines.[120]

As in India, other courts have addressed separation of powers disputes over legislative parole and remissions and the executive clemency power. The Supreme Court of Pakistan has considered such a clash between a remissions scheme and the pardon power, noting that "the pardoning powers of the President under Article 45 of the Constitution are part of the constitutional scheme and cannot be circumscribed by any subordinate legislation or executive instrument. In the event of conflict between the two, the former has to prevail."[121] A court in Micronesia has also delineated the boundaries between the judicial power to modify a sentencing order and the executive pardon power.[122]

In the United States, the clemency and pardon power has been a site of contested control between Congress and the president. At the US Constitutional Convention in 1787, Federalists and Anti-Federalists disagreed over whether a strong executive should possess the kingly mercy prerogative. Anti-Federalists expressed deeply-held reservations, preferring to involve the Senate in pardon decisions. Roger Sherman, a delegate from

118 Poornima Sampath and Priyadarshini Narayanan, *Mercy Petitions: Inadequacies in Practice*, 12 Student Advoc. 72, 78 (2000), *citing* Maru Ram v. Union of India, (1981) 1 S.C.C. 107.

119 Ashok Kumar v. Union of India, (1991) 3 S.C.C. 498.

120 Kehar Singh v. Union of India, (1984) 4 S.C.C. 693. According to the Court in that case, "it may not be possible to lay down any precise, clearly defined and sufficiently channelised guidelines, for we must remember that the power under Article 72 is of the widest amplitude, can contemplate a myriad kinds and categories of cases with facts and situations varying from case to case in which the merits and reasons of State may be profoundly assisted by prevailing occasion and passing time." *Id. See also* Kumar, *supra* note 69 at 19.

121 Nazar Hussain v. State, Crim. Pet. No. 426 of 2009, Crim. App. No. 383 of 2009 (Aug. 2010) (Sup. Ct. Pakistan).

122 Kosrae v. Mongkeya, [1987] FMKSC 2; 3 F.S.M. Intrm. 262 (Kos. S. Ct. Tr. 1987).

Connecticut, motioned to drop the phrase "power to grant reprieves & pardon" and substitute the phrase "to grant reprieves until the ensuing session of the Senate, and pardons with consent of the Senate." Though the Connecticut delegation supported the change, the other eight delegations defeated Sherman's motion.[123] At the US Constitutional Convention, delegate Rufus King of Massachusetts made the case against legislative pardons, arguing that a legislative body was "utterly unfit for the purpose" as it was "governed too much by the passions of the moment," and in turn he suggested that the Senate concur in acts of pardon. Anti-Federalists and Virginia delegates Edmund Randolph, later the first US attorney general, and George Mason opposed giving the Senate this power, as the Senate was already powerful under the US Constitution.[124] Although this exchange only concerned the pardon for treason, it is a strong indication that the drafters of the US constitution did not intend for Congress to issue individual reprieves.[125] Impeachment remains the only legislative check on the plenary executive clemency power, although Congress can regulate the administration of the mercy process.

In *United States v. Klein* in 1871, the US Supreme Court definitively held that the president's pardon authority was not subject to legislative restriction or control, either directly or indirectly, such as by precluding expenditure of funds.[126] However, the US constitution does not necessarily make the pardon power *exclusive* to the president: Congress appears to have at least some power to grant an amnesty. During the Civil War, the constitutional question of whether the president could proclaim a general amnesty was a subject of sharp dispute, with the Senate Judiciary Committee taking the position that the president had no such power. The president probably possesses an amnesty power, but Congress can also grant general amnesties.[127] Unlike the president, however, Congress probably cannot grant individual pardons. Congress can impose procedural regulations on the president's ability to pardon, and it can adopt legislation to regulate subordinate officials who perform duties related to the pardon process, such as the US Pardon Attorney, an office created by Congress. In general, the Supreme Court has assessed the validity of legislative interference with presidential powers by weighing the extent to which the legislative restriction infringes on the president's ability to carry out his

123 Jeffrey Crouch, THE PRESIDENTIAL PARDON POWER 15 (2009).

124 Quoted in, Max Radin, *Legislative Pardons: Another View*, 27 CAL. L. REV. 387, 393–394 (1939), *citing* DOCUMENTARY HISTORY OF THE CONSTITUTION OF THE UNITED STATES OF AMERICA 753–754 (1900).

125 Radin, *supra* note 124 at 394.

126 US v. Klein, 80 US (13 Wall.) 128, 148 (1871).

127 Weihofen, *supra* note 115 at 373–374.

constitutional duties, and regulating the pardoning power would probably have little effect on its exercise.[128]

Most state legislatures also do not clearly possess the power to issue an individual pardon. In 1938, the California legislature introduced a bill to grant a pardon to Tom Mooney, a labor leader convicted for a bombing 20 years earlier. The lower house passed the bill, but it failed in a close Senate vote, though Mooney was later pardoned by the governor.[129] At issue in that case was a former provision of the constitution of California, since amended, that stated, "[n]either the governor nor the legislature shall have the power to grant pardons, or commutations of sentence, in any case where the convict has been twice convicted of a felony, unless upon the written recommendation of a majority of the judges of the supreme court."[130] The current amended version of the California constitution states that the "Governor may not grant a pardon or commutation to a person twice convicted of a felony except on recommendation of the Supreme Court, 4 judges concurring."[131] The former provision implied that the governor and the legislature *could* grant pardons or commutations of sentence where the convict has *not* been twice convicted of a felony if the negative wording were changed to affirmative wording. Consequently, the intention of the amendment appears to remove any doubt and ensure that the pardon power is exclusive to the executive in California. Some states have emphasized that the clemency power is exclusive to the governor. The Tennessee Supreme Court has found that the governor's clemency power cannot be reduced or dictated by the legislature.[132] This does not mean the legislature is irrelevant to the use of the pardon power. Some US states require legislative confirmation of members of the mercy commission and one state (Rhode Island) requires the state senate to approve all grants of clemency.[133] All states have a legislative scheme governing a wide variety of clemency issues, ranging from procedural rules governing a board's handling of clemency hearings, to notice provisions requiring the applicant to notify the prosecuting attorney, sentencing judge, and/or victim. In

128 Todd David Peterson, *Congressional Power over Pardon and Amnesty: Legislative Authority in the Shadow of Presidential Prerogative*, 38 Wake Forest L. Rev. 1225, 1250–52, 1256 (2003).

129 Weihofen, *supra* note 127 at 371.

130 Cal. Const. art. VII (1879). For the full text of the original unamended constitution of California, see the California Secretary of State website at www.sos.ca.gov/archives/collections/1879/archive/1879-constitution.pdf (last accessed November 13, 2014).

131 Cal. Const. art. 5 § 8 (1879, *as amended to* 2012).

132 Dwight Aarons, *Adjudicating Claims of Innocence for the Capitally Condemned in Tennessee: Embracing a Truth Forum*, 76 Tenn. L. Rev. 511, 546 (2009), *citing* Carroll v. Raney, 953 S.W.2d 657, 659 (Tenn. 1997).

133 *See* R.I. Const. art. 9 § 13 (1842).

addition, twenty-seven states require that the governor report his or her clemency actions to the state legislature.[134]

Conclusion

Under the traditional conception of the prerogative of mercy, the exercise of the clemency power was not reviewable in court as it was a personal and discretionary prerogative of the executive. In the last three decades, however, a new majority trend has emerged that allows judicial review of clemency proceedings – though not of the decision itself – in order to prevent injustice. Unsurprisingly, it appears that those jurisdictions with the most explicit constitutional procedures and the most heavily regulated clemency structures are the ones that are the most susceptible to judicial review. One would expect, therefore, that a court is more likely to intervene in defense of a petitioner's rights where the clemency authority is required (as opposed to merely permitted) to consult with a mercy committee or receive a recommendation from a justice ministry. In jurisdictions where an applicant has the right to seek clemency, an executive typically has the duty to listen, one of the minimum due process standards that have developed around a traditionally unfettered discretionary power.

The traditional conception of the pardon power held that mercy was not the subject of legal rights; it began where legal rights ended. A series of decisions in the United Kingdom and around the Commonwealth, however, began to open traditional royal prerogatives to judicial review, beginning with the seminal case *CCSU v. Minister for the Civil Service.* Slowly, Commonwealth jurisdictions including Australia, Canada, Caribbean nations, Hong Kong, New Zealand, and others began wrestling with the application of *CCSU* to the mercy prerogative. In countries where the prerogative of mercy has been constitutionalized, countries such as the United States, India, Singapore, South Africa, and South Pacific islands have determined that the pardon power is subject to at least some constitutional due process minimum requirements. Finally, this chapter also explored the ways in which legislatures influence the clemency power through passing amnesties or general pardons, setting guidelines or regulations on the mercy authority, or even by granting individual pardons in some jurisdictions.

134 Kathleen M. Ridolfi and Seth Gordon, *Gubernatorial Clemency Powers: Justice or Mercy?*, CRIM. JUST. 31 (Fall 2009).

9 The future of executive clemency

The clemency and pardon power appears to be declining in most countries. This is due in part to an increase in political populism that views the clemency power as contrary to the rule of law or that is overly lenient in serious cases. The decline of the death penalty contributes as well, rendering dormant specific capital punishment provisions in many constitutions and reducing the urgency of pardon decisions in general. The rise of parole boards or alternative sentencing authorities also removes some pressure from executives to provide clemency, as is the case in the United Kingdom and the United States. Finally, skepticism in international law of clemency and pardons is increasing where these powers could shield human rights abusers from accountability. This chapter will assess some of the characteristics of the apparent decline of the mercy power and the purposes of mercy in the future.

The case for clemency

A variety of rationales have been advanced for the exercise of the clemency power. Clemency could be backward-looking, raising doubts about the validity of the conviction itself, or it could be forward-looking, considering instead an offender's rehabilitation or remorse for a crime.[1] Clemency allows individualization, which becomes important when judges lose authority to tailor sentences, especially as a result of mandatory or mandatory minimum sentencing schemes. The same safety valve that was critical to spare controversial or sympathetic cases from the gallows during the era of the mandatory death penalty are equally important in the present era with the decline of parole and probation and the harsh collateral consequences of incarceration.[2] In addition, executive clemency, like jury nullification, can prompt attention to systemic failures in the criminal justice

1 David M. Zlotnick, *Federal Prosecutors and the Clemency Power*, 13 FED. SENT'G REP. 168, 168 (2001).

2 Rachel E. Barkow, *The Ascent of the Administrative State and the Demise of Mercy*, 121 HARV. L. REV. 1332, 1360–1361 (2008).

process that make the need for individualization even more pressing. Jury nullification has sparked reforms in police practices, criminal law, and sentencing, while grants of clemency have brought about reforms in the law of self-defense and insanity and in the death penalty.[3]

The risk of arbitrariness in grants of clemency is the price of having an opportunity for individualized justice. Executives already face political disincentives to exercising clemency. If they also had to provide reasons and face a judicial review process, it is likely that the already depressed numbers of pardons and commutations will fall still further. The cornerstones of administrative law – reasoned decision-making and judicial review – are costly tools if applied to clemency because they would act to depress mercy.[4] The risk of one bad apple – an individual who benefited from clemency and reoffended – is the greatest deterrent to use of the clemency power. Nonetheless, the general pattern masks some notable exceptions. Some individual executives have bucked the trend, even when facing reelection or seeking higher office; others have focused on the lower-level forms of mercy relief, such as restoration of rights. An executive may have an incentive to pardon out of religious faith or constitutional duty, using themes of redemption and forgiveness. As Barkow writes, the same political forces that discourage clemency could be marshaled to support a more generous clemency approach as well.[5]

The mercy process involves different individualized attributes than either the sentencing or post-conviction review phases of a criminal proceeding. Though capital sentencing allows for limited moral individualization through the weighing of mitigating and aggravating factors, the mercy process emphasizes contrition, remorse, penitence, and atonement to a much greater degree than in the sentencing phase of a trial.[6] Mercy lawyers may emphasize an offender's religious devotion or conversion in a mercy petition, for instance, which may in turn reinforce restorative justice goals by allowing an offender to play a role in healing the private pain of victims and their families through a process of remorse and apology.[7] "Like other sentencing determinations, clemency decisions must negotiate the modern politics of crime in order to be exercised with any frequency."[8] Even if the mercy process is shrouded in secrecy, this does not necessarily mean that it is uncontrolled or that it fails to adhere to a structure or regularly observe and apply consistent legal standards.[9] It may be that clemency is infrequent

3 *Id.* at 1361.
4 *Id.* at 1364–1365.
5 Rachel E. Barkow, *The Politics of Forgiveness: Reconceptualizing Clemency*, 21 FED. SENT'G REP. 153, 153–55 (2009) (hereinafter, "Barkow, *Politics*").
6 Anthony V. Alfieri, *Mercy Lawyers*, 82 N.C. L.REV. 1297, 1308–1309 (2004).
7 *Id.* at 1316–1317.
8 Barkow, *Politics*, *supra* note 5 at 155.
9 David Caruso and Nicholas Crawford, *The Executive Institution of Mercy in Australia: The Case and Model for Reform*, 37 U.N.S.W. L.J. 312, 323 (2014).

in some jurisdictions because those jurisdictions have more lenient parole or remissions mechanisms or fewer disabilities as a result of a criminal conviction.[10]

The role of victims in clemency decisions

One reason for the long-simmering controversy over clemency is that the process tends to neglect individual crime victims. That is starting to change, as victims themselves begin to play a more prominent role in the clemency decision. Restorative justice jurisprudence has spurred a new critique of executive mercy. Restorative justice refers to the array of non-adversarial, reconciliatory mechanisms for dispute resolution that purport to emphasize the healing of the victim after trauma. Victims want an offender to own responsibility for the harm and feel genuine remorse, something that punishment may not be able to deliver.[11] Kenya's constitution indicates that the advisory committee "may take into account the views of the victims of the offence" when deliberating a recommendation to the president.[12] Virtually every state in the United States has provisions in its constitution, code, or rules that require notice to the victims of crimes for which clemency is being sought, and an opportunity to be heard. As the Lieutenant Governor of Delaware Matthew Denn writes, mandatory waiting periods for unsuccessful applicants help reduce the number of times that crime victims relive their traumas by formally opposing the clemency applications.[13]

Involving victims in the clemency process does not only serve restorative justice goals; it may also provide political cover to an executive and thereby encourage grants of clemency. Governor Bob Ehrlich of Maryland, for instance, sought input from victims before granting a clemency application in order to neutralize political opposition. As a frequent granter of clemency, this helps explain why his clemency record did not figure heavily into the political debate when he stood for reelection.[14] In announcing the largest mass clemency in American history, Illinois Governor George Ryan relied heavily in his speech on the language of victims and victimization. He noted that he had discussed the mass commutation of sentences with victims' families and he spoke hauntingly of the murderer of a close neighbor in the small town where he grew up, incidentally one of the beneficiaries of his grant of mercy.[15] Nonetheless, victims' families lamented the governor's decision, especially after Ryan publicly acknowledged that nine

10 Barkow, *Politics, supra* note 5 at 155.

11 Robert Weisberg, *Apology, Legislation, and Mercy*, 82 N.C. L. Rev. 1415, 1419–20 (2004).

12 Kenya Const. art. 133(4) (2010).

13 Matthew Denn, *Clemency in the State of Delaware: History and Proposals for Change*, 13 Del. L. Rev. 55, 64 (2012).

14 Barkow, *Politics, supra* note 5 at 155–56.

15 Austin Sarat, *Putting a Square Peg in a Round Hole: Victims, Retribution, and George Ryan's Clemency*, 82 N.C. L. Rev. 1345, 1364–65 (2004).

days of emotionally-charged hearings from victims' families caused him to reconsider his plans to grant the clemency. Some victims stated that the decision denied them the closure they sought in an execution.[16]

What works best?

Though the image persists, modern clemency is no longer a personal and lonely decision of a sovereign wielding mercy as a fortuitous act of grace. In short, it is no longer a charismatic process. Especially in the very largest jurisdictions, clemency is bureaucratic, often housed in a ministry of justice or legal affairs. Such procedure allows the application of formal criteria and expeditious handling of large numbers of cases, though inefficient processing, as in India, affects the quality of the final recommendation. In smaller jurisdictions – particularly in Africa, the Caribbean, and the South Pacific – clemency recommendations or decisions are made by a specially-appointed committee. This involves more actors in the clemency process and resists "capture" of the clemency mechanism by law enforcement or prosecutorial interests, but it lacks the political and due process safeguards of a routine and defined process. Both constitutional structures have relative advantages and disadvantages and possess almost unlimited variation across the English-speaking world. Piecemeal evidence from the United States suggests that the most active clemency mechanisms are those that are most insulated from political considerations, such as an independent board of experts. Balancing the interests of victims, the public, the justice system, and the clemency-seeker befits no single clemency structure. This inherent tension has made clemency perpetually controversial from the very earliest times, but it nonetheless survives in every common law system.

16 Stephen P. Garvey, *Is It Wrong to Commute Death Row? Retribution, Atonement, and Mercy*, 82 N.C. L. Rev. 1319, 1320 (2004).

Index

For Product Safety Concerns and Information please contact our EU
representative GPSR@taylorandfrancis.com
Taylor & Francis Verlag GmbH, Kaufingerstraße 24, 80331 München, Germany

www.ingramcontent.com/pod-product-compliance
Ingram Content Group UK Ltd.
Pitfield, Milton Keynes, MK11 3LW, UK
UKHW021720240926
475702UK00029BA/1700

* 9 7 8 0 8 1 5 3 5 5 3 6 6 *